MW01485633

The Business of Science Fiction

Two Insiders Discuss Writing and Publishing

Mike Resnick *and*
Barry N. Malzberg

McFarland & Company, Inc., Publishers
Jefferson, North Carolina, and London

For Alvaro Zinos-Amaro:
scholar, critic, writer, friend

The chapters of this book were originally published
in the *SFWA Bulletin* as entries in the column
"The Resnick/Malzberg Dialogues."

LIBRARY OF CONGRESS CATALOGUING-IN-PUBLICATION DATA

Resnick, Michael D.
　　The business of science fiction : two insiders discuss writing
and publishing / Mike Resnick and Barry N. Malzberg.
　　　　p.　　　cm.
　　Includes index.

　　ISBN 978-0-7864-4797-8
　　softcover : 50# alkaline paper ∞

　　1. Science fiction — Authorship.　　2. Science fiction — Authorship — Marketing.　　I. Malzberg, Barry N.　　II. Title.
PN3377.5.S3R47　　2010
808.3'8762 — dc22　　　　　　　　　　　　　2009052946

British Library cataloguing data are available

Front cover images ©2010 Shutterstock

Manufactured in the United States of America

*McFarland & Company, Inc., Publishers
Box 611, Jefferson, North Carolina 28640
www.mcfarlandpub.com*

Table of Contents

Preface

Science fiction writers love to say that the most frequently asked question they encounter is "Where do you get your crazy ideas?"—and when speaking about the reading public, that might even be true.

But when writers speak to each other, the subject invariably turns to the profession of writing, and it seems that each new generation of writers comes into the field virtually clueless. Their questions are more along the lines of "What do I look for in an agent, and how do I get one?" or "How do you make foreign sales?" or "An option clause means the publisher wants my next book ... so why do established writers hate them?"

And it's pretty much up to the established professionals (we're both a little sensitive these days about the term "old-timers") to answer their questions and point them in the right direction.

We both broke into print in the 1960s. We've both won major awards. Barry has written two books about the field of science fiction: *Engines of the Night* (1982, a Hugo nominee), and *Breakfast in the Ruins* (2007, a Hugo nominee). Mike has written three: *Putting It Together* (2000, a Hugo nominee), *I Have This Nifty Idea ...* (2001, a Hugo nominee), and *The Science Fiction Professional* (2002).

In addition, Barry has written regular columns on science fiction in *Pulphouse*, *Science Fiction Review*, *Jim Baen's Universe* and elsewhere, and Mike wrote a regular column on the subject in *Speculations* for twelve years.

As fiction writers, we have each sold over one hundred novels, collections, and edited anthologies. Barry had sold close to four hundred stories; Mike about two hundred and fifty, plus a pair of screenplays.

We have been friends for more than thirty years, and occasional collaborators. Despite that, we view the world — and especially the world of publishing — very differently. We are fond of saying that we agree that God outdid Himself when He created Sophia Loren, and we have agreed on nothing since. Not quite true, but closer than you might think.

So when the revamped *SFWA Bulletin*, the official publication of the Science Fiction Writers of America, approached Mike a dozen years ago and asked if he'd like to write a regular column, he suggested that he and Barry have a "Dialogue" on a different facet of the business every issue. They agreed, and after forty-seven dialogues, many of which are collected here, we haven't run out of steam or subject matter. The dialogues have become, by consensus, the most popular feature in the *Bulletin*, and these days many of the members write to us suggesting new topics they would like to see us attack in our Siskel-Ebert mode. We've covered many of the traditional areas — promotion, conventions, awards, collaborations, publishers' abuses, and more — as well as new problems that keep popping up as publishing evolves, such as print-on-demand, e-publishing, piracy, and so forth (and our most recent dialogue was devoted to the pros and cons of the Google Settlement, which is still *un*settled as we write these words).

So what makes this different, and more useful, than other books on the subject?

— We have more than ninety years aggregate in this field. We have each written for just about every major (and minor) publisher around. At this late date, no one is going to blackball us for speaking our minds ... and speaking our minds is one of the things we do best.

— We have both been magazine editors. We have both been anthology editors. We have both collaborated with numerous partners. Barry has been an agent. Mike has been a book editor, and (in another field) a mass market publisher. There is *nothing* we haven't seen from both sides of the fence, and very little we don't have opinions on (including dangling participles).

— We're not interested in repeating what all the "how-to" books on writing and getting published say. There are a couple of decent ones, but most of them remind us of elephants in a circus ring, each holding the tail of the one ahead of him. We truly believe that the reason there are so many clueless newcomers is because they can't get the professional advice they need out of any of the "how-to" books (or at least they can't get enough of it), and we take it as our obligation to "pay it forward" to the next generation by telling the unvarnished truth as we see it.

Anyway, that's who we are, those are our qualifications, and that's why we continue to write the dialogues and are pleased to bring a number of them out in softcover. Now, if you want to see what we *think* — and we'll present both sides of both issues, with a certain degree of passion — start turning the pages.

— Mike Resnick and Barry N. Malzberg
Spring 2010

SECTION 1
Writing and Selling

1 The Specialty Press

MIKE: Today's subject is the specialty press. They've been with us since the 1940s, and indeed discovered science fiction a few years ahead of Doubleday and Ballantine. There was Arkham House, which is still around, and Fantasy Press, and Gnome Press, and over the years there have been literally hundreds of specialty publishers. Some, like Phantasia Press and Underwood-Miller and Axolotl Press and Donald M. Grant, managed to put out a lot of titles; some published just one or two and then vanished. But they have always been an integral part of the science fiction field, so it seems that perhaps we should consider their advantages and disadvantages.

First, the good stuff:

1. They make it possible to get hard-to-sell books (and especially single-author collections) into print.

2. They make it possible to keep some or all of your backlist in print, which is just about impossible in mass market if your name isn't Heinlein or Asimov or Bradbury.

3. If your book's original publication was as a mass market paperback, sending an impressive-looking hardcover to those foreign markets that have not yet purchased it may very well sway at least a few overseas editors.

4. This isn't exactly a financial consideration, but dealing with the specialty presses allows you to support that very important segment of the community in a very visible way — and I persist in believing that we need the specialty publishers.

5. The specialty presses will be more willing to take a chance on publishing some clearly non-commercial books — poetry, essays, experimental fiction, whatever. After all, they only have to sell 300 or 500 or 750 copies to a community that is already predisposed to buy what the author writes.

Now, the bad stuff:

1. The obvious: by virtue of being a small press, the publisher hasn't got very much money. Which means you're not going to get very much money for

your book. I know of no small press that pays as much up front as a beginner would make for a mass market paperback original. Or anywhere near that, to be honest.

2. The corollary: since they don't have any money, they're not going to be able to afford a big print run, or much of an ad budget, or any serious publicity. That's why they are small presses and not big presses.

3. If this is your book's first publication, your eligibility for the Nebula and the Hugo will probably be used up before a mass market edition appears. Now, theoretically that shouldn't matter; theoretically 200 or 300 (or even 50) motivated readers should be able to put a brilliant limited-edition novel on a ballot — but in the real world that just doesn't happen.

4. Speaking of mass market, a specialty edition could make it more difficult to sell mass market rights, since some mass market publishers will insist on first book rights.

—⟨∘∘∘⟩—

BARRY: Specialty press is a complicated topic, uncovers the usual duality or ambivalence with which I regard all too much. I respond to this in two ways: as a historian (however presumptuous or uncredentialed) of science fiction and fantasy, and as a writer who has had his difficult adventures within and without the genre.

As a historian — the specialty press is essential to the present state of the art. In the early postwar period Random House and Crown came out with enormous anthologies of so-called Golden Age stories (*Adventures in Time and Space, The Best of Science Fiction*), edited respectively by Healey/McComas and Groff Conklin, proving that there was a post–atomic bomb audience for this work, that science fiction as Asimov wrote retrospectively "wasn't only for a bunch of crazy kids." But the first systematized effort to get the novels and short stories of this period into print came not from Random House, Crown, or Simon & Schuster, but from fan presses created to fulfill just that mission: Gnome Press, FPCI, Shasta Publishers, etc. It was they who published Asimov's *Foundation* and Heinlein's *Beyond This Horizon* and Bester's *The Demolished Man* and Kuttner's *Robots Have No Tails* and dozens more of what we take to be the classics of science fiction: through small advertisements in the science fiction magazines, through mail order, and through a good deal of private industry these presses put into permanent form — and proved modestly profitable — work about whose viability the trade houses and mass market publishers were still not sure.

God's work certainly, and in his first book review column for *Galaxy* in 1965 Algis Budrys wrote about it all with a Proustian precision and remorse — but all of these specialty publishers overextended, exploited, and in many cases simply failed to pay the writers and went out of business. Part of this was due to their own incompetence and venality, part of it had to do with the fact that the trade houses, persuaded by the evidence of the specialty press's modest success, decided that they could have a better-than-modest success if they were to factor out the incompetence. (No one ever gets around to factoring out the venality.) Doubleday, Ballantine, Avon, Bantam Books got themselves science fiction specialists to advise and edit and moved into the field in a systematic fashion. By the mid–1950s the specialty publishers were used up, finished, bankrupt, among the missing, although many of the titles they had first published — think of *Foundation*— remain in print half a century later and have generated a continuing audience and income. (Arkham House is the sole exception; it remains a profitable publisher to this moment ... but Arkham, concentrating upon the works of Lovecraft and associated writers for most of its existence, was willing to work a territory which no trade publisher could be persuaded to undertake until "horror" became a category of its own in the 1980s.)

There is no science fiction market as we understand it without those specialty presses of the 1950s. Any contemporary specialty press, many of them coming into existence in the last ten to fifteen years, partakes of that tradition and should be supported, both in the abstract and as a practical matter. Furthermore, with the trade markets progressively closed to collections (other than by the most successful writers), backlist items by almost all of us and eccentricity of all kinds, the specialty press has a more important place in publishing; the small publishers are willing to commit to print work which Avon, Bantam or del Rey might have undertaken ten to fifteen years ago but are no longer willing, for economic reasons, to publish. This fusion of tradition and practicality makes the specialty press a laudable institution, one which should be on the submission list of almost every writer with an ad hoc determination to negotiate the best deal realistically possible with publishers, many of whom simply don't have the time, money or commitment to approximate the trade deal.

That's the historian speaking. The historian is the guy to whom to listen.

The writer has an unsurprisingly more equivocal take on all of this. The writer — or at least this writer, the person writing this, me, I — started serious life wanting to publish in the mainstream equivalent of what we now take to be the specialty press—*Epoch, The Hudson Review, Prairie Schooner*, etc.— moving on from there, I would hope, to collections published in trade and mass market but certainly originating in these small-audience outlets. A concatenation of misfortune in placing my work in these markets, and — as I came to actually study the magazines to which I was submitting — a disgust with the arcane, self-serving, insular nature of most of the work which I found there, led me to flee the writing fellowship and to take the form rejections of *Epoch* seriously. I went to work for Scott Meredith in June 1965 and made my signatory statement to my friend Arlene Heyman a few months later. "As between selling *The Hudson Review* which pays 2.5 cents a word on publication and selling *Alfred Hitchcock's Mystery Magazine* which pays 5 cents a word on acceptance, there is no contest: I want *Alfred Hitchcock*. If I can't make it in the commercial marketplace, find a wide or at least wider audience, I don't want to make it at all." I pretty well exercised that principle (or lack of principle) for the next quarter of a century. Well, we see how all of that worked out.

Most of the novels and collections published by the contemporary specialty press—well, a lot of it, maybe not most of it, I exclude reprints of the kind you discuss—shudderingly reconstruct for me the marginalized nature of the so-called "literary" markets which I fled such a long time ago. Practically, I know that for many of us, it's not only a good place to go, it's the only place to go. Privately and in a private way I wouldn't recommend for anyone else, I shudder.

———

MIKE: Okay, there's another advantage, or at least a serious consideration, that I want to discuss, and that's avoiding competition — not with other writers, which is both healthy and unavoidable, but with yourself.

I hear a lot of writers complaining that they can't keep their backlist in print, and they blame everyone and everything from their hostile publishers to their spineless editors to the Thor Power Tools decision. And yet, I'm not so sure that having all your works available in mass market paperback at Barnes and Borders and Dalton's and the rest of the chains is the brightest idea in the world.

Let me give you an example, and an explanation.

From 1991 through 1994 I edited about 20 anthologies. It was fun to do, and I got to bring a lot of new writers to the attention of the field.

And, I guiltily admit, I really liked the notion that in 1993 and early 1994 I could walk into a bookstore and find maybe 22 Resnick books on the racks— 5 or 6 novels, which was par for the course, and 16 or 17 anthologies. Made a nice display.

Didn't make a nice royalty statement, though.

Oh, I sold as many copies of Resnick books in 1992 and 1993 as I had in 1988 and 1989—maybe even a few more—but they were the *wrong* copies.

That's when I learned that just selling 5,000 or 50,000 or 500,000 copies of books with your name on them didn't matter. What mattered was how your most recent books—the ones for which you'd just cashed substantial checks, and which had not yet begun to earn out their advances—sold. And with 20 or 25 books on the stands, the Resnick readers were frequently choosing the wrong Resnick book.

My advances went down. They didn't nosedive, but they were cause for concern, because I hadn't figured out what I was doing wrong. I was winning awards, I knew I was writing better books than I had a few years earlier, I knew I was known and read by more people each year.

Then I picked up some screenplay assignments, and because I was already working at capacity, I had to let something go, and I dropped the anthologies.

And lo and behold, I sold as many copies of my 5 or 6 novels as I had sold of my five or six novels plus my 15 or 20 anthologies. My advances went right back up, and I realized that I had stumbled on a Hidden Truth. I didn't *want* to compete against all my old titles.

But I still wanted my backlist in print. I wanted fans who had missed my earlier books to be able to read them ... and I wanted foreign markets that had passed on them one and two decades earlier to have another shot at them.

And here came the specialty press to the rescue — a trade paperback press in this instance. I made a deal to reprint *Birthright: The Book of Man*, a 1982 title that had been out of print for 13 or 14 years.

It would sell for $17.95, so it couldn't possibly compete with my current mass market paperbacks.

It had a new cover, and a 1998 cover price and look to it, so I wasn't sending around a $2.25 paperback from 1982 to foreign markets.

It printed 2,500 copies, and has since gone back to press for another 1,500. Enough for fans, enough to send to 30 or 40 countries ... but *not* enough to harm the sales of the mass market hardcovers and paperbacks that *have* to sell in order for me to make a living.

In other words, it did exactly what it was supposed to do, and I just signed a contract that will allow the publisher to do a number of 3-in-1 and 4-in-1 editions of my old novels. The first 30 of each to come off the press will go directly to foreign markets who, 15 or 20 years ago, saw the mass market originals of these books and said, "Resnick? Never heard of him. Let's buy someone we know."

So, yeah, I guess you could say that's another argument, however obtuse, in favor of the specialty presses.

—◦◦◦—

BARRY: The specialty press is unequivocally, inarguably the proper outlet for backlist items, for the restoration to print of those novels or collections we published 15 years ago and which — unless we are in the golden 15 or 20 writers in our genre — would be less likely (or not likely at all) to be taken on by the trade publishers. Specialty press does not in any way compete with the mass market or trade publications, it has different outlets for the most part (science fiction specialty stores will carry both items but the chains will not and the airport newsstands never), and it's possible that not only a given work but a writer could find an entirely new audience through the specialty press. Nothing obtuse about that.

—◦◦◦—

MIKE: Let's move away from commercial considerations for just a moment and point out that a lot of specialty press books are *fun*.

For example, I edited a hardcover called *Shaggy B.E.M. Stories* a few years back. It consisted of 31 sf parodies, and even though it had stories by Asimov and Clarke and Poul Anderson, there was no way I could have sold it to mass market, because the problem with parodies is that you can't appreciate them unless you know *what* they are parodying — and you're simply not going to find 15,000 or 20,000 paperback readers who are that well versed in the field.

Since then I've edited *Alternate Worldcons* and *Again, Alternate Worldcons*, and Patrick Nielsen Hayden and I co-edited *Alternate Skiffy*. A couple of years ago I brought back some stuff from the old *Marvel Science Stories*, stuff that was so terrible it was wonderful, in *Girls for the Slime God*. All four books went to specialty presses. Delightful experiences and delightful books, and about the time each of them sold its 600th copy, it had almost certainly reached 75 percent of its potential audience.

Bob Bloch's Lefty Feep stories would never have found a mainstream publisher. Neither would Dick Lupoff's Ova Hamlet stories. I doubt that any mass market publisher would have taken a chance on John Betancourt's *Swashbuckling Editor Stories*.

So never overlook the fact that, along with trying to make a buck, there's nothing wrong with having a little fun as well, and specialty presses are simply more willing to go along with your crazier notions.

—◦◦◦—

BARRY: I'd add George Alec Effinger's Maureen Birnbaum collection to your list, or the 1994 NESFA Press collection of my own "recursive" science fiction, 160,000 words of novels and short stories about science fiction itself which would never have been taken on in that form by any trade publisher. There's still sometimes a place in mass market for craziness — Baen's *Carmen Miranda's Ghost Is Haunting Space Station Three* anthology of some years ago, for instance — or at least craziness of a certain kind, but not much of it, and the great collections of John Clute's criticism which are not crazy at all would not have been made available by other than the specialty press.

It's very important, always has been, we need it, it's irreplaceable. I don't want anyone (including me) to confuse my emotional reactions with what is a difficult and encroaching circumstance ... idiosyncratic work is less likely each year to appear in mass market, and yet it is work originally perceived as idiosyncratic — Henry Miller, *Lolita*, *Ulysses*, *Finnegans Wake*, *The Story of O* — that really marks the stations of the true way. Science fiction's equivalent of *Ulysses* today would have been far more likely to have been published by White Wolf or Mark Ziesing than by Tor or del Rey. That doesn't discredit anyone but it's a fact.

—◦◦◦—

MIKE: I've dealt with a lot of specialty presses over the years: Don Grant, Misfit Press, Axolotl Press, NESFA Press, WSFA Press, Wildside Press, Phantasia Press, Obscura Press, Nolacon Press, Farthest Star, Old Earth Books, Dark Regions Press, a handful of others, and I've learned a few things about dealing with them.

The main thing you have to remember is that most — not all, but most — of them are operating on a shoestring, and most of them are doing it as a hobby.

This means that you can turn in a book in 1992 and have it appear in 1996 (it's happened to me). But because they're usually one-man operations, it also means that if they're motivated you can turn in a book in mid–July of 1997, and have it appear at the 1997 Worldcon six weeks later (that happened to me, too.)

It means that you can be contractually promised a certain amount of money, and wait a long time — and I'm talking *years* here, not weeks or months — before you see it.

The thing you must always keep in mind — and sometimes it takes some work, I'll admit — is that these amateur and semi-pro publishers are spending their lunch money and their vacation funds to bring *your* book into print. If sometimes the project crashes, or extends into the next year or two, or if they promise you a Michael Whelan dust jacket and give you Joe Unknown ... well, if you were selling first rights to *Dune* or *The Space Merchants*, you wouldn't be dealing with a specialty press in the first place, right?

—∞∞—

BARRY: Well, yes, that's another fact. No one — not the publishers either — gets involved with specialty press in the hope of quick profit or much profit at all. Some places are, as we like to say, "businesslike" and reasonable — Arkham House notably — and quite a few are not. The publishers are indeed paying out of their lunch money or child support; if it's you or the courts in line for the money guess who's going to get paid? (Lawsuits aren't going to do any more good now than they did in the early 1950s. "Judgment proof" are the last words that many of us will hear as our final confessions and complaints are taken.) But the money from mass market and trade doesn't come that quickly either, and the conglomerates are no more eager to meet the terms of their contracts than the specialty publishers who were the subjects of Budrys' exquisite first review column for *Galaxy* back in 1965. The conglomerates are *not* judgment proof, but do you want to undertake the time and expense and bad kharma involved in serious legal threats only to get marked as a troublemaker?

Thinking about this discussion I find myself at a slightly different place than I was at the beginning, which may be one indication of a remarkable dialogue ... as the landscape for all but a narrowing range of mass market media-related science fiction and fantasy darkens, the differences presented to most writers by specialty press or the trade publishers are ever narrowing ... and the specialty press publisher is less likely to have the voice mail permanently in an ON position.

But I'd still rather sell *Hitchcock* than *The Hudson Review* ... (I did sell *Hitchcock* quite a lot through a very brief period almost twenty years ago. Never placed anything in *The Hudson Review*. Je ne regrette rien.)

—⌒∿∿⌒—

MIKE: Time for an ounce of summary. I have on my desk a copy of the August 1998 issue of *Locus*— the one that contains the annual *Locus* Poll.

Twenty-eight novels got enough votes to be listed for Best SF Novel. Every single one of them comes from a mass market house.

Twenty-two novels got enough votes to be listed for Best Fantasy Novel. Twenty came from mass market houses, and one of the other two is by Stephen King, who is going to be read no matter *where* he appears.

Sixteen novels got enough votes to be listed for Best First Novel. Fifteen came from mass market houses (though one house — Farrar, Straus — is not exactly known for category sf.)

But when we turn to non-novels, the numbers tell a strikingly different story.

Twenty-one short story collections got enough votes to be listed as Best Collection. Sixteen of them were published by specialty presses.

Ten non-fiction books got enough votes to be listed as Best Non-Fiction Book. It's difficult to separate specialty presses and academic presses, but suffice it to say that seven of the books were *not* from mass market houses.

Eight art books got enough votes to be listed as Best Art Book. Four of them were from specialty presses.

And, to cap it off, 3 of the 13 publishers with enough votes to be listed as Best Book Publisher were specialty presses.

I'm not saying to run right out and sell your magnum opus to a specialty press. That's not what they're there for. But I think the *Locus* Poll confirms a number of the conclusions we've reached here: the specialty publishers serve some meaningful and clearly-defined purposes, and I think the science fiction writer who disdains them is doing himself and his career a disservice.

2 Foreign Sales

MIKE: One of a writer's most important sources of income is the foreign sale. Actually, I shouldn't use the singular; if you make only one foreign sale on a book, you're barely scratching the surface of the vast overseas market.

I remember the first foreign sales I made, back in 1982. The Germans offered me about a thousand dollars less than I'd made for the American sale, and a week later the Japanese actually offered me a thousand *more* than I'd gotten here. It was then that I counted up how many countries were in the United Nations and realized there was gold in them thar hills.

I would consider it a given that any midlist writer, when the dust finally clears, will have made more money from foreign sales than he will make domestically. (One caveat: this doesn't necessarily hold for bestsellers, people making, say, $100,000 or more per U.S. advance. But they don't need to worry about foreign sales, anyway; if they just stand still, they'll be surrounded by foreign editors eager to throw money at them.)

Now, I'm not saying any *single* foreign advance will equal the American advance; it won't. But — and let's price these things reasonably, not at the high or low end — if you sell Japan ($5,000), England ($6,000), France ($4,000), Germany ($4,000), Poland ($1,500), Russia ($1,500), and Italy ($4,000) ... well, hell, that's $26,000 for a midlist book and you've still got more than 100 countries to go.

(Yeah, I know ... it'd be nice to make even more, and some people do on some of their titles. But most foreign publishers pay royalties. In fact, I have *never* sold a book to France, Italy or Japan that *didn't* pay royalties sooner or later, a blanket statement I cannot make about my American editions.)

Of course there's a minus side as well as a plus side. The first foreign title I ever sold was *The Soul Eater*, a story that was as close as I ever came to hard science; most of the book is set on a spaceship, and takes place inside a lonely man's head. And the cover of the first foreign copy of it that I saw had a barebreasted warrior woman brandishing a sword. Kinda makes you hope the translator paid more attention to it than the art director.

And yes, your works can get pirated, and yes, you often don't find out about that for years thereafter.

You can also get paid in full and spend the next five years trying to get the author's copies that the contract calls for.

You can also — and this is incredibly frustrating — sell two or three books to a country, earn out your advance and then some, and fail to sell them the next four books. Or you can have a foreign editor buy only the middle book of your trilogy, leaving the audience just a tad confused about how it all began and where it will all end. And you can go nuts waiting for an explanation for same.

But anyone who ignores or disdains the foreign markets does so at his (very real) financial peril.

—◀๛▶—

BARRY: Of course, you need an agent for foreign markets. I suppose it's possible to make contacts and sell directly — the Internet and e-mail have made previously inaccessible foreign markets quite reachable — but it's still difficult to make cold sales on the basis of correspondence. (Maybe it's a little easier with short stories; there are less levels of approval through which to pass a short story ... and less money of course.)

Getting an agent isn't all that difficult if you've already had one on the domestic sale: all USA agents have cooperating foreign agents who are routinely sent copies of clients' work on publication. Some USA agents have part-time or full-time foreign rights people who make these submissions, some simply function as a remailing service to Agence Lenclud in Paris or Paul Fritz in Switzerland, but all will accomplish coverage.

If you've published a book domestically, however, and you don't have an agent, the foreign markets would constitute the strongest reason to now get one (and with a creditable novel sale you'll find it much easier, of course, than you would as an unpublished writer). Agents and cooperating agents vary in their efficacy in the foreign markets, just as they do with everything else, but all of them are essentially dealing with the same overseas publishers, the same cooperating agents, and the variance in outcome, advances and so on, may not be as great in the foreign market as it is domestically.

These are strange, quirky markets as you indicate. I have never been able to assess or predict them. (This may have more to do with my work than the market, of course.) In the 1970s I managed six or seven novel sales to England over a period of five or ten minutes; I've never subsequently sold a book there. I sold four or five novels to France in about 15 minutes in the 1970s, and have not placed a work there since. My best-known novel sold to Japan in the 1970s for a $300 advance (less tax and 20 percent commission) and paid out about $80.00 in royalties over the next ten years; the only other Japanese sale was a knockoff novel which Bill Pronzini and I wrote in a couple of weeks in 1980, which sunk out of sight on publication here, and which received in Japanese advance and royalties about 50 times what *Beyond Apollo* did. I can't claim to understand any of this, or why Finland stopped after the acquisition of the first three *Lone Wolf* novels—but Norway loyally, insistently, published all fourteen. (Hard to get excited in either case; Scandinavian advances in the 1970s for paperback originals were about $200. Haven't improved all that markedly since.)

In the old, bad days, foreign rights were additional, discretionary income; genre novels sold for remarkably low prices and rarely earned royalties. In the 1960s and 1970s the Scott Meredith Agency was selling science fiction novels to Germany for $300–$400, to France for about the same, to Spain or the South American countries for barely three figures. Italian advances weren't much better and British advances were only a little bit better than that. That's not the case now, of course; there was a period recently, and it may still exist, when British advances for medium-level science fiction novels were higher than domestic advances and there were careers and reputations which were being driven by the foreign markets. (Gibson has always been a bestseller in Japan; Germany has paid out much more over the years than her own country for Marion Zimmer Bradley's overwhelmingly successful *The Mists of Avalon*, and that novel has been on German bestseller lists continuously for more than a decade and a half.)

We're talking for the most part, of course, about the old NATO group and our own hemisphere. The Westernization of the Communist countries this decade has opened up a huge market which is no longer pirating (Phil Dick was a bestselling writer in the 1970s in places like Czechoslovakia, Bulgaria, Hungary: never got a cent) but paying. I know you've had remarkable success in the Iron Curtain countries. Tell me about it.

—*ww*—

MIKE: Back at the beginning of the decade, just after the Iron Curtain turned to Kleenex, a lot of magazine editors from the Soviet bloc hit the Worldcons—especially Chicago and Orlando in 1991 and 1992 (and later Scotland in 1995). Most of them didn't have two dimes to rub together; their countries were destitute, and they didn't have any publishing industry to speak of.

Well, these editors came around at the Worldcons, shyly approaching a number of writers, and asking for free gifts of stories, or perhaps offering a whole $25 apiece for them. I unloaded a couple of dozen stories, including some Hugo winners and Hugo nominees. A couple of friends—I won't name them, since they're still friends and still SFWA members—took me to task for my inept business decision, explaining that I was a *pro*, and pros didn't let major stories, even reprints, go for such pittances.

I replied that as I read the situation, there was no book publishing industry in these countries, but there soon would be. And when that happy day arrived, it made sense to me that the book editors would be most interested in those Americans who had already established a local fan following. And the only way to establish it was to let those stories go for a few cents or a few dollars or perhaps only a hearty handshake. They told me I was crazy, that these were little more than fanzines I was selling to. I explained that, whatever their appearance, they were currently the top of an expanding market, and that was good enough for me.

So okay, half a dozen years have passed. I've sold 26 books to Poland, none for under $1,500; I've sold 19 books to Russia, none for under $1,500, some for more than double that; I've sold 7 books to Bulgaria, 6 to the Czech Republic, a few to Lithuania. Croatia hasn't got a book publishing industry yet, but I sold them three Hugo-winning short stories, and one of them recently won their highest award, so I feel reasonably confident that when a book publisher finally arrives on the Croatian scene, I'll have a receptive market.

As for my two friends who would never let a reprint go for under $100, I don't believe either of them has yet made a single sale to an Iron Curtain country.

(Okay, so you don't get rich on any one of these sales ... but $2,500 here and $1,500 there and $2,000 the other place, where there were never any markets before, begins to add up quickly — and there's no heavy lifting involved.)

You have long said that this remains a field of personal cachet, and I think that holds for foreign sales as well. This is why I try to hit at least one foreign convention every year or two: so that I can meet with my foreign editors and agents face-to-face.

I was just guest of honor at a convention in France, where I not only met my editors, but *nine* of my translators— and while it probably doesn't hold true in France, it's a fact of life in many countries that the translator has as much influence over whether you sell or not as the editor. (So I always make a point of visiting with my Japanese translators at Worldcon, and I've had my Russian translator stay as a guest in my house when he was touring America. A nice side effect was that he not only continued to buy my books, but after meeting my daughter one evening at dinner, he bought some of her romance novels as well.)

I find that the more established Western countries run their business pretty much the way we do, and while I'm always happy to meet my English, French, German and Italian editors, the initial contact, negotiations, and contract goes through my domestic and foreign agents. But in many Second and Third World countries, they're re-inventing the wheel, and I find I can do more business personally, via e-mail and computer conferences, than through the normal channels. It's enjoyable — I mean, hell, I enjoy the company of *anyone* who wants to spend money on me — but it's also about as efficient as Second and Third World publishing gets, circa 1999.

—⟋∿∿⟍—

Barry: You're being kind. I'd probably have been one of those people telling you, "Whatta you, crazy? Whatta you doing, selling stories to fans or would-be publishers for $25 or for nothing at all? Aren't you the guy who keeps telling us, 'Let's get this straight: if you're a writer they're supposed to pay you. You don't pay them. You don't give away your work.' I wouldn't have dealt with these people until they had something other than hope, until they could put up something other than a token payment or no payment at all."

And in so doing, you have already reminded me, I would have taken myself out of tens of thousands of dollars, a flourishing exposure of my work in the Eastern European bloc, with far more to come. I can't quarrel with that: you have the evidence and the outcome.

But I still don't know if I'd do it, granted that the opportunity came to me. You have to understand that my perceptions of the foreign markets are based not only upon my own difficult experience but upon decades of observing foreign publishers, overseas fans, their ambitions and their ethics, while employed at the Scott Meredith Literary Agency. Some of these folks have worked out okay and some haven't worked out at all. The problem is that you don't know the difference going in and I'm not smart enough, unagented, to make that judgment.

I've already noted that Phil Dick learned toward the end of his life that he was a bestselling writer in Hungary, Poland, other parts of the grand and unlamented Soviet Union. This was news to him because he had never seen any money at all from those countries. Stanislaw Lem, Phil Dick was told, was a great fan and had translated several of Dick's novels into Polish. "That is interesting, because I have never heard a word from Mr. Lem, much less received a contract," Dick noted.

Okay, that was then, this is now: capitalism is about to flourish, may already be flourishing, and those bad old stories about Poland belong to the south forty along with the discarded shoes and plumbing equipment for the outhouse; we are moving into One World International Internet Publishing. Good enough, Mike, except that my own perceptions were formed in a hard and grimmer school. (It took me months to collect a five dollar payment for the translation of a story into Esperanto, for heaven's sake. An Argentinean publisher sent me contracts for rights in that country to *Beyond Apollo* and subsequently a $300 check drawn on an Andorran bank ... the check bounced because, I was informed many months later, Andorra had the fetching and pleasant habit of allegedly not putting any money into private hands located outside the country. Do you note that? No money. To any human being. Not in the country of Andorra.) The Argentinean editor became and remained mute. I have many similar narratives. (And I also don't have stories. Like so many of us, I have been pirated utterly without my knowledge before, during and after.) Do you think the freelance writer is often helpless when her interests are juxtaposed against the interests of domestic editors and publishers? Try to gauge the helplessness when the editor is in Argentina. Or Andorra.

Okay: I am a traumatized child, dysfunctional home, all of that, telling bad stories about bad times; it has changed. But I have a deep and abiding suspicion of the foreign rights situation. It varies, of course. I don't mean to generalize — the British are more equitable today than most of our conglomerates; Paul and Peter Fritz are sensational in extracting royalty statements, royalties, and renewed licenses from German publishers; there are some wholly equitable publishers everywhere; and European publishers can be trusted, more or less.

But I still wouldn't give Hugo-winning stories for $25 or less to people I meet at conventions or online expressing only good intentions; I wouldn't sell six or three books to an unknown Polish publisher before I had been paid for the first. At least, I wouldn't do it unagented. If I had an agent I trusted who in turn had a cooperating agent in the Eastern bloc who she trusted, well, then, maybe. And then again maybe not, because your domestic agent can be no less helpless in the face of distant venery than thee or me.

Too much caution, a failure of trust leading to many lost opportunities? Very possibly. But let the opposition be heard. Caveat emptor and all that.

All this being said, I congratulate you on the quantity of your sales to the former Eastern bloc and the size of the advances. You done splendid. But most of us don't — by virtue of your intelligence, awards, and overwhelming competence — have your leverage.

MIKE: You forgot to mention my manly good looks.

Look, it wasn't all that bold and daring a thing to do. I didn't give any *books* away. The whole purpose was to make the books worth something in an emerging market that probably hadn't heard of any American science fiction writers except Heinlein, Asimov, Bradbury, and maybe two or three others. And seriously, what do you think a reprint of a short story, even a Hugo-winning short story, is worth? The way I saw it — the way I still see it — is that you've got a hell of an upside (i.e., lots of book sales), a tiny downside (i.e., maybe you'll lose a couple of hundred dollars' worth of stories that no one else in that country wants anyway), and it's an easy call.

I should add that while I may have made the initial contact, or plotted the strategy, I do have agents in all these countries, and *they* negotiate the contracts.

I suppose, while we're on the subject of foreign sales, we ought to talk about payment. Right now (and I'm writing this just before the Euro goes into circulation and perhaps changes the whole set-up), the only major markets that pay in their own currencies are England, France, Germany, and Italy ... and because of that, there's extra money to be made from those countries *if you know what you're doing.*

One of the first things I did when I started making foreign sales was to have my agents in each of those countries set up local bank accounts and deposit my checks there. Then I started studying the foreign exchange rates. (I'm no expert, so I went to an expert for advice.)

What's this leading up to? Let me give you an example.

In 1989, I sold *Ivory: A Legend of Past and Future,* to my British publisher for an advance of 10,000 pounds. The afternoon I signed the contract, the pound was trading at $1.53, which means my advance was worth $15,300 *as of that day.* By the time they finally cut the check and my British agent deposited it in my London account, the pound was trading at $1.61. I waited until my expert felt the rate had peaked and was due to come down, and brought it to America when the pound was trading for $1.92. That made my advance worth $19,200 — a profit of $3,900 simply because I waited out the exchange rates.

Almost no one pays in "soft" currencies anymore, but once upon a time they did. My first Polish book sale was in zlotys (all my subsequent Polish sales have been in dollars). Now, zlotys weren't worth the powder to blow them to hell if you tried to import them and exchange them for dollars, so I left them in a Polish account. In the States, converted into American dollars, these millions of zlotys were worth about $350; in Poland, they were worth about $1,600 at the time. So I waited until I found a friend who was touring Eastern Europe, and sold him my zlotys for $1,200. He was happy, I was happy, my Polish bank was a willing accomplice, and all was well that ended well.

Which is simply another way of saying that it can sometimes be very profitable to deal creatively with foreign funds.

———*⁓⁓*———

BARRY: Currency speculation, playing with the varying strength of the dollar against foreign currencies ... that's all beyond me. I'm a simple, one-celled organism as my collaboratrice, Kathleen Koja, used to note, consistent right down to the bottom. All that concerns me is collection: if it comes through a USA agent, the agent takes care of the conversion; if it comes from an overseas agent, then my bank will (although the German agent with whom I've worked for decades now makes the conversion at his end and pays, eventually, in American funds). You are talking to a man, remember, who took months to collect a $5.00 payment for Esperanto rights. And who, when it at long last emerged, was glad to get it.

Send me the money, that's my mantra. Not *show* me the money, the catchphrase which came out of *Jerry Maguire* a couple of years ago, that's different. "Show me the money" implied "...and then I'll decide what to do." "Send me the money" means exactly that: "Send me the money." Five dollars for Esperanto? A hundred dollars for Portuguese rights to a novel? Two hundred for Italian rights to *The Men Inside* or *Beyond Apollo?* No problem. Ship it in, take them out. If you'll send it by next Thursday, you can deduct 20 percent for the consideration. You can understand why currency speculation might be a topic of lesser concern to the lovable and ever hopeful Kid, here.

I know enough about the foreign markets to know that I can neither predict nor control; they are not to be understood. The German agent to whom

I referred earlier — Thomas Schluck, he's represented my work for 27 years, as long as I've been in this house — told me a long time ago, when I was pleading with him to get me a sale, any kind of sale, I needed the money, "You don't understand what the situation should be. Anything I do for you should be seen as good news, as something extra. You cannot count on me to do anything and you cannot budget the money." Reasonable, and I've tried to accept that.

David Goodis, wholly out of print in the USA (with the exception of *Down There*, which sells a few copies in trade a year), still receives by his Estate's proxy (he's been dead 12 years) tens of thousands a year from France and Germany, and has had at least 15–20 films produced in those countries based on his work. Cornell Woolrich, virtually the same situation, is revered in France, his work kept alive by the Truffaut and noir cult. Jim Thompson sold nothing in the USA in his last five years; his only sales were to Series Noir/Gallimard in France. The foreign markets have a great role in the career and long-range visibility of some writers. But they can neither be managed nor predicted. I'll cite myself as a paradigm.

How could — or, working in the present tense, how can — I have improved/improve my chances in the foreign markets? Get a good agent, get on the Internet, sure. But how about the work itself? Is there any quality to your work which you think has made you successful overseas? If there is, is such a quality transferable to the work of others?

—◦◦◦—

Mike: "That's all beyond me... I'm simple... Just send me the money."

That's defeatist talk, Barry. This field — and hopefully even our dialogues — can provide tools for making *more* money. Do you just want them to send it yesterday like the penny-a-word pulp writers of old — or can you bring yourself to wait a week or a month and cash a bigger check?

You know, one of the things we haven't mentioned, here or in any prior dialogue, is that the word "No" is just about the sexiest word in the world of bargaining. Say it and mean it, and you'd be surprised at the nice things that can happen. For one thing, the offer you've rejected invariably remains on the table, just in case you change your mind. For another, you frequently receive an even better offer. You make it sound like every publisher's offer is take it or leave it, and that's just not the case — at least, not any longer — here or abroad. (Though of course you must be prepared to leave it; cave in even once, and you're marked for life.)

(I have to add, based on my little tale of the Eastern bloc editors, sometimes you also have to know when *not* to say No, no matter how poor the offer.)

Now, as to your last question: I think that the well-structured plainly-told story probably translates better than the novel that aspires to be a 100,000-word prose poem, and of course if the translator makes you read better than your competition, you're ahead of the game. But I would never suggest that anyone write in an unnatural style just to increase foreign advances.

There are many other strategies that have nothing to do with writing. Probably the most effective of them is to collect every review you can get your hands on. Yes, I know that syndicates often pick up a review, so that the same one may run in ten different newspapers. No problem. Send out copies of your books to fanzines—especially those that run regular reviews—and you should get another 20 to 50 reviews.

So what do you do with your 50 or 60 favorable reviews? Make copies and package them with each copy of your book that is submitted to a foreign editor. Maybe it won't impress the Brits, who are very aware of our fannish community. Maybe it won't help you beat out a Hugo nominee. But I am convinced that if an editor who isn't too fluent in English — and that's *most* foreign editors— gets two American sf books on his desk, and one of them comes with 60 good reviews and one comes with three or four, it doesn't matter that 45 of those good reviews were written for fanzines, and 12 of the others are identical except for where they appeared. He's got 60 reviews of one and a small handful of the other, and it's an easy call.

Writing for foreign fanzines—or giving them reprints of American fanzine articles—also doesn't hurt; it gets your name known.

Going out of your way to meet foreign editors and fans at the major cons, especially Worldcon, isn't a bad idea either, and for the same reason: the more exposure you can get, the better.

Another suggestion (and one your agent won't like): wait until you have a few books in print before submitting overseas. Most of the countries you're trying to sell want to know that you're not a flash in the pan, that if they're going to spend serious money buying and translating and promoting you, you're going to stick around.

It's a business. You've got to run it like one — and foreign revenues are an increasingly important part of it.

3 Awards

MIKE: We toil in a field that gives out awards. *Lots* of awards. There's the Hugo and the Nebula. The Sturgeon and the Clarke. The Campbell and the Campbell Memorial. The Locus Award and the Science Fiction Chronicle Poll. The Lambda and the Tiptree. The Dick and the Tour Eiffel. The Prix Apollo and the Ditmar. The Ignotus and the Seiun. The Rebel and the Phoenix. The Balrog and the Skylark. And if I were getting paid by the word, I could go on and on.

Now, we all agree that they're not of equal value. My own experiences would put the Hugo at the top, but I realize a case can be made for the Nebula. I think the only truism about awards is that if you stay in the field long enough, you're eventually going to win one.

You and I have both seen people sweat blood trying to win a major one — and that sweating usually begins sometime after the story is written and published. They contact their friends. They hold up copies of their book at convention panels. They make their book or story available for free to any potential voter. They push it on the convention circuit. They beg their publishers to send copies out to all likely voters.

I don't know for a fact that it works; in point of fact, I tend to think that it doesn't. It's never subtle, not in a field that's so used to spin, and it's often off-putting. It can also be expensive.

So here's the operative question: is it worth it? Which is to say, more explicitly, is an award worth having for anything beyond simple ego gratification? Is any award worth a couple of bucks more on your next contract, or are they all just pretty objects to put on your trophy shelf?

—⁓—

BARRY: Well and again, as with your all-purpose query some columns back on fee-paying literary agencies (I applauded your disingenuousness which was a lesson in kharma to us all) this is one of those questions. As AA says about drinks to a drunk, one is too many and a thousand aren't enough. A short response is saying too much and the longer version — well, the longer version can't wrap the territory. Hardly approaches.

Let me begin by taking issue with your truism that anyone who hangs around long enough in the sense of producing some volume of published work is going, eventually, to win an award. Not so. I won't embarrass the living — you know who you are out there — but will talk only of the departed; here are some major science fiction writers who never won an award of any kind: Rick Raphael, Robert F. Young, Zenna Henderson, David R. Bunch. Mack Reynolds, I suppose, doesn't quite qualify; Fred Pohl announced that a *Galaxy Magazine* poll of the readership for "favorite writer" put him on top in 1968. Randall P. Garrett. Tom Godwin. L. Ron Hubbard.

None of these writers seemed to suffer particularly for lack of an award ... one cannot construct, for example, a career for Robert F. Young which would have been much different if he had won a Hugo in short fiction in the 1950s; certainly Garrett (not really well known today, of course, he died in 1987, had been silent since 1979) was so prominent in the 1960s that most readers would have been surprised to learn that he *hadn't* won an award. It's possible to get through hundreds of thousands of published words (forget unpublished) and obtain no sanction from the readership base or fellow professionals and to live or for that matter die happily ever after.

Still, awards don't hurt — I don't think that there's anyone around cynical enough, and that includes me, to attempt an argument that awards are career-damaging. They have their uses, some of them, and even those that don't can leave the nights a little less cold than they tend to be in northern Wisconsin from November through May. (Or so said the non–award winning crime writer Jack Ritchie in 1976; a great short story writer, endlessly admired within the genre, he won only one Edgar, in 1982 for the short story "The Absence of Emily," and celebrated by dying six months later.) "It's good to be the king," Mel Brooks tells the court in *History of the World, Part I*. It's good to win an award or at least it's less bad. Ask anyone who's been through the experience as winner or loser. Mike, you've won four Hugos and a Nebula and been on final ballot for each, what, twenty-five times? Which outcome was more fun?

But how about that career sense? Any practical good? For certain writers at certain points of a career, absolutely so; the relationship between Samuel R. Delany's four Nebulas and one Hugo in the 1960s and his income and prominence was direct. Similarly for Roger Zelazny. Then again, how much practical good was Katherine MacLean afforded by her Nebula in 1972 for "The Missing Man" best novella? Ed Bryant and Charles Grant both won two Nebula Awards for short story, Bryant in consecutive years, in the 1970s, and neither of these writers went on to have any significant career in science fiction. (Grant has been fairly prominent in the mystery and horror fields, Bryant similarly has had as very high profile in the field of horror as writer and critic ... but neither has done much significant work in science fiction in more than twenty years.) I'm sure that in both cases this near-abandonment of science fiction writing was voluntary and self-willed. But what effect did winning those Nebulas have in terms of retaining them in the field?

There are a lot of awards out there, certainly, so many that I was able in early career to win one myself. (Small help, bigger tsouris, since you so kindly ask.) In the 1950s the International Fantasy Award for best novel and the Hugos across the category were certainly the significant awards (they were in fact just about the only awards for writing in the 1950s). The International Fantasy was abandoned in the mid–1950s and the Hugos were alone until joined by the Nebulas in 1965. The two awards were for a long time regarded as roughly equivalent; for a number of reasons—probably unseemly to say this in the SFWA publication but here he goes again — the Nebula has been significantly devaluated in the last decade and most writers privately if not publicly will say that given a choice of one or another for the same work they'd rather have the Hugo.

Sales figures? Neither Hugo nor Nebula other than in the novel category, publishers know (if do not admit), has any effect on sales at all. A Nebula or particularly Hugo for novel is modestly helpful in the years immediately succeeding, can raise sales slightly (and advances considerably). Even in the long category, however, their relevance to sales is significantly overrated.

I've been rich and I've been poor and rich is better as the late Joe E. Brown said many years ago (that it's now a cliché makes it no less valid); I've won and I've lost and it's better to win. It's almost always better to win. (I am modestly eliding any comments on the election, people.) John F. Kennedy and his friends always felt that losing the 1956 vice presidential nomination — in the famous open balloting — to Estes Kefauver was the basis of his national career; he had the prominence of the near-miss but was saved the task of running on a ticket which lost badly.)

He didn't feel that way at the time, though.

—◦◦◦—

MIKE: I was kinda sorta hoping for some more specifics in your reply, so I didn't have to be the first. However...

Let's begin with the cash awards, because as far as I'm concerned they're ends in themselves. I've been fortunate enough to win Spain's UPC contest for Best Novella (about $8,000) and France's Tour Eiffel Award (about $14,500), and when they toss around money like that, you don't have to ask if it will help your career. You write for a living, so it just *did* help you in a very meaningful way.

As for the biggies— the Hugo and the Nebula — I'd have to say the Hugo will probably do you a bit more good. Now, neither will increase your word rates because, award winner or first-timer, your short fiction goes to markets with posted rates, and they're not inclined to change them just because you won an award. I think there was a time, back in the late 1950s and most of the 1960s, when winning a Hugo *did* add a few thousand dollars onto your next advance

... but in these days of computer returns, your advance will be predicated only on what your last couple of books sold.

What changed? Well, back in 1958, if you won a Hugo for Best Novel, you were only the fifth person ever to do so. If you won the 1968 Nebula for Best Novelette, you were the third. But move the calendar up to the year 2000, and there are so damned many Hugo and Nebula winners walking the Earth that you almost get the feeling, at a large convention, that they outnumber those who haven't yet won one. Look at it this way: we give out eight fiction awards each year—four Hugos, four Nebulas. We've been doing so for over 30 years in Nebulas, close to 50 in Hugos. Do the math. Ask yourself whether advertising that a new book is by a Hugo winner has quite the exclusivity you want when you're promoting an award winner.

I'm sitting here with the current *Science Fiction Chronicle* (Oct/Nov 2000) on my desk. I'm going to look at October releases and see just how many Hugo and/or Nebula winners have books (not short stories, just *books*) out that one month:

Kim Stanley Robinson. Esther Friesner. C. J. Cherryh. Michael Bishop. Jane Yolen. James Morrow. Ursula K. Le Guin. Fred Pohl. Anne McCaffrey. And me.

A fluke month? Let's look at November:

Joe Haldeman. Charles Sheffield. Anne McCaffrey. George R.R. Martin. Bruce Sterling. Charles L. Grant. Lois McMaster Bujold. Isaac Asimov. Jerry Oltion. Robert A. Heinlein. Lawrence Watt-Evans. Larry Niven. Terry Bisson. Gene Wolfe.

There were also a handful of Campbell winners in the same months' releases, and a Dick winner, doubtless a Sturgeon winner, even a related Hugo winner (Ben Bova, whose Hugos came for editing) and a Nebula-winning author who edited an anthology (Gardner Dozois, who is also a multiple Hugo winner as an editor.)

Kinda dilutes the commercial value of the Hugo and Nebula when you come up with this sort of quantity month in and month out.

So ... if that's the case, is any award, other than a cash prize, really worth anything except in terms of ego gratification?

Well, my experience is that you can capitalize on the Hugo. You just can't do it in the science fiction field in America.

The New York Times, Lord knows why, feels compelled to run the Hugo winners on Sunday or Monday of each year's Worldcon. Three of the four times I have won Hugos I have been involved in long, intensive, occasionally antagonistic negotiations with movie studios ... and every time my name appeared as a Hugo winner, they gave in on almost every point of contention within a week. This was not the same studio, mind you, but three different studios for three different Hugos.

What else? Well, after my first Hugo, I was actually paid a dollar a word by a Japanese magazine to write an article about a Hugo winner's day. (About the same as a Hugo loser's day: you wake up, you write a bunch of pages, you go to bed.)

I find that being an award winner helps most when you're trying to sell overseas. All other things being equal (which is to say, incomprehensible — at least to an editor who has a problem speaking or reading English), the Hugo winner (and to a lesser extent, the Nebula winner) has a major advantage over the non-winner. After all, it's proof (of a very subjective sort, to be sure, but proof nonetheless) that you are a Class Act and a Quality Author. The Hugo also implies that you have a fan following, since it's voted on by fans — and fans are the people who buy books.

It's hard to sell a collection, here or abroad ... but it becomes a bit easier if you can offer a couple of Hugo or Nebula winners that the publisher can brag about on the cover. No one gets rich off a collection, we're not talking huge money here, we're talking a minimal sale or no sale at all, and sometimes having an award-winning story will make the difference.

And then there's the stories themselves. If I win a Hugo, I can count on selling that story again — to reprint anthologies, to foreign markets, to audio and electronic markets — perhaps 12 to 15 times over a 5-to-8-year period. (I'm afraid I can't speak for a Nebula winner, as mine was also a Hugo winner). I also find that even a Hugo or Nebula nominee will sell from 8 to 12 more times in the next decade.

So I suppose it might even be worth your while to campaign for an award. I hear people complaining about politics and campaigning all the time ... but since the Hugo and Nebula final ballots are (and remain) secret, I honestly don't know how you go about politicking, or, more to the point, how you would know if your politicking was having any effect at all. Would you have won anyway? Was your campaigning so off-putting that people voted against a book or story that should have won based just on its quality?

So ... would you care to draw upon your 30+ years in the field and comment on any of the above?

———◆◆◆———

Barry: Campaigning.

That's another broad area; it cries for generalization and I can do no less than fall into that abyss. The usual stipulation: all generalizations including this one are probably untrue. But some are less untrue than others.

The Nebulas and the Hugos represent a different electorate, somewhat different conditions. The voting base for Hugos in the professional categories now is, I would guess, about a thousand votes, maybe 1200. It's less than half that for the Nebulas. Because the Nebulas have a smaller base it is easier to campaign there than it is for the Hugos. Probably considerably easier because through the SFWA address book and the Internet, any SFWA member can have access to the entire electorate. Not so easy with the Hugos.

In the old days—from, say 1965 to 1975 — the Nebulas drew on a very small voting base indeed. "Twenty votes will get you a Nebula," was the truism. I don't know the exact figures for those early years with one exception which has in tribute to Cordwainer Smith burned itself upon my brain: "Final War" was a finalist in the novelette category in 1969 and received 12 votes, finishing third. Poul Anderson's "The Sharing of Flesh" (won the Hugo, incidentally) had 13 votes to finish second. Richard Wilson's "Mother to the World," the winner, had 19 votes. A switch of four Wilson votes to me or vice-versa gives me the gonfalon, similarly eight fresh and eager bidders if I can recruit them does the same. That's not a heck of a lot of people. I don't know if winning the Nebula that year would have made any difference in the short or long run, yes and no are the answers, I suppose, but I would like to have learned instead of speculated. (I don't begrudge Richard Wilson the award. Good writer, nice man, difficult final years, died too young and had plenty of literary frustration.)

Nowadays, I suppose—figures are no longer released or rankings—that forty or fifty first place votes (it's not clear to me if the Nebulas, like the Hugos, work on the Australian ballot) would win a Nebula, at least in the shorter categories. That still isn't a heck of a lot of votes and less than that are needed to achieve the preliminary and then the final Nebula ballots in SFWA's increasingly Byzantine system which I have never fully understood and don't want to understand. Obviously campaigning under these conditions can work. I'm not saying that every winner or final ballot work has reached that because of campaigning, but I'm not saying that such works haven't. It's my inference — I'm just a distant spectator now, folks— that campaigning goes even beyond merit to mark the most significant factor in the entire Nebula process. Of course some voters won't respond to campaigning at all, a few voters in fact will reflexively disqualify any work with the whiff of self-promotion. And of course campaigning, if everyone does it, can to a certain degree be self-obviating, if everyone's somebody, then no one's anybody. (But those who won't campaign at all are almost certainly excluded.)

The Hugos: larger, more scattered electorate, less compact, more difficult to manipulate now. Again, in the old days, in the 1950s and even the 1960s the Hugos were predicated on relatively few votes, and there are credible rumors— name I no names— that a few of them might have been bought for minor considerations. That's doubtful now — I think that the Hugos in the professional categories, if not unimpeachable, represent the outcome of a more honest and less biased process than that surrounding any other literary award. Perhaps any award at all. (The Edgars, the National Book Awards, the Pulitzers, all decided by small committees in subterranean fashion, are obviously more manipulable than the Nebulas, let alone the Hugos.)

That's a relatively long answer to a short but charged question: in sum, campaigning works. Or, in sum, while campaigning for the Nebula is absolutely no guarantee of an award, it is now almost a certainty that no work without campaign has a chance.

(There's the jury system adding a work in each category and a juried work, apparently, even won recently, the only time in 20 years, but the jury system doesn't prevent or minimize injustice, it's what they call a cosmetic reform. And, of course, it's easier to lobby three or four jury members than a voter base of some 400, isn't it?)

The latter part of this sermon might then pass on to consider the exact nature of a "campaign" ... what constitutes this process? outright currying of votes? Sending on a solicited or unsolicited basis copies of the stories at issue? Trading nominations and votes? But other than saying "all of the above and some things not part of the above" I guess I'll pass.

—◦◦◦—

MIKE: I suppose if you send every member of SFWA a copy of your new hardcover with a note suggesting they might recommend it for a Nebula if they like it, you're probably going to get on the ballot. After all, it costs nothing to recommend a book; you can recommend 300 a year if you've a mind to ... and if you recommend a guy who sends you a $26.95 hardcover that you can trade in to your local bookstore, why, he might send you another next year. (There was a time when the best thing about SFWA, other than the Grievance Committee, was that the membership got free monthly mailings from various mass market publishers ... enough to more than cover your dues if you re-sold them or traded them in.)

The operative question is this: is it worth $32,340 (1,200 members times $26.95) to be a Nebula nominee? Of course not. Even if you get the book at a 50 percent author's discount, is it worth $16,170 (plus postage; never forget postage) to make the ballot?

I don't care how great your ego is, and I don't care how gullible your editor and publisher are, the answer is still a resounding No.

Short fiction? Well, that's a different ball game. For years the digests sent copies of all nominated stories to the voters; then came the internet, and now *Asimov's* and *Analog* post them on their web page. (I don't remember if *F&SF* does.) But that's all *after* the fact; no one's posting every story that was published during the year so the voters can read it for free. So you're looking at sending out 1,200 copies of a $3.95 magazine to hopefully make the ballot. Is it worth just under $5,000 to lose to Connie Willis? (Remember: if you've got an outstanding, award-quality story, you don't *need* to campaign just to make the ballot.)

So much for campaigning. Now let's be perfectly honest. We live in a microcosm of writers and editors and fans, and the man or woman with a few Nebulas or Hugos to his or her credit verges upon superstardom.

But walk out the door of the hotel right after you've won one of those wonderful awards, and ask the first hundred people you see if they know what a Hugo or a Nebula is.

I guarantee that their answers will make you humble.

———《》———

BARRY: Humbling all right. Brings you to heel right away; certainly induces what the counselors call "perspective." In 1983, again, I was on a final ballot; Nebulas were in New York but Doubleday was too cheap or uninformed to pay for a banquet ticket and I had no disposition to spend $50 to eat bad food and lose. (I can do that at considerably less expense every day of the week.) I hung around the hotel in the afternoon, went to a couple of panels, talked to this friend and that, then took a walk to the car which would take me home. Two blocks from the hotel, the friend who was keeping me company (before himself returning for the banquet) pointed to an attractive woman and said, "Look at her. *She doesn't know you've lost a Nebula.* She doesn't even know what a Nebula is. She probably doesn't even know what science fiction is." Well, you never know — maybe he was pointing at Cecelia Holland who just happened to be in the territory — but then again you probably do. Worth keeping in mind.

Or Patricia Cadigan, who was around at the Baltimore World Convention in 1983 where I lost in my category and collected Richard Geis's 12th or 15th Hugo in his. I carried the Geis trophy on a long, solemn walk around Baltimore Harbor after the ceremony, thinking of this and that. "How much do you think I could get, cash money, for this Hugo from anyone strolling the Harbor at this hour?" I asked. "Try twenty-five cents," Patricia said. "If you offer to carry it home for them."

So all right, everything is relative and as you might confirm, Mike. Most of the population of Kenya or Zaire aren't concerned with Nebulas and maybe one out of ten thousand could tell you what an Oscar is, let alone a National Book Award. "Drink is good, it musters indifference," that master of perspective, Dr. Johnson, said. While we're on the subject I might as well note in passing and conclusion that the extended eligibility rule, now extant for about a decade or a little more, has in my opinion severely discredited the Nebulas. Best of the year? "Well, uh, it was the best in the last two years." But last year's winner was also published within the two-year limit. "Well, it's one of the two best stories of the last two years. Or maybe the best of the year before last." There *is* no "best of the year" thanks to the extended eligibility and this change — which came from some members exploiting an obscure loophole permitting the withdrawal of a story or novel if a "better version" would subsequently be published — has done the award little good. (I don't think that X or Y or Z who have won through the use of this give a damn nor should they.)

Richer is better than poorer, sure. But the awards process often seems designed to create little but pain (always more losers than winners) and make competitors of colleagues, sometimes bitterly. But this is where we are and it's not going to go away; where it all ends knows God as Woolcott Gibbs pointed out. (And where did Woolcott Gibbs end?)

———*/\/\/*———

MIKE: Time for an attempt at a summing-up, I suppose.

First, I don't think a truly bad story or novel has ever won a Hugo or Nebula. I'm less convinced as you move to the plethora of minor awards.

Second, most people don't know it, but more people vote for most of the Hugo categories than for most of the Oscar categories. Winning an Oscar gets you a few million dollars and a ton of prestige; winning a Hugo certainly *ought* to get you a free drink from your editor, though I can testify that it frequently doesn't.

Third, we have so many lesser awards that I doubt anyone can name them all. I have one that possibly nobody has ever heard of: the Golden Pagoda Award, which comes not from Beijing but from Oklahoma. I've got another nonentity of an award called the Alexander, and an equally obscure one called the Bookworm. I hope they impress foreign editors because I've never quite had the nerve to add them to my credentials when pushing a project in this country. (Probably I just don't want to deal with a mystified "Huh"?)

But good or bad, major or minor, awards are here to stay. And here comes the crux of it: I think they're a good thing, especially for writers who don't regularly earn out, let alone hit the bestseller lists (and that probably includes a third to half of the award winners.) If you can't convince your publisher that you're going to make him rich, awards will at least go a long way toward convincing him that your name, while it may never top the bestseller list, will bring prestige to his list.

4 The Marketplace

MIKE: One of the questions I'm asked most often by beginners is: "What kind of science fiction sells best?"

Now, why they should ask me, instead of people like Anne McCaffrey or Ray Feist, who live on the bestseller list, is a mystery, but an even bigger mystery is: What kind of science fiction sells best?

My first inclination is to answer: Good science fiction. But that's ridiculous. Just look at what Trekbook #308 or Wookiebook #79 does to any year's Hugo-winning novel in head-to-head competition. In fact, look at what generic seven-book trilogies do to works of literary ambition. There are mighty few totally unoriginal fantasy quest books that can't whip a well-conceived beautifully-written science fiction novel in straight falls.

Has it always been like this?

I have a horrible feeling that it has. Let me share an experience with you.

Back in 1970, I was given a tour of Charles Levy's warehouse. (Levy was the major — indeed the only — distributor of books and magazines in Chicago.) As we passed by the Gothic section — Gothics were wildly popular back then, and invariably had a cover illustration of a girl running away from a foreboding house on a hill — the warehouse manager pointed to a just-arrived title and told me it would sell 57 percent. I must have looked interested or impressed (I was both), because he began going through the Gothics, announcing that this one would sell 53 percent, this one 48 percent, this one 50 percent, and so on.

I remarked that he must have a remarkable knowledge of all the authors and books to be so well-informed, and I wondered where he found the time to read them all. (Okay, I was young and innocent then. Sue me.)

He laughed, and explained that the average Gothic sold 54 percent. If there was a light in the house on the cover, you could subtract 3 percent. A high neckline on the girl, subtract another 2 percent. Yellow letters for the title, add 4 percent. If cover blurb implied that the curse on the house (there was *always* a curse) was English, add a point; American, subtract a point; French, subtract 7 points. If she was running away in the daylight, subtract 10 points; on a moonless night, and you could still make out her features, add 2 points. He listed 20 or 25 factors that determined the sale of the book, and every single one concerned the packaging; the quality of the writing had absolutely nothing to do with it. It was a revelation.

I was afraid to ask him to take me to the science fiction section and do the same trick. I wanted desperately to believe that quality mattered. I *still* want to believe it, but I'm 32 years older and just a tad more cynical.

I'll go this far: I think a quality *package* sells. But of course, that has a lot more to do with the artist and book designer than the manuscript.

Please tell me I'm wrong. Then we'll go to work on Santa Claus and the Easter Bunny.

—⌇⌇⌇—

BARRY: Does quality sell? I'm not quite as cynical as you — I have flushes of hope and universal acceptance which persist for as long as 15–20 seconds — but I'm prey to the same feelings and emotions which you suggest. If quality was the sole determinant of sales, then the Star Trek or Star Wars franchise novels would not — as you point out — outsell the Hugo or Nebula winners 2–1, which they do, nor would Sturgeon's *More Than Human* have been out of print for more than a decade (Vintage brought it back a few years ago.) Alfred Bester's sales figures would have been greater than those of Robert E. Howard's; fine and promising writers like X, Y and Z would not have given up writing, voluntarily or otherwise, in early or mid-career because of low sales.

But of course there are anomalies. Good work can sell very well (although never better than the best-selling not-so-good work). *Neuromancer*, an outstanding and ambitious novel, has never been out of print in its 18 years and has certainly sold well over two million copies in all of its editions. Kim Stanley Robinson's Mars trilogy is both distinguished and commercially successful. Sometimes good work is indeed rewarded. But that is an anomaly; it is by no means a pattern.

I'd go this far: good work lasts, not-so-good work doesn't. Cumulative sales of *The Demolished Man* or *A Canticle for Leibowitz* must be well below the cumulative sales of *Conan the Conqueror*. But the Alfred Bester and Walter Miller novels keep on coming back; if they fall out of print, they return to print and their audience is self-renewing. (The same is true of Conan, of course. To say good work lasts doesn't exclude the fact that some not-so-good work can last too, and in lasting raises the question as to whether it may be good work after all ... but that is for three other columns.) My *Beyond Apollo*, never a commercially successful novel, has kind of hung around: an electronic edition last year, a mass market paperback in 1991, reissues in foreign markets. Disch's *Camp Concentration* and Phil Dick's *Do Androids Dream of Electric Sheep*, bestsellers neither, have more presence than almost any other novel published in 1968 (*Stand on Zanzibar*, published that year, did pretty well too). Good and innovative work persists. It may even prevail. But we are not talking of immediate sales figures and — as we well know — we are living in a market geared as never before to immediate sales figures.

———✸✸✸———

MIKE: All very true, but merely persisting, sticking around, somehow making an occasional resale, is begging the question. I've resold books, too—but never for top dollar. If your name isn't Isaac and we're not discussing the Foundation Trilogy, I don't know of anyone who ultimately makes six- and seven-digit advances for reprints of books that originally sold for three digits.

Which is to say: if an editor likes your work, it's no great gamble for him to pay you a beginner's advance to reprint it. And it's no great triumph either, not in this year of 2002 where our very top authors (King, Clancy, Steele, Koontz) regularly make eight-digit advances which were undreamed of 15 years ago, and where million-dollar contracts are no longer so rare, even in science fiction, that they make national news.

All the titles you named, and all their reprint sales, and all their aggregate sales figures combined, don't equal what one best-selling generic fantasy novel sells in a week.

Is it the packaging? I know if I was concerned only with sales, and I could choose between having a Frank Frazetta cover or a brilliant novel, I'd take the Frazetta cover every time. Is that the key?

Is it — as I like to believe, when I fail to make the bestseller list, which is most of the time now that I come to think about it — that when you do not genuflect to the lowest common denominator, when you write for adults, when you go out of your way *not* to tell the same story every time you write, that you immediately alienate 80 percent or more of your potential audience? That it's the boneheads and not the discerning readers that make you rich?

Or is it something else, something subtler? Heinlein didn't shoot for that lowest common denominator. Neither did Herbert, or Bradbury, or Clarke, or Asimov. Didn't stop them from selling zillions of books. Did they finally make their millions (and "finally" is the operative word here) because, as Herbert once said, they had primed 10 or 15 generations of magazine readers who could finally afford hardcover books by the 1970s?

———✸✸✸———

BARRY: I don't think there's anything profound here. Heinlein didn't aim for the lowest common denominator, nor do you, nor I, nor —come to think of it — Robert E. Howard or Mr. Lovecraft. All of these writers did their work as best they could more or less and took their chances in the marketplace. It took Howard and Lovecraft many years of death to reach a large audience; Heinlein was reaching a large audience well within the first ten years of his career. Did any of them plan it that way? I doubt it very much.

It seems easy to say that work aimed at the lowest common denominator will always sell better than work not aimed at & etc., but the reasoning behind this when examined will often prove to be remarkably circular. Look at the *New York Times Book Review* bestseller list, start working your way down from Grisham to Koontz to Anita Shreve (Anita Shreve?) and point out that this one appeals to the masses for that pandering reason, another appeals for another pandering reason and so on. But this excludes the fact that every year hundreds of novels are published for the mass market, some of them with large advances and heavy advertising budgets which fail utterly; it ignores the fact that the Harry Potter books made their way in two countries and then the world without large advances, print orders or publicity; that works like *Blue Highways* or *Zen and the Art of Motorcycle Maintenance*, published in someone's garage decades ago, sold so many copies without advertising or publicity that one of the commercial trade publishers took it over and sold millions of copies. (Same thing to be said of Castaneda, of *The Whole Earth Catalogue*.) There's no formula for a bestseller; there is no formula even for a lowest common denominator. If there were, this would not be a business in which 90 percent of trade books fail, in which almost half the print run of the magazines (the most successful magazines, mind you) are returned unsold from the newsstand).

A business predicated on failure, I think. *Dune*, published serially in *Analog* in 1963 and 1964, was rejected by forty or fifty hardcover publishers before Chilton took it on for a $1,500 or $2,000 advance and published it almost invisibly. Terry Carr described in a memoir how he and Don Wollheim had finally decided to buy paperback rights for Ace after all the science fiction paperback publishers had declined. "We decided that it was a very long novel," Carr said in effect, "and that would be something unusual; there had been very, very few long science fiction novels and this would be something unusual and *Stranger in a Strange Land* was a long science fiction novel, albeit by Robert Heinlein, and maybe we could do something here. Anyway, we didn't have to pay much at all." Scientific publishing. I do want to remind us all that *Stand on Zanzibar* in all of its USA editions over 33 years has sold less copies than a new Janet Dailey or Nora Roberts novel will sell in the first 30 days after its publication. Perspective is important.

————

MIKE: I know, I know — if a publisher knew what made a blockbuster, it's all he'd publish.

But science fiction, while it was born in the pulps, has a half-century history as a book field (no, don't remind me of Wells and Verne and Burroughs; I mean as a clearly-defined category field), and now that a number of books have hit the bestseller list, and many have sold well, and many have sold poorly, there must be some hint of a reason.

For example, how much does a Whelan or Eggleton cover boost your sales? Or doesn't it?

How about raised metallic type? Does it really do any good?

How about ads in *Locus* and *Chronicle*? Do they help sales, or are they counter-productive since the average subscriber knew about your book six months before the publisher advertised it?

We tend to say reviews don't add to sales, except perhaps for pre-pub reviews in *Publisher's Weekly* and possibly *Kirkus Reviews*— but is it true?

Do autographings at bookstores help? Or are they just plain humiliating to 90 percent of the sf writers who consent to them?

Do book club sales introduce you to a huge new audience, or merely under-cut your own paperback sales?

In other words, the field — and its methods of selling — have been evolving for half a century. Can we, after all these tens of thousands of examples, make any definitive statement as to what helps or hurts?

—◦◦◦—

BARRY: "The field and its methods of selling have been evolving for half a century." Hollow, Woolrichian laughter to that one. Yes, our beloved field has evolved (not as much as we'd think, however: need I remind you that "No Woman Born," "That Only a Mother," "Clash by Night," "Thunder and Roses," "Private Eye" were all published more than half a century ago? "Fondly Fahrenheit," *More Than Human, Solar Lottery* almost half a century ago?), but the "methods of selling"? Methods of selling, Mike, haven't evolved in the last half century; they haven't, in fact, evolved significantly in the last one hundred years. (Read George Gissing's *Grub Street* set in late Victorian England.) Get quotes from friends or eminences or both. Put quotes on front cover or back cover of book. Send out review copies. Take out advertisements (sometimes) in publications associated with the subject of the book. Have readings, perhaps autographings. If science fiction, publicize at the major conventions, send copies to dealers. That was what publishers did (or against authors' protests failed to do) in 1950 and that is what they are doing today.

"Well, what are they supposed to do?" you might ask, "Put the book on shelves in supermarkets? Buy advertising time during the Super Bowl?" Well, no, that wouldn't make any kind of economic sense. It does, however, make a kind of practical sense because the thrust of selling books has always been based upon selling them to an audience of book readers ... targeting those who are self-selected. That there is an entirely different way of looking at this— marketing the work to people who are *not* habitual readers or readers of the kind of book at issue — has almost always been dismissed out of hand.

When it hasn't been so dismissed, the technique has worked. There are a number of works marketed outside of customary channels ranging from the romance novels of Janet Dailey to *Fire Island* by Burt Hirschfeld to the novels of Jacqueline Susann which were enormously successful and whose procedure of marketing defied all of the accustomed, inherited non-wisdom of the business.

Indeed, part of the resentment toward Jacqueline Susann and her promoter husband, Irving Mansfield, in the 1970s had to do with the fact that these people were breaking the rules, working against the common wisdom of marketing and succeeding ... and by so doing making fools of the publicity and promotional departments. It wasn't that Susann's books were lousy that lay at the heart of this anger — they weren't all that lousy in my opinion but we can leave that debate for the *Bulletin of the Jacqueline Susann Society*— but that the marketing circumvented, and in so doing proved practically useless, conventional promotional methods. This might have pointed a direction, but publishing, as any reader of *Grub Street* will quickly understand, is a 19th century business still, even after all of the conglomeratization, in the hands of people who want it to stay that way.

So, no, I don't see much of an "evolution" in methods of selling (better termed "methods of not selling"). Part of this for the reasons above, another part rooted in the fact that no one, not publicity directors, not editors, not writers, not critics, not even Larry King or the late Sam Moskowitz knows what sells or why. This is what flummoxed the new conglomerate owners in the 1960s and 1970s; this was not a rational business; it did not respond to accepted wisdom or the kind of methods which the conglomerates had used in other fields. It was unpredictable. It is still unpredictable, even in the age of King, Grisham, Koontz, Nora Roberts, Robert Parker. From where did Harry Potter come? Who hyped Harry Potter? With what expectations were the first two Potter volumes published? If a British-based conglomerate were to conceive a marketing plan for the Rowling novels in the early 90s, exactly how would they have proceeded? (Blurbs from fantasy writers and a few advertisements in *The Magazine of Fantasy & Science Fiction* or *Nickelodeon?*)

Here is my secret: I don't know what works. I don't know why something sells. And with equal bewilderment: I don't know why something doesn't sell. A novel of which only three people have ever heard, *The Movement*, by Norman Garbo, reached Don Wollheim's desk from William Morrow in 1968 when I was doing paperback coverage for that sainted man and I read it. "This is our big fall book," the subsidiary rights flyer said. "Bestseller," I said. "The book of the decade. Takes us inside the student riots. Will sell and sell." Sure it did.

—◦◦◦◦—

MIKE: I persist in believing that some people can tell the difference between a seller and a non-seller right at the outset (though I don't know if it's an instinct or a learned response).

Take Judy-Lynn del Rey. I may not have agreed with her taste very often, but if I were investing my money in a publishing company (and hence more interested in the bottom line than in anything else), she's the editor I'd have wanted. Nothing in this field, before or since, ever sold like her line of books. And yet she didn't turn every book into a bestseller, or even every monthly leader; just enough of them to shake up a science fiction field that had seemed unable to reach the bestseller lists before she arrived on the scene. How did she know to promote this book and not that one?

Take an author, one I've never met — Terry Goodkind. I know he got a six-figure advance for his first novel, and I know it earned out. I must also assume his editor sees dozens of 2000-page fantasy manuscripts every year, manuscripts that couldn't earn a twentieth of Goodkind's advance. How did he know that *this* manuscript, a first novel by an unknown writer, was worth that kind of money?

Or, on the flip side, take mostly-hypothetical author X. He's been around for a decade, won a Nebula, been up for a couple of Hugos, wrote and sold two novels that did okay, not great, not terrible. Now he delivers a thousand-page manuscript showing him at the absolute height of his literary powers, a knock-out, a likely bet for the Nebula and Hugo ballots. And the odds are that, brilliant as it is, he's not going to pick up a six-figure advance or anywhere close to it.

So the book goes out and gets on the ballots, and doesn't earn out its $22,500 or $30,000 advance. Whose fault is it? The author delivered what he promised — an award-quality novel, of greater length than any contract is likely to call for. It was an even better novel than anyone had dared hoped. And it didn't sell as well as it should have.

Do they fire the editor? The art director? The cover artist? The road men?

We know the answer. Of course they don't. It's easier to blame the writer, even though everyone admits that the book was exactly what they'd contracted to buy, that in fact it exceeded what they'd contracted for.

But exactly *what* are they blaming him for, and what can he do on his next book to overcome that jaundiced eye with which his publisher now views his output? Is there an answer, other than to write endless generic series under pseudonyms?

—⌘—

BARRY: I don't think there's an answer. Should there be an answer? Are sales in the millions the only goal? John Simon, not a lovable man, has been writing for 40 years of the folly of corruption; why have a *Man of La Mancha* anyway? Why dumb down *Don Quixote*? Leave *Don Quixote* to the small population which can appreciate the novel as Cervantes wrote it, leave it in peace rather than abomination. This was an argument in a 1974 issue of *New York* magazine. I found him at a New Year's Eve party a month later, the only time I've met him and asked him, "Isn't it better to get a little bit of a masterpiece, even a dumbed-down masterpiece, into the hands of a population which wouldn't otherwise read it? And isn't it possible that a few of them might go from *Man of La Mancha* to the original because they became aware of it?" Simon was having none of it. "Think of chamber music," he said. "It's great art and it's for a small audience and that is intrinsic to its greatness." I don't agree then or now but it is, as the family counselors like to say, a position.

Look: it's a position. Maybe our not-so-imaginary Hugo-and-Nebula-finalist with the masterpiece and the relatively low sales doesn't want it any other way. Maybe the right book done for the right audience, earning necessarily less than the wrong book for the wrong audience, is the way our writer wants to go. Maybe a large royalty statement and a small percentage of returns are not the only desired way. Judy-Lynn del Rey brought to the marketing of science fiction the same mind-set and practices which had in earlier generations been given over to the marketing of toothpaste, of hair-coloring, of the Cadillac deVille. Her methods worked brilliantly. She was brilliant. She wanted to prove that writers like Anne McCaffrey or Stephen Donaldson or Terry Brooks could reach as wide an audience — or wider!— than the brand-name bestselling writers. She proved it with lengths to spare. Late in her career (it shouldn't have been "late"; she was 40 just two years before the stroke that killed her), she said to me with fury, "Malzberg, I want you to know that I didn't destroy science fiction!" This flabbergasted me. "I never said you destroyed it, Judy-Lynn," I said. "In fact, I think you love it. You might have corrupted it a little..." If she had been given another ten years to edit out of the unassailable security she had by then earned, she might have reached that conclusion herself. Not everything had to be on the *New York Times* bestseller list. In fact, there were some very fine writers who might lose their minds and careers out of the misguided attempt to fit themselves into a suit they could not wear.

That's a digression, I suppose, but a digression built upon an assumption which has been the underlay of a good many of these columns and a preponderance of the articles which have appeared in this Bulletin ... the assumption that more is always better. More pages, more sales, more readers, more dragons, more apocalypse, more hard science or soft science or no science or medium science. More more more. But the most concentrated run of the greatest work science fiction has ever known occurred in the mid–1940s *Astounding Science Fiction*, a magazine whose circulation at that time was about a third of the figures Raymond Palmer was achieving for *Amazing Stories*. Shaverism outsold Kuttner, Van Vogt, and Sturgeon by three to one. Where is Shaverism today? (We could also ask where those three writers are, but at least one of them has books in print from the most prestigious Vintage line which is more than Shaver or Palmer could claim.)

"The ethos of this field valorizes sales at any cost," John Clute has written (or something very close to that). I suppose there's no other position a professional journal can take but I'm not really comfortable with that.

And I don't think you are either, Mike.

—∿∿—

MIKE: There's so much to disagree with here I hardly know where to begin — but let me start by briefly noting that John Simon is an elitist snob who has trashed more good plays than any three critics extant. One almost gets the

feeling that if Simon is present when the audience gives a play a standing ova-
tion, he instantly concludes that it's no good.

I'd also argue that *Galaxy* from 1950 to 1955 and *Astounding* from 1939 to
1943 were both superior to the *Astounding* of the mid–1940s.

But the main thing I'd argue is your supposition that fine writers would
rather sell less copies than more. Remember: no one is suggesting that they sell
out, that they write fat eight-book trilogies about elves and swords and magi-
cal quests. They would simply like to know how to increase their sales without debasing their plots and their prose. They look at Heinlein and Herbert
and Asimov and Clarke and Bradbury, and they *know* it can be done, that none
of those authors was catering to the lowest common denominator ... so they
are unquestionably justified in wondering *how* they did it, what the secret might
be.

I submit to you that if you walk up to any Hugo or Nebula winner, and
say: "Would you like to receive and earn out a trio of million-dollar advances
for your next three books without having to change anything about your
approach or style?," the only ones who would say "No" are probably already
wearing nifty little jackets with wraparound sleeves.

I suppose what I'd really like is to resurrect Judy-Lynn del Rey for a decade,
give her a dozen brilliant writers who have yet to hit, or even approach, the
bestseller list, and turn her loose. And yet, while her methods worked better
than anyone else's, they weren't unique, and they weren't original, and they
weren't copy-protected, so isn't it about time someone picked up the torch?

Or are we wrong, and was that guy in Levy's warehouse right all those
many years ago? Is the package everything, or can the writer somehow make a
difference?

"Sigh"—I still don't know. And, to paraphrase the pundits of the ad biz,
where only 20 percent of what they do is effective but nobody knows *which* 20
percent and hence they have to work like hell at all aspects of it, until we know
for a fact that *all* that counts is the packaging and the hype, we'd probably better keep writing the best books we can. You never know...

5 Anthologies

MIKE: I seem to find myself back in the anthology business again this year, after a half-decade hiatus. I'm not quite sure how it happened. I know that in the early 1990s I edited more than 20 of them in something less than four years. Then—although a 3-year lag time on a pair of them would lead you to think otherwise, I was out of it for six years. And now, as I write these words, I'm editing four original anthologies.

And hearing screams of "Unfair!" from quite a few writers.

Why?

Because my anthologies are by invitation only.

Still why?

Because there's a difference between charity, which is the way I view my editing gigs, and poverty, which is the way I (and my creditors) would view them if I edited open anthologies.

Maybe it's time to discuss just what goes into putting an anthology together, and just how much money it costs the editor to pursue anthologies rather than more lucrative work (which includes writing novels, writing short stories, writing screenplays, writing articles, writing comic books, in fact writing just about anything but poetry).

Let's take a good, hard, honest look at it.

Let's say an anthology I'm editing pays a $7,000 advance, which is about par for the course for original anthologies these days. (Yes, I've written for some that pay far more, and edited a couple which ditto, but they are the exceptions, not the rule.)

Let's say I decide to pay 6 cents a word, which again is pretty much the average. I've paid more on a few occasions; only once—a current one with all kinds of complications—have I paid less.

Let's further say that the contract calls for 100,000 words worth of stories, not including all the editorial introductions.

And let's say that every writer delivers exactly the length I ask for, that none of them come in too long (which, I might add, has never happened; somebody, or usually a group of somebodies, *always* come in too long.)

Okay. I must pay out $6,000. That leaves $1,000 for the editor. Except that it doesn't. *I* don't sell the anthologies; Marty Greenberg does. Marty is the man behind more than 90 percent of the anthologies that get sold in this field, even when his name doesn't appear anywhere in the book. It's his specialty, he's damned good at it, and for his partner in a project there is an extra advantage: you get half the money up front and half on delivery, but your authors want to be paid *now*. Assume that you're spending more than half the advance on stories—and you always are—and having Marty handle the money and paperwork means you don't have to dig into your own pocket to pay for stories and then wait until they're all in to recoup your expenses from the publisher.

Back to number-crunching. If everyone delivers the right length, Marty and I will make $500 each.

It takes about two weeks of my time to do this—and that's dealing with writers who hopefully don't require extensive revisions. Two weeks for $500.

If I can't make at least four times that much writing, I'm in the wrong business.

So I'm already taking a huge loss by editing an invitation-only anthology.

If it was an open anthology, I would do all that *plus* read maybe 300 to 600 slush stories, most of them terrible beyond imagining, for that same $500. At that point, it gives new meaning to the words "economically counter-productive." And *that* is the reason almost all anthologies are by invitation only.

(Now, this doesn't necessarily mean they're closed to newcomers. Over the course of more than 25 anthologies, including the ones I'm currently editing, I have averaged four or five new writers in each. Which helps explain why I take such a financial hit to edit anthologies: my proudest achievement as an anthology editor wasn't making a couple of Hugo ballots as Best Editor, or putting seven stories [including a winner] on the Hugo ballot; it was putting eight beginners [including a winner] on the Campbell Ballot for Best New Writer.)

You've edited 15 or 20 anthologies yourself. Are your financial findings different than mine? And have you any insights you'd like to share with an outraged public that knows beyond any shadow of a doubt that you edit by invitation-only for the sole purpose of excluding them?

—*∿∿*—

BARRY: You're talking of original anthologies, of course. I've co-edited just two of those: *Final Stage* with Edward L. Ferman and *Graven Images*, also with him; these were invitation-only anthologies and the first of them was truly problematic. All of the others have been reprints (although my co-editors and I did put an original in *Arena*, another one in *Dark Sins, Dark Dreams*). So the problems you've incurred in the original anthology are not problems which I was forced to encounter other than on those two occasions, both more than a quarter of a century ago.

Fred Pohl once wrote—a long time ago—that anthologies were a misunderstood pursuit: they were actually quite easy to conceive and not particularly hard to put together; they were, however, quite difficult to sell ... for every anthology idea or proposal which he had placed, there were several multiples of that which he had not been able to sell. Pohl edited the *Star* original anthology series, of course, eight or nine volumes through the 1950s, the others were all reprints. He was a prolific anthologist and I think I know exactly what he means.

The economics of the original anthology, as you point out, are usually ridiculous ... the anthologist's share rarely recompenses the time, at least not at the level that one's own work does. There are, as always, exceptions, there have been some original anthologies which have been startlingly remunerative for all concerned — Greenberg's Tolkien tribute, *After the King* in the early 1990s, of course, and Robert Silverberg's first *Legends* anthology of original series fantasy stories (a sequel has been announced and is well in progress). But these are atypical and the more customary economics of the original anthology are relatively low; they are even lower if the anthology — like the old *Orbit* or *New Dimensions* or *Nova* series — are indeed open submissions. Screening and selection if one is being fair take a great deal of time. Where this is leading, I suppose, is toward the statement that for the functioning fiction writer, anthologies are no career, should not be a career ... they have their purposes and audience and they can be fun, sometimes relatively a great deal of fun to edit. But no one — not Groff Conklin who was an editor at Collier Books for decades, not Martin H. Greenberg who was a full Professor of Political Science at the University of Wisconsin/Green Bay — can make a career or a living from these things. Judith Merril might have been the only anthologist to have made a try at self-sustentation from anthologies alone but she lived frugally and by 1968, after a dozen years of her *Year's Best* she had had more than enough.

—————

MIKE: Okay, we seem agreed upon that. Hell, everyone who's ever edited an original anthology must be agreed upon it.

So let's get on to the next question: why must every damned anthology these days be based on a theme, some of them incredibly silly? I think I put out some pretty good anthologies, a lot of the stories won or were nominated for awards, still more have been reprinted here and abroad — but one was entirely about Kennedys, and another about dinosaurs, and a third about Sherlock Holmes, and a fourth about witches, and so on. And I confess that the whole time I was editing them, I was envying Robert Silverberg and Terry Carr and Damon Knight and Fred Pohl, who got to exercise a little more editorial taste and judgment.

You see, when you invite someone to, say, *Alternate Secretariats*, you are telling them to write a science fiction or fantasy story about a precise subject — in this hypothesis, the racehorse Secretariat. It is a story that would never have been written had you not assigned it. If you bounce eight or ten of them, they'll of course be sent to the magazines—and how many Secretariat stories do you think Gardner Dozois or Stan Schmidt are likely to buy?

So I think the invitation-only editor has a moral obligation *not* to reject a story he assigns, a story that otherwise would remain unwritten. You can (and should) send the writer back to make it better if it's not up to par, but in the end you either buy a not-quite-right story and bury it in the middle of the book (easier to do with a 25-story anthology than a six-story magazine), or you pay a kill fee.

But it sure would have been nice to see the best each writer had to offer on *any* subject. Oh, it would still be an invite-only anthology, but without a theme. I'd invite 20 or 30 writers and say, "Let me have a look at your best work" (which is, in essence, what the magazine editors say to the contributors, albeit silently), and if I didn't like it, why, I could return it with no moral obligation to buy it.

Do you know how long it's been since such an anthology appeared? The four editors I named above didn't just do it once; they each edited a series of them. How did we get from *New Dimensions* and *Orbit* to *Alternate Secretariats*?

——————

BARRY: I don't know exactly how we got from *Orbit* and *New Dimensions* to *Alternate Cat Stories* or *Future Impotence*. The theme anthology did not overtake the market until the 1970s. I suppose that we can thank Roger Elwood for that (and for so much else). But you can see the theme anthology foreshadowed early; Groff Conklin's famous first three anthologies—*Best of Science Fiction, Treasury of Science Fiction, Big Book of Science Fiction*—were general anthologies but shortly thereafter *Invaders from Earth* and *Possible Worlds of Science Fiction* followed and *Great Stories by Scientists* and all the rest of them. William Tenn's *Children of Wonder* was published in the early 1950s. I think that publishers—particularly those who were not familiar with science fiction, who were just entering the field —were more comfortable with theme anthologies, packaging was easier, targeting of the audience. Perhaps readers were more comfortable as well ... if you wanted to read about cats, then a theme anthology brooked no surprises. (Surprise, as James Blish pointed out in *The Issue at Hand* almost fifty years ago, is among the lesser emotions the science fiction reader wants ... the science fiction reader in the main wants her thrills pre-packaged and of the stimulus-response variety.) General anthologies—even best-of-the-year compilations—also tended to vary widely in the quality of their contents in a way that theme anthologies did not; or at least publishers so rationalized.

But the problem with theme anthologies is that the effect of stories can be lost. If—for instance —the surprise ending of a story hinges upon the fact that the protagonist is secretly a cat, the impact of that surprise will be considerably lessened if it appears—as Stephen Vincent Benét's *The King of the Cats* probably has appeared—in an anthology of stories about felines.

Or, as Dave Langford, put it, and even more eloquently, consider the plight of the editor of an anthology called *Great Vampire Stories in Which the Lead's True Love Turns Out to Be a Vampire* rereading a story she is about to include in the work and thinking, "Somehow the ending here doesn't have quite the impact it had on me when I read it years ago in *Infinity Science Fiction*." The mere appearance of a story in a science fiction magazine assures that the denouement will be linked to something other than contemporary realism. (This for me destroyed the power of Reginald Bretnor's "The Doorstop," a story of alien intervention which appeared first in *Astounding* in 1956; if it had been first published in *Harper's* the ending would have been unexpected and far more powerful.) And the appearance of a surprise-ending cat story in an anthology of cat stories wholly undercuts not only the ending but the work itself.

On the other hand, theme anthologies are comfortable to read, certainly more comfortable to edit and work against precisely that sense of wonder which Blish felt so overrated among readers and writers of the genre. There were a lot of original series anthologies in the 1970s—*Orbit, Quark, New Dimensions, Universe, Chrysalis*—so many that most readers felt that they would utterly displace the magazine; then suddenly in the 1980s there were almost none at all. The original, unthemed anthology is never a series work now and these one-shots have not been successful. (The fantasy original anthology on the other hand has yielded at least one bestseller, Silverberg's *Legends* and one near-bestseller, Martin Greenberg's Tolkien tribute, *After the King*.)

Stories rejected by the original themed anthologies are difficult to place, yes. Editing *Amazing/Fantastic* in 1968 I was gifted by a Fritz Leiber story which Sam Moskowitz had foolishly rejected for his original anthology *The Man Who Was Poe*—but that was Fritz Leiber ... and his saver sale was for all of two cents a word.

———❦———

MIKE: I'd like to briefly address a point that writers ought to consider before blindly contributing to any anthology that asks.

You mentioned the *Legends* and *After the King* anthologies. There was another that made a mint, and that was the *Batman* anthology that came out to coincide with the release of the first Michael Keaton *Batman* movie. I was in *After the King* and I was in *Batman*, and while *After the King* still delivers a royalty check every six months come hell or high water and I haven't seen a cent from *Batman* in about a decade, I think I probably made more money per word from the *Batman* anthology. Not up front, but when you added in the royalties, it came to something better than $3.00 a word before the public moved on to the next movie anthology/adaptation. (Never saw a penny's worth of royalties from the *Joker* or *Superman* anthologies. Go figure.)

So what's wrong with that? Nothing, and I have no regrets about writing for the *Batman* book.

But when it came time to put together a collection of my short fiction for which not only that story and stories I did for the *Joker* and *Superman* anthologies would have been perfect fits, I ran into a certain voracious hunger on the part of the copyright holders—DC Comics and the book publishers—who insisted that *I* pay *them* for the right to reprint my stories.

Now, they had every legal right to request that (we'll argue about moral rights some other time), but no one else whose copyrighted characters I had used (with permission, of course) from the Conan Doyle estate to the Chester Gould estate had ever tried to extort money from me for reprinting my stories. I refused to pay, and to this day the stories have never been resold, though my average story gets reprinted/resold from five to eight times here and abroad.

So when writing for sharecrop or shared-world anthologies, you might inquire on the front end what their position is on reselling your story.

Now, before we get too far along, I'd like to talk about the anthologies I most enjoy editing (and reading, too, for that matter)—and those are the reprint anthologies.

As an editor, I feel (and I'm sure the writers agree) somewhat constricted by theme anthologies—but even more to the point, when I'm editing a theme anthology, I have absolutely no idea what the stories will read like until they're delivered. At that point, I may suggest that Author A tweak her ending a bit, and Author B lose the info dump, and so on ... but they are essentially the stories that the authors wanted to tell, and only hopefully the stories the editor wanted to read.

But a reprint anthology ... ah, that's a whole different ball game. I am in essence saying to the audience: "I have been a devout reader in this field for half a century, and a professional author/editor for a third of a century. In that time, I have come across a handful of truly memorable stories that I want to share with you, stories you probably missed because demographics say I was writing this stuff before your father met your mother and I may well have been reading it just about the time your grandfather met your grandmother. No matter how well-read you are, you can't possibly have read *all* these masterpieces, and now here they are, assembled with love from a reader and writer who wants to share them with you, and who envies you the thrill of reading them for the very first time."

Name the great anthologies ... and what you get are the early *Astounding* and *F&SF* and *Galaxy* anthologies, and the Groff Conklin and Healy & McComas anthologies. No Alternate this or Children of that. Just compilations of great stories.

Of all the two-dozen-plus anthologies I have edited, only five have been reprints. And two of those five are my two very favorite anthologies for the very reasons I mentioned.

I can't be the only editor who feels this way — and as a reader, I can't be the only one who loves to find truly brilliant stories I've missed along the way.

And certainly a reprint anthology — even a themed one — is far less expensive to put together than an original anthology, and will invariably have bigger names to put on the cover...

...so why are they so goddamned hard to sell?

—◦◦◦—

BARRY: They are so goddamned hard to sell for several reasons: one is that anybody conversant with science fiction can compile a good anthology; not everybody conversant with science fiction can write a good novel. There are very few people alive who can write a novel at the level of a Fred Pohl, but there are several thousand who could assemble an anthology just about as good. (Of course Fred Pohl's anthologies will sell better ... he has far more name value and recognition. But the quality of the book will not in any way vary in the way that the quality of a Fred Pohl novel and the quality of a novel by science fiction fan and scholar X are likely to vary.)

The competition is extraordinary for this reason and, in fact, it is for this reason that most reprint anthologies — not all of them, but a larger proportion than ever — are edited by writers of the first rank, who have modest fame. And of course editing a reprint anthology is easier than writing a novel. It's even easier, most of the time, than writing a short story.

"Anything is better than writing," Jimmy Breslin once said when asked why he was running a hopeless race in 1969 for president of City Council. So editors wallow in anthology proposals, are sunk in them and of necessity gravitate toward the big name writers or the brand-name anthologists who they know will deliver good work with a minimum of difficulty. But even the brand-name anthologists like yourself are competing with the other brand-names; even famous writers like yourself are competing with the other famous writers.

(An anecdote in that regard: at the very beginning of his career as an anthologist, around 1972, Marty Greenberg and his then collaborator, Joseph Olander, submitted a proposal and a proposed table of contents to Sharon Jarvis, the science fiction editor at Doubleday. Sharon told me what her response had been: "You people have great ideas but I can't sell this. Find a big-name writer to be the third anthologist and I probably can get you a contract.")

And then of course is the indisputable fact that anthologies do not sell as well as novels. Looking at the process of assembling a list, an experienced mass-market editor knows that a novel will sell perhaps twice as many copies as an anthology. Why publish the anthology at all? (This was Judy-Lynn del Rey's theory of mass market publishing for the early years of her career; it was close to inflexible and it changed everything. Later on, as she became more secure, she relented a little.) Of course anthologies usually require slightly lower advances and are more dependable in their delivery than novels but not really enough to offset the balance.

And finally there is the simple and perhaps most salient of all reasons: after 55 years of furious anthologization in science fiction, beginning with Healy-McComas *Adventures in Time and Space* and Conklin's *The Best of Science Fiction* in 1946, after thousands of anthologies, the reservoir has been pretty well drained. There are only so many times one can reprint "The Cold Equations," "That Only a Mother," "The Tunnel Under the World" and on and on, and indeed these stories have been reprinted within the borders of the field alone 15–20 times over those 55 years. The stock of masterpieces has long since been culled, and the near-masterpieces and the could-have-been masterpieces. A contemporary reprint anthologist is faced with a Hobson's Choice: a) recycle the familiar, b) seek the non-familiar while understanding that there are pretty good reasons for this. There are very few buried masterpieces out there now. In 1985, Greenberg, Piers Anthony and I compiled our Avon anthology, *Uncollected Stars*, and among some pretty good stories was Kuttner's "Time Enough" but it's now 17 years later. Yes, of course, stories are coming out all the time, it's an ongoing, not a static, field, and 1200 new short stories (according to one count) are being published every year. Some of them deserve anthologization, many of them do not, and the factor of recency works against them.

I wish the damned things weren't so hard to sell but as Damon Knight once wrote more about writing altogether, "If it were easy, everyone would do it and you and I couldn't make a living." Got a good gimmick? *Great Time Machine Stories About Cat-Vampires*?

—◆◆◆—

MIKE: I like your Sharon Jarvis story — and for the one or two readers who don't know how it ended, Marty found a pro named Asimov. And found him maybe 100 more times over the years as he established himself in the anthology market.

I'd take issue with a couple of your points, though. One is that the average anthology gets half the advance of the average novel. Given — and I don't debate it for an instant — that an anthologist has to be a brand name to sell, I'd say that the average science fiction anthology gets an advance of between a quarter and maybe a twentieth of the editor's novel advance. (We're not talking *Legends* or *After the King* or, turning back the clock a bit, one of the *Dangerous Visions* books here, but rather the *typical* anthology.) And, at between 5 percent and 25 percent of the editor's novel advance, I don't see that publishing an anthology constitutes that great a gamble. In fact, all credit to the ladies at DAW Books, who publish an anthology every month and don't seem headed to the poorhouse because of it.

I do agree that the stockpile of unmined classics is getting awfully small — but here is where the theme anthology notion actually becomes useful and meaningful. When I edited *Shaggy B.E.M. Stories*, for example, a reprint anthology of science fiction parodies, I mined not only the prozines but also the fanzines and found some wonderful stories by fans who later became famous writers, including a kid named "Ego" Clarke who was knighted a couple of years ago.

I would further submit that some of the reprint anthologies I've done (and others as well; I can only speak authoritatively for myself) required such a specialized knowledge, or such special access, that *not* everyone could have done them. The parodies anthology and the recursive sf anthology, to name just a pair.

Back to the main point. The thing we always must remember is that you and I have about a century's worth of reading science fiction between us, so yes, it's pretty hard to come up with a brilliant story from history's dustbin that we're not acquainted with. But today's average science fiction reader is under 30 years old, probably under 25, and is hardly as voracious a reader as you and I were and are. So most of the stories we know — this one that was anthologized a mere 17 years ago (when our hypothetical reader wasn't yet ten years old), and that one that we got tired of when X and Y and Z all anthologized it during a 5-year period back in the 1970s — these are mostly unknown to those young men and women who form the bulk of our readership. Reprint the first *Galaxy* or *F&SF* anthology and you and I and most of the people we associate with will roll our eyes and say, "Good ghod, not again!" — but I'd wager that 90 percent of the contents of each would be brand-new to 90 percent of the people who keep publishers in business.

There's one last thing I want to address, and that goes back to the impetus for this discussion: the feeling, on the part of newcomers and unknowns, that all invitation-only anthologies are closed to them.

Not so. I bought more than 40 first stories in a four-year period in the early 1990s, as well as a fair batch of second and third stories. I've bought a batch more for the anthologies I'm editing right now. Seven of "my" discoveries made the Campbell ballot for Best New Writer — and you can't do that if you're not buying from new writers.

It's really not difficult to find new writers. Let it be known that you're even considering editing an anthology, or that you've edited one in the past and may possibly edit another in the future, and you'll be whelmed over with samples of their writing whether you want them or not. Teach Clarion or another of the better workshops, and you'll find quite a few promising new writers. Talk to other pros who run workshops and you'll get still more newcomers recommended to you. Or read some promising debut stories, and contact the authors and ask for more of their work; I've never come across one who said no.

I just wanted to note for the record, before we cut this off, that an invitation-only anthology is not a clubby way of excluding newcomers, but rather a way — to my way of thinking, the *only* way — of making the editing of the book an act of charity rather than economic insanity.

6 Conventions

MIKE: There's some debate about whether the first convention was the 1939 Worldcon, or whether it occurred a year earlier when Don Wollheim, Cyril Kornbluth and a few other New York fans took a train to Philadelphia to meet a handful of Philly fans. (The total number of fans that got together came to 12, but if you read the fannish history books, most of them insist that it was a convention and pre-dates the Worldcon.)

Worldcon wasn't exceptionally prepossessing at the outset. NYCon I drew 200 attendees in 1939. You have to move ahead all the way to Portland in 1950 to find a larger attendance, and it fell below 200 again in 1951, which is a roundabout way of suggesting that not a lot business got done at the early conventions for the simple reason that hardly anyone showed up at them.

That is demonstrably not the case today. Worldcons tend to range from 4,500 to 9,000 attendees; even the foreign ones regularly top 3,000. World Fantasy Convention draws almost as many pros, editors and publishers as Worldcon, just a lot less fans. The Nebula Weekend usually draws a few hundred people who are intimately involved in the field. Conventions all around the country — Boskone, Westercon, Windycon, Balticon, Lunacon, and others — regularly top 1,000 attendees.

Obviously a lot of business gets done at conventions. But there are a lot of writers who hardly ever attend, and they still make a living. So there are clearly two sides to the issue.

Now, it just so happens that I've attended more than 30 Worldcons, and perhaps 150 other conventions. You have attended one of the last 19 worldcons, and rarely attend conventions more than a couple of hundred miles from your home, on those infrequent occasions that you attend them at all.

I make no secret of the fact that I try to line up the following year's business at Worldcon. You clearly have done no business at at least 18 of the last 19 Worldcons. As a writer and anthology editor, I've assigned, bought and sold dozens, perhaps hundreds, of stories at smaller cons. I rather suspect you haven't.

Okay, we each hold diametrically opposite positions, we've each been work-

ing in the field for more than a third of a century, and neither of us has filed
for bankruptcy yet, so it might be interesting to compare and contrast our
views on this subject.

Be my guest.

—◦◦◦—

BARRY: You're right. I've attended one World Convention in the last 19
years (Philadelphia 2001) and a total of four, one of which (New York 1967)
might be called a Special Guest & Flee attendance. I met Judith Merril and Isaac
Asimov, watched a legendary sf pro whose name I shall suppress invite 10 people to dine with him and then run out on the bill, and generally had a wonderful time for two hours. Kept me away from the Worldcon until Boston in 1980,
that did. (I know that your own thoughts on the 1967 World Convention are
even less affectionate than mine.)

Hasn't seemed to hurt me in any professional sense, this non-attendance.
On the other hand you never miss that which you never see and it was at that
1980 Noreascon that I sold *Engines of the Night*; in Baltimore at 1983 I was able
to bridge the gap with Judy-Lynn del Rey and sold her *The Remaking of Sig-
mund Freud* a month later. (I sold nothing in Philadelphia but then I wasn't
trying.) My advice to every nascent science fiction and fantasy writer for the
last thirty years has been "Get to the World Convention if it is anywhere in your
neighborhood or at all financially practicable." This provides the quickest access
to editors, to writers at all stages of development and (through the panels) to
some real sense of the market. I'd call the experience irreplaceable. I was able
to make my way around and about the World Convention (or even local Conventions; it was Lunacon in the spring every year between 1972 and 1984 and
that was about it) but I lived in or near New York, still do, was able to connect
with the editors who could help me, had a strong sense of the market. (Worked
at Scott Meredith for that matter, the most important factor of all.) If I had not
been in the Metropolitan area I don't think I could have done whatever I managed without regularly attending at least two of the major conventions a year —
the Worldcon and one of the major regionals like Northwestcon, Balticon,
Boskone, etc. Part of that True Unwritten History of Science Fiction is how
much of it has been sold through direct contact between writers and editors
(who were likely to switch roles or occupy both roles often enough). More than
half of it, I would guess.

So in the area of career advancement that is my opinion. That leaves out
(and probably all for the best) the social advantages or disadvantages of convention attendance: the friendships, the hatreds, the late-night parties, the
early-day parties, the feuds, the passion, the sex! More of all of this per capita
than one would find at a Democratic National Convention and you'll find plenty
of it there. (And not nearly as much mean-spiritedness and a much more interesting program.) But if you're thinking of attending the conventions only for

the fun of it, career or business considerations being of no account, then I would suggest that there is as much fun available elsewhere although not more talk of science fiction.

In relation to conventions I find myself eager to go and — after about six hours — eager to leave. Mr. Bad News and Mr. Good News, a package deal "I'm always early at the dinner party but then again I'm among the earliest to go." You've tried nobly for a long time to show me how to (apart from all professional considerations) enjoy the conventions; I am a singularly poor, if not ungrateful, student.

—*ᴗᴗ*—

MIKE: Well, as the advocate of doing business at conventions, I suppose the first thing I should do is explain which conventions (and why), and a couple of ground rules for going about it.

There are three major conventions that most of the editors and publishers attend: Worldcon, World Fantasy Con, and Nebula Weekend. I know a lot of pros prefer the smaller, more intimate atmosphere of the latter two (I disagree for esoteric reasons that have nothing to do with this dialogue), but for doing business, there's simply no comparison: Worldcon is by far the best venue.

For one thing, it's much the longest. Worldcon is officially five days — Thursday through Labor Day (or, overseas, Wednesday through Sunday). But these days, almost everyone gets there on Wednesday, and probably a third to half the attendees are there by Tuesday night, and stay until the Tuesday after Labor Day. For the pro who is not in great demand, who isn't fighting editors off with a stick but actually would like to sit down and talk to some editors, that gives him a whole week to make contact. World Fantasy is three days, four at the outside, and Nebula weekend is really just two if it's in New York (those hotel rates!), three elsewhere.

Second, Worldcon is huge. It draws thousands. World Fantasy tries to limit attendance to 750, and Nebula weekend rarely draws as many as 350. Furthermore, Worldcon has parties. *Lots* of parties. Maybe 75 of them going on simultaneously Friday, Saturday, and Sunday nights.

Why is that a good thing? Simple. It spreads people out, and it spreads editors out. The problem with World Fantasy Con is that of those 750 attendees maybe 500 or so are professionals: writers, editors, artists, publishers — about the same total that you'll find outnumbered 10 to 1 at Worldcon. But since there are hardly any fans at World Fantasy (and none at the Nebulas), there aren't 75 or 50 or 25 parties a night. There are one or two, given by publishers. That means you've got 300 to 500 hungry writers (no, not for food) crowded into a suite with a handful of editors and barely enough room to inhale and exhale. Have you ever tried to have a private conversation under such circumstances, or talk a little business without dozens of competitors being able to overhear, join in, and try to steal your precious Audience of One?

So I think its size and its duration both favor Worldcon for doing business.

There are other considerations, as well. You don't really want to sit down in the lobby or coffee shop of the convention hotel to discuss business with an editor. It's too public, too accessible. Every time you start to deal, fans will walk up and interrupt to ask you for an autograph, or pros will come up and strike up a conversation with your editor, which precludes her doing business with you. So the trick is to get the editor off the premises, preferably for a meal. Now, most editors are reluctant to leave the hotel for a couple of hours during a 48-hour Nebula weekend, or even a 72-hour World Fantasy weekend ... but a few hours out of a week-long Worldcon? Most of them (and most of us) are thrilled to get away for a little while.

Other advantages? Well, I defy you to find any convention room that costs as much as a room in midtown Manhattan, where you'll likely stay if you go to New York to visit editors. And very few convention meals cost what a Manhattan meal will cost if you're not being treated by an editor (and how many of them are available to treat for breakfast or dinner?).

And still more. If you're dealing with the small presses for reprints, collections, non-fiction, or whatever, you'll never find as many small press editors and publishers assembled anywhere else as at Worldcon and World Fantasy Con (in that order).

And more again. The odds are about 20-to-1 that your agent (assuming you have one) will be at Worldcon ... so if a deal is offered, it can be negotiated right there on the spot, before the editor or publisher has time to go home and have second thoughts. (Yes, most agents will be at World Fantasy and the Nebulas as well, but it's almost impossible to pitch a project, get it accepted, and have an agent negotiate it, all in 48 or 72 hours.)

And yet more. The only time I've seen foreign editors and agents in any number is at Worldcon. There's no better time or less expensive way to meet them.

And another thing. You'll find more foreign fans—and translators—at Worldcon than anywhere else. And frequently they are the ones who will petition (well, nothing as formal as that; substitute "nag") a publisher in their country to buy the rights to your books. I'd guess that translators are responsible for almost as many foreign sales as editors. Worldcon is the perfect place to meet and befriend them at your leisure.

At Worldcon you're not trying to cram everything into two or three days, and just being able to sit down and visit with people you want to do business with is a proper prelude to actually doing the business. You're not as rushed, things aren't as frantic, you have time for some social amenities, and believe it or not, social amenities are noted, appreciated, and remembered.

I think the only other cons I'd recommend for trying to do business (unless, of course, you know a certain editor is going to show up at Podunkcon because his mother lives there, or some such thing) would be Boskone and Lunacon. There are bigger cons, but those seem to be the two regional conventions (the three I mentioned before are all national or international) that draw at least a handful of editors and publishers.

So how about it? On those rare occasions that you actually show up at Worldcon or the Nebulas, do you just schmooze with friends or do you actually try to do a little business? Or is one of the reasons we're on opposite sides of the fence here the fact that you work in Manhattan and can see editors whenever you want, and I live a thousand miles away in Cincinnati?

—⟨∿∿∿⟩—

BARRY: Norwescon in Seattle used to draw a huge crowd of New York editors and the annual Philcon has in my time always done the same, so Lunacon and Boskone hardly have the sub–Worldcon monopoly on doing business. Balticon and Discon similarly are both close enough to and far away from New York to make them provocative and I would think that some business gets done there. (I have no firsthand experience; I've never been to either.) And of course the Massachusetts Readercon in July attracts about 400 attendees and 20–30 editors, not a bad ratio, and with programming centered on so-called sercon matters it is possible to live the illusion for a little while that Science Fiction Rules The World. (Rumsfeld and Spielberg probably feel that way all the time.)

My own experience with conventions is obviously atypical of most professional writers and hardly functions as a working model. I don't particularly like them, I don't do much business there (above I mentioned sales initiated at the Boston and Baltimore World Conventions but these constitute the only business or pre-business I have ever contracted at any Convention) and I find myself becoming uncomfortable early and often.

The wonderful and terrible enclosure of the convention, at least the science fiction convention, is that it destroys time. I have written of this. By staying at one fixed point — hotel bar or lobby, Con Suite or the largest panel room — one may live the amalgamation of one's life, a sudden and terrible (and occasionally stricken) phenomenon. Past this fixed point swirls last year's editor and the enemies of one's youth, various centers of sexual yearning or more than yearning, some from the deep past, some from the not-so-deep past, all of them gathering, making intersection. In the old days one could see three or four of one's wives zooming in perspective like aspects of the Doppler Effect. When science fiction was a compact field it was possible in the hermetic world of the convention to indeed live that synchronicity of past, present and future which has made science fiction such a wonderful outlet for some of us.

This phenomenon of collapsed time may have very little to do with the making of business and then again it may have a great deal; certainly it intensifies the editorial process. Novel and anthology proposals can be floated through three or six markets in a night. (Other processes may also be intensified and accelerated but this is a very solemn dialogue for a solemn and business-oriented audience and there is no need to verge into that area.) Careers can bloom in a weekend. Multi-book contracts can explode like time-delayed photographs of flowers blooming. Everything happens more quickly at conventions; even slow is quick in those forests of the night.

Apart from business, conventions can be addictive. Professional careers which have bloomed there can also be dissipated or destroyed. I know that you spend most of your free time at conventions being a fan but you are no less a pro for all of that. Tell some stories, Mike. Discuss X, Y and Z. Explain how Z (a wonderful, paradigmatic example) could be said to have Lost It At Conventions as definitively as Pauline Kael Lost It At The Movies.

We're all waiting.

—◦◦◦—

MIKE: Sorry. I do anecdotes as a toastmaster, not as half of a dialogue.

Quick update for you: Norwescon doesn't draw the New York editors any more. Neither does Balticon—certainly not in enough quantity to justify flying in to schmooze with them, anyway. As for Disclave (which is the con you meant; Discon was the name for the 1963 and 1974 Worldcons), I don't think it even exists any more; I know they had to cancel it after that incident where some bondage freaks—not fans, though the hotel refused to acknowledge that fact—hung a (willing) girl from a sprinkler nozzle, after which the pipe burst inside the ceiling and flooded out a couple of floors before they could get to it. (Okay, you got an anecdote out of me after all.)

I'm sure all the tales of sex and ex-wives and such are fascinating, and Lord knows plenty of writers mention such things in their memoirs, some *ad nauseam*, but they really don't have much to do with the subject at hand, which is: are conventions useful in the pursuit of your profession?

Well, so far I've pretty much used the standard definition of editors—someone who edits a line of books or a magazine for a particular publisher—but there is another type of editor you'll find at conventions, and that is the freelance anthology editor. He often looks just like you or me. In fact, he occasionally *is* you or me.

I think just being present and alive will result in an occasional sale. If you're an editor who is putting together an anthology, there are a couple of hundred qualified pros to choose from — and it's a lot easier to see one you know at a con and invite him than to go home, hunt up addresses, write letters of invitation, discuss money and deadlines, and wait for a reply. (No, it's not difficult at all; it's just not as easy as inviting someone face-to-face — someone who might have slipped your mind until you encounter him at a con. And of course you encounter more writers— and, the flip side of the coin, more editors— at a Worldcon than anywhere else.)

As an editor, I've probably assigned over 200 stories at conventions. Mostly at Worldcons since that's where most of the writers are, but also at World Fantasy Con, Nebula weekend, Rivercon, Tropicon, Lunacon, Windycon, Armadillocon, and a handful others, including the one I most recently attended two months ago in San Diego.

Okay, off with one hat, on with the other. I just checked my records, and found that in the past decade, I have received 27 short fiction assignments at cons (mostly Worldcons, for all the reasons already mentioned), have sold two regular columns at cons, and have sold eight articles at cons. I won't count books, because while I certainly pitch and discuss books at cons, and I'd guess that 90 percent of my book sales are initiated at cons, I've never officially concluded a mass market book deal at a con, since at some vital point my agent steps in and does the negotiating. (Although I *have* concluded a trio of small-press deals, one at a Windycon, two at Worldcons.)

Conventions are the very best places for new writers to make contact with editors, to put themselves forward, to make a lasting (and hopefully favorable) impression. And again on the flip side, cons are equally good places for anthology editors to meet new writers, sound them out, and see which of them they'd most like to work with.

So I think I'll ask again: do you think you avoid all this at least partially because you work in Manhattan and see too damned much of the editors without going afield to conventions to see them yet again? Or would you prefer to destroy my premises with a brilliant and incisive piece of logic?

———

BARRY: "Brilliant and incisive logic" is beyond me, at least in relation to conventions.

Commentary, I guess, is not. For instance, the Lunacon, held in midtown New York City for all of its decades, moved to the Sheraton at Hasbrouck Heights, New Jersey, sometime around 1980 and was there for five or six years. Then, suddenly, it wasn't there any more; it moved to Rye, New York, where it has now been for almost a couple of decades. The reason for the sudden transfer to Westchester had to do with the energetic couple who one of the hotel staff found enthusiastically collaborating in a stairwell ... their shrieks of satisfied collaboration and general athleticism permeated the stairwell and the ears of other cleaning staff who had looked in on the party. Sheraton's management, for reasons I cannot possibly discern, became rather stuffy about the event and ordered the Lunacon out.

And then of course there were the series of fire alarms at a huge Boskone sometime in the 1980s (attendance at this regional had leapt to an almost uncontrollable three or four thousand) which emptied rooms, put people in corridors and outside the premises not once but three or four times on one February night, leading the Boskone to downscale suddenly and severely. Attendance figures have never gotten to that level again which all seem to agree is a damned good thing. (The identity of the alarmists was of course never deduced but as always the convention staff blamed it on other guests. You know those riotous hardware and banking people, they'll do it everywhere.)

So I have a couple of anecdotes too although in neither case first hand. (Hasbrouck Heights' Sheraton was very much in my neighborhood but I was staying out of stairwells then and for the immediate future.) In the old days which aren't so very old at all conventions were far more raucous than they are now. "The only reason I go to these things," the author of a dozen science fiction novels and at least as many short stories said to me in the early 1980s, "is for the sexual stuff." (I am euphemizing what he said; I am sure that no one will mind.) While the science fiction convention even in its long-departed heyday could never compete with the MLA or state police conventions for sheer expanse of unprintability, it certainly had its remarkable aspects. I could add some more secondhand information but I will not. This is a businesslike dialogue and I am a gent of some advanced and perilous age.

I don't go to conventions, mostly, because they bring on a fight-or-flight reaction and I am indeed of too advanced and perilous age to do the former and find the latter somewhat circular ... I mean, if I'm going to flee almost as soon as I enter the hotel or at least struggle with the impulse to flee, why go there at all? I have never had to transact business at conventions, indeed the fact that I live in the New York City area and can see editors easily enough (mostly I did and do not) makes the convention unnecessary; I have clearly missed some foreign sales or contacts by not attending the Worldcons but the first *and* second Law(s) of Freelancing are that you do not miss what you never had.

If you lived in New York or its environs—perish the thought, I know— would you attend as many conventions as you have? Or would you do your editorial business in Manhattan, attend almost every Worldcon because you love them, and otherwise let it all go?

—*rtr*—

MIKE: I'm not provincial enough to live in New York. I believe that real live people of real merit live between the coasts, so I'm disqualified right there. But in answer to your question, even if I were forced by a malicious deity to live in the New York area, I'd still prefer to do my business in the friendlier and more relaxed atmosphere of Worldcons.

When I was younger and hungrier and less established, I used to fly to New York a couple of times a year to meet editors and hawk my wares, and yes, it worked. But even then I preferred to meet with them at Worldcon. I always felt that every hour I spent with them in their offices meant they would have to take home an extra hour's worth of reading and editing that they didn't get done during the workday. At cons, they're more relaxed, as am I, and their way is paid by their publishers for the express purpose of meeting and courting writers. I just find it a more congenial atmosphere — not that every editor wasn't congenial in New York, but there was always that knowledge that they had a hundred tasks waiting for them the instant I left their offices.

Okay, I see by the word-count on the wall that it's time for your summing-up.

———*ᴧᴧ*———

BARRY: Here is my summing up ... if I were trying now to get started, perish the thought and hush your mouth, I would force myself to attend at least four conventions a year — the Worldcon of course, the World Fantasy Convention and two major regionals. I'd also get to the Nebula banquet every other year, going to that banquet which involved less travel. But I'd go. I'd go because I see no alternative now; it may be possible to make a career from a post office box and through judicious one-on-one meetings with editors in New York, but it is extremely difficult; you'd have to be better than good, and the editors when in New York, as you so properly point out, aren't so thrilled to see you most of the time unless you're Robert Heinlein or Isaac Asimov (who aren't likely to be showing up any time soon).

You'd probably correct me on the Nebula banquet and the World Fantasy Convention — too many professional or close-to-professional writers, too much competition for the attention of the editors. Hard to capture the attention of editors at those functions when they are outnumbered by the writers fifty to one. But I'd still recommend them because there's a lot of market information going around, a lot of collegiality, and there are now so many writers commissioning stories for anthologies (as have you over the past decade) that just hanging tight with your colleagues can produce enough leads and possible assignments to cover the expense.

I see conventions now as integral to the plans of anyone trying to start a serious or even a part-time career in science fiction. It's always been an insular field, nepotistic and clannish as the New York State Legislature; now, when there are so many competent writers fighting desperately for shrinking space (and after the franchise work and the series and the fantasy trilogies are all booked, the available space for new science fiction by new writers has been sharply reduced in the book market as well as the devastated situation for magazines) you need, at the beginning or even the early middle, every bit of advantage to be found. That means the convention circuit. (It may also mean workshops but that's another column and there we ran the issue pretty well to ground.)

Conventions are a business necessity; they can also be a great deal of fun. I've managed to find five or ten minutes of such at every convention I've attended and you, a merrier and far more congenial soul, can find five or ten days worth of fun in any three-day weekend. There are worse places to be. Isaac Asimov, writing of the Cleveland World Convention of 1955, called conventions "three days of heaven carved from necessity." Not my idea of heaven but I can understand his position and if I had been or was Isaac Asimov I'd feel the same way.

In fact, next time around I am going to be smart. I am going to be Isaac Asimov. I don't think anyone had more fun being himself than our late, great friend (well, maybe Arthur C. Clarke) and Isaac was never more himself than in company. He attended conventions because he loved them. And for those I advise to find them in early career: you can learn to love them, too.

—◦◦◦—

MIKE: A quick observation: editors *are* thrilled to see you if you visit them at lunchtime, because then you both go out to lunch on the publisher's nickel. It's damned expensive to eat in Manhattan if no one's picking up the tab.

I think Worldcon is the one essential convention for the reasons I've mentioned, but I agree, the more national and regional conventions you can go to, the more market information you'll pick up — and as we know from prior dialogues, 95 percent of all anthologies are by invitation only and don't openly solicit contributions. Much the same is true of any new publishing venture: magazine, specialty press, even (occasionally) mass market book house.

As for enjoying conventions, I'm on Isaac's side. I look forward to Worldcon like a kid looks forward to Christmas, and if I average four hours' sleep a night during Worldcon week, that's a lot. But as much as I love seeing old friends and attending parties and browsing the huckster room, I never forget what I'm there for: this is, when all is said and done, a business convention. The fact that it's the most pleasant business venue around in no way alters the fact that it's also the most productive.

7 Works for Hire

MIKE: There's a practice that seems to be getting more and more popular with publishers, and certainly more lucrative for writers though it's hardly new, and that's the work-for-hire.

Now, it comes in many forms—movie novelizations, shared worlds, "collaborations" when the lesser-known writer writes a novel based on the outline of a much-better-known writer, franchised worlds and universes, the whole bag of wax. What they all have in common, unless I'm missing something, is that the writer is not the copyright holder. Sometimes, in fact quite often these days, if he's writing a novel or novelization, he gets a royalty, but it's never a full royalty—usually it's more like a quarter of the full rate (2 percent on an 8 percent rate and so forth).

There are reasons for writing works for hire, and reasons for not writing them. I have, in my time, done many if not most of the variations, and I have rather strong opinions about each. But since I know what they are, and I have no idea what yours are, I think I'll let you expound first. I think it'll work best if we consider each type separately, as there is a considerable artistic and financial difference among them.

———

BARRY: Well, let's begin by discussing that aspect of the work for hire with which I have the most (in fact the only) direct experience: the movie novelization. Decades ago I wrote a number of these, only two of which—*Phase IV* based on the 1974 Saul Bass film and *The Sign of the Tiger, The Way of the Dragon*, a novelization of the pilot script for the 1973 David Cassidy Kung Fu Series—were published. Advances were respectively $3,000 and $2,000, the movie novelization provided for a small royalty (2 percent, I think), the television pilot novelization was for a flat fee. Pocket Books in fact did pay me a few hundred dollars of royalty money over the years; Warner Paperback Library having no obligation to pay me anything never did. (The latter novel was the basis of my only involvement with anyone's bestseller list ... #7 for a couple of weeks on the *Publisher's Weekly* list and it sold, I learned, over half a million copies.)

(The novelizations which I wrote and for which I was paid but were never published are, in fact, a more interesting group than the brace of published novelizations. I novelized 1972's *A Touch of Class* for which Glenda Jackson won a Best Actress Oscar; I novelized Lindsay Anderson's *O Lucky Man!*, something of a cult success by the (now forgotten but at the time acclaimed) director of *If*. The producers of *A Touch of Class* did not have enough faith in their film pre-release to subsidize the Berkley printing, which would have been the only terms under which Berkley would have released it. Lindsay Anderson, as I wrote in *Engines of the Night*, wanted to have his own trade paperback of the film script with clips from the film and stated that he would sue to block a novelization. I was pretty sullen about both at the time. I was also paid $1,500 for a novelization of the pilot episode of a British series, *The Protectors*, which was supposed to be re-released on USA television but neither that nor the book itself ever happened.)

The two published novelizations—for that matter all of the novelizations—were extremely easy work. I was writing with great rapidity at that time but even by those standards they went quickly. *Phase IV* was done in four or five days, the Kung Fu novelization in perhaps a week. I ran into external trouble on the latter—turned out that the pilot script which I had novelized was an earlier draft, not the actual film pilot, and I was asked for substantial rewriting. Since I felt that I had fully met the terms of the work for hire, I refused and a quick patching job was done in-office by the senior editor, Robert Abel. Neither, however, was at all difficult.

Not at all difficult! I said as much in a symposium on novelizations which George Zebrowski edited for this *Bulletin* about a decade and a half ago. "Novelizations are as close to a legal method of stealing I know," I wrote rather uncharitably, thereby opening the secret of every writer who had done these. "Not testing work. Open the script, start at the top of the first page and just crank it out," was Robert Hoskins' advice. "Just run the dialogue and fill in the space between the dialogue with description." That—after my first fumbling attempt to reconstruct the film as a true narrative and wasting five pages on internal monologue—was brilliant and needed advice and off to the races I went.

It was easy or relatively easy or relatively pleasant work, somewhere between the exigencies of a "real" novel and a typing exercise, and I regretted the adventure not at all and wish there had been a good deal more. On the other hand, the Kung Fu novel had been published under a house pseudonym ("Howard Lee") and once the series was sunk it sunk and certainly its half million copy sale was not transferable anywhere; editors didn't care. *Phase IV* had been published under my own name but was always treated as a kind of public faux pas—the Duchess taking violently ill at a seaside restaurant and raining dinner upon the cutlery, the kind of thing everyone simply looks past and gently ignores.

I went into all of these projects with no expectation whatsoever and am happy to say that my lack of expectation was met completely and satisfyingly in a way that was never afforded me otherwise. That is the signal benefit of work for hire (particularly pseudononymous work for hire); like Kevin Spacey's guy in *American Beauty* there is no goddamned responsibility. It is high wire work above a soft and utterly enveloping net.

———*∿∿∿*———

MIKE: I loathed my first few work-for-hire novel experiences. The first three were in the sex field, back in the late 1960s. My job was to novelize a nudie movie of the Russ Meyer type (but infinitely worse) that hadn't yet been released. There was nothing rash like a videotape or a script that I could work from. They would send me the dummies of a four-page publicity brochure, which contained perhaps a 200-word synopsis of such plot as existed, and a cast list so I could learn the names of the characters, and that was all I had to go on. You really have to love writing to stick with it after jobs like that.

My next experience wasn't any more enjoyable. I did a *Battlestar: Galactica* novelization back in 1980. To this day I have never seen an episode of the show. I hope to go to my grave without ever learning what a Cylon is, and based on the script I was given I can't imagine why the show lasted all the way to the first commercial break of the first episode without being cancelled. There were more science errors, English errors, and plot errors than you would think anyone could possibly put into a 65-page teleplay. I tried Bob Hoskins' method: just transfer the dialog (after you convert it into something resembling conversational English), put in the descriptions, fix what laughably passes for logic, and presto, the book is done. But it didn't work that way; when I hit page 25 of a 275-page manuscript I was already on page 33 of a 65-page script. I wrote the book in four days, on the reasonable assumption that if I took any longer my brain would turn to porridge and run out my ears. A week later I had so thoroughly put the whole thing out of my mind that I couldn't have told you a single incident that was in the book. I knew the readers would hate it as much as I did, and that would be the end of my career as a science fiction writer. Sigh — of course it became my bestselling book.

That's when I began hating the notion of work-for-hire novels, both for what they force the writer to do and for some unpleasant truths that are revealed about the readers. I turned down more than half a dozen over the next 23 years, including a Star Wars trilogy ... and it wasn't just because of my own experiences. I remember the late George Alec Effinger, who desperately needed the money, backing out of a Star Trek contract and crying on my shoulder because he couldn't put up with a bunch of non-writers telling him that Spock couldn't say this and Kirk couldn't do that and that a ship traveling at light speeds could make a right turn as easily as a car and so on. I was not encouraged.

I figured —falsely, as it turned out — that every writer who committed works for hire did them solely for the money and had a certain contempt for the subject matter. Kevin Anderson and Kris Rusch and a number of others put me straight. Some of our very best writers choose to write these books simply because they love the characters and the universes every bit as much as the fans do. It was a revelation to me, and I began to reconsider my hard-and-fast position. After a 23-year absence, I tried another work for hire in 2003. It was the first Lara Croft book to be based on the game rather than the movies. The reason I chose that one — I've never played a computer game, and despite Angelina Jolie's bustline I fell asleep during the first movie and didn't go to the second — was that rather than novelizing a movie or a game, my task was to get Lara, who's kind of a female Indiana Jones, from the end of one game, in which she is buried under a tomb in Egypt, to the beginning of the next game, where she shows up, alone and embittered, in Paris 10 months later. I didn't have to use any other characters from the games, I didn't have to use any locations (and the manuscript was jokingly referred to as "the mildly-fictionalized Resnick travel diaries"), I was able to put her in countries and hostelries and restaurants and game parks that I myself have visited, and it turned out to be a lot of fun. Okay, it was no *Kirinyaga* or even a *Santiago*, but I enjoyed writing it and I'm proud to have my name on the book. I still don't think I'd want to novelize other people's work, or have a bunch of copyright holders tell me what I must or cannot do with their characters, but I have now had a pleasant experience with a work for hire novel, and I expect I'll do more from time to time. They pay a lot more than they did in your day. I know a couple have actually earned the authors seven-count-them-seven digits when the dust cleared, and one of the offers I turned down about a decade ago was a lot closer to six digits than to four, so there are sound financial reasons to consider writing such books. Now, I had more than 40 science fiction novels in print before I wrote the Lara Croft book. Your reputation was established before you wrote the books you referred to.

I suppose before we get on to discussing other forms of work for hire, we really ought to address the obvious question, which is: if you are not yet an established writer in the field and you start writing works for hire, do they accrue to your benefit or your detriment? Are you known as a writer who makes deadlines, does what is required, and is thoroughly professional — or are you known as someone who isn't good enough to sell his own original works and is best utilized as a work-for-hire writer?

—◦∿◦—

BARRY: What I neglected to note about the *Phase IV* novelization is that there was so little to Mayo Simon's wretched script (this was by the way the first and last film the noted titlist Saul Bass directed and it is easy to know why) that I faced your problem; running out of story on page 23. So what I did was to improvise a diary for the protagonist; interpolated chapters in which he commented on The Horror of It All. (And of course, this being the author of *Beyond Apollo*, his sexual frustration, overall angst, cosmological paradox, etc., *Phase IV*, a downrent 1974 version of *Them*, was about giant alien ants in the Southwestern desert eating everything. And everybody. And eventually themselves.) That diary seemed to work pretty well or at least it enabled me to lurch on to page 150 and so the manuscript was delivered.

The film — which had been completed and for which a release date had been announced — went subsequently into an inexplicable limbo, finally being premiered (it lasted three days in theaters) ten months later. At the screening in the Gulf & Western Building, the Pocket Books editors and I noticed that my diary had become a voice-over; every five minutes or so the action froze while the disembodied voice of the actor playing the lead commented on his sexual frustration and the angst and The Horror of It All. "They ought to give you a screenwriting credit and a lot more money," Bob Gleason, my editor, giggled. "Now we know why they postponed the release." No screenwriting credit and no more money — but the film still plays on early-morning television and my younger daughter said a classmate at Rutgers had pronounced it his favorite film of all time, had taped it so that he could see it several times a year, and was flabbergasted that her father had written the film. "No," she corrected, "He didn't write the film, he wrote a book based on the film." He insisted upon remaining impressed. Ah, the vault of memory!

Your question of course is a good one, although it might have had more relevance twenty years ago than today ... today many writers at the top of this field, including several award winners, have done franchise and novelization work and have suffered no loss of prestige, nor presumably have these people felt they were slumming. But then again writers in early career face a different and more ominous situation. Yes, one can become identified with franchising or novelizations (identified that is by the publishing community; I don't think that most readers even note the authors of franchises, buying on the basis of the title and the originating author which are always far more prominently billed on the cover) and this can affect the chances of one's own work being taken seriously or perhaps of one's work even selling. Certainly there is no carryover — the otherwise unknown author of a very successful franchise or novelization will find that her name is not only not known to the public but it is barely known to editors at other houses. To approach an editor with a proposal or completed novel by saying, "My franchise novel for the *Boomer's World* series sold 500,000 copies so you know I am a big success" is more likely to get you negative feedback ... the editor will feel that if readers recognize your name at all it will be only for the purpose of another *Boomer's World*. Still there is limited choice in the market as it has evolved or devolved and many writers struggling for publication may find that their only credible chance at publication is through this kind of sublicensing.

Another story: in 1967 the late Michael Avallone (1924–1997) was contracted by Ace to write the first novelization of the pilot script for *The Man from U.N.C.L.E.* television series. $1000. The series was top of the charts in its first season (David McCallum, anyone?) and Avallone's novel sold well over a million copies. Avallone was approached for another novel but said instead, "I wrote you people a bestseller. I want a bonus and I want a lot more money. It's a bestseller!"

Donald Wollheim told me that he had transmitted this request to A. A. Wyn, the publisher. Wyn's response had been prefaced with and ended by two different obscenities; in the middle he said, "Any hack could have written that book and sold a million copies. I'm not giving him a dime. Get me another hack."

With suitable adjustments for inflation and the passage of time, the same dialogue is likely to occur today. This is one reason why an ambitious young writer might want to consider her options carefully before plunging into the work for hire racket. Then again, this is the reason why there is such turnover and more opportunity than available elsewhere. "I like science fiction writers just fine," Damon Knight once wrote, "But they do have a way of rolling over at the first sign of a check."

———

MIKE: Yes, it's true that some very popular award-winners have done media books. Joe Haldeman did a Trekbook, Kris Rusch has done media books, Tim Zahn won his Hugo before writing the first bestselling Star Wars trilogy. Hell, even Isaac Asimov novelized a movie—*Fantastic Voyage*. None of them, I hasten to note, did it very often.

I would take issue with the fact that no writer has ever found a way to carry his media audience over to his own novels. I think Alan Dean Foster was probably the first to show it could be done. Kevin Anderson is the most recent, and I suspect there have been one or two others in between (though if pressed I couldn't name them).

But on the flip side, I can name more than two writers, more than half a dozen actually, who got labeled as media/sharecrop specialists and simply cannot sell their own books for love or money. Well, not for money, anyway.

And ah!, the days when you could hand in a 150-page book manuscript. These days there are chapters than go more than 150 manuscript pages. Lots of them.

Well, media books are just one side of a many-sided work for hire coin. Another would be franchised worlds. These can range from "tribute volumes" like *Foundation's Friends* and *The Williamson Effect*, where a long-established superstar invites a number of professional friends to write in his universe, to more traditional franchise work.

And the franchise work can vary, from stuff that was clearly designed to be bestsellers, such as the Foundation novels by David Brin, Greg Benford and

Greg Bear, to what I would call the "absent collaborator" book, where a major author writes a two-page outline, a beginner turns it into a novel, and when the dust clears they share a byline equally and an advance very unequally. There's other stuff between the extremes, but I'd be interested in your opinions of these first.

———♒︎———

BARRY: Well, there are the big-deal franchise books (I'd add to your examples the Silverberg-Asimov expansion to novel length of "Nightfall" and two other famous Asimov novelettes published in the 1980s) and there are the small-deal franchise books, *Isaac Asimov's Robots* and the financial distance between the two is certainly extreme, but for the authors there is a commonality: Just as James J. Walker noted famously that "No girl was ever ruined by a book," no writer's career was ever improved by a franchise.

None of the writers of the big-deal books, the *Foundation* extensions and so on, raised their advances, audience or prestige through those novels. They were paid a considerable advance, probably equivalent to what they were receiving for their own work and they may well have enjoyed writing the novels but they did so to no increase of reputation. And at the bottom end the writers who scrambled for the franchised universe improved their bank accounts, some of them considerably, but none of them could have been said to have increased their stature in the field. (Or lowered their stature. It was just work.) It's easy to infer from that kind of information that franchising — or novelizations — are not the way to build a career of anything other than franchising and novelizations. Such work can and usually does lead to more assignments of this kind, but none of it has anything to do with building a career. And of course there is close to no critical recognition. If franchise novels are reviewed at all the reviewers will say things like "Good of its type" or "Really doesn't seem to have gotten the spirit of the original books." Reviewers (and editors) don't say, "This is really great and the author should be signed for a novel of her own at the earliest opportunity." It's product, pure American product, that's all it is and there's that famous William Carlos line about what happens to the pure products of America. (John Kessel published a well-known story about what happens.)

So — as a writer with at least minimal credits, the beginning of some kind of market presence and that's stipulated because you can't get the work without such — should you do it? Putting aside the question of money which is for this kind of assignment work the central motivation most of the time and we know that this is central, will the non-effect or even possibly deleterious effect that franchise work will have upon a career mean that one shouldn't do it?

As with almost every other aspect of this business, that's an individual's decision. This kind of work can be fun (or as much fun as writing gets to be).

It can pay adequately, not derisorily, and it enables the writer to shape, exploit, expand skills through their practice. Hard to turn it down. But be advised: if you're going to get heavily into this kind of work you're likely to be in the same position ten years from now that you are today: your proposals for your own novels are likely to have languished, and you are facing a professional future which will look very much like the past. It's not really a decision I had to make. There were no franchise novels in the 1970s and I pursued no film or television novelizations after *Kung Fu #1* because the whole experience had been so repellent. I couldn't have done any more of this. If the huge franchising/sharecropping market of the 1990s had been available to me then I can say that it is clear I would have had a great deal of difficulty refusing. I am glad that I was never given that choice.

—◆◆◆—

MIKE: I would argue that there is at least one major exception to the notion that you can't capitalize on novelizations and franchise work. Kevin Anderson was not a major seller when I first met him, though he was a very talented writer. But then he started writing Star Wars books, and an L. Ron Hubbard book, and then the Dune books with Brian Herbert, and suddenly he was living on the *New York Times* bestseller list — and he just got a bestseller-type contract for his new series, a series that had he written it before he wrote all the above I am certain would have gotten him a modest advance, modest handling by a publisher, and not much more. And where there is one exception, there can and will be others. (For all I know, there already are and they've simply slipped my mind, which can get pretty slippery at 4:00 in the morning, which is when I'm writing this.)

Whoops! Before I forget, I ought to mention that there is one kind of novelization that I am so opposed to that I never sign a contract unless it is expressly forbidden — and that is a novelization of a screenplay based on one of my novels.

Over the years I've optioned a number of properties to Hollywood, even sold them a couple of screenplays, and, who knows, maybe someday they'll even keep their promises and make a movie. But when they do, the only book bearing the title of that movie and carrying the keyline art (i.e., "movie poster" art) will be my original novel. I've seen it happen, not often, but a few times, where a popular movie that didn't have all that much to do with the source has been novelized — usually the movie changed the book's title, and the novelization of course uses the movie title and the keyline art — and the novel that formed the basis of it all gets re-released and sells maybe 15,000 extra paperbacks, and the novelization, however dreadful, sells 450,000 in its first month of release.

For that reason, I have never signed an option contract without a clause forbidding novelizations. (Well, let me amend that. No one in Hollywood will sign a contract forbidding *anything*. What they *will* sign is a contract stating that there can be no novelization without the author's approval, and I guarantee it'll be a frigid day in hell before they get it.)

That doesn't apply to short stories, of course. I may reserve the right to expand the story into a novel (and I do), but it wouldn't serve any purpose forbidding a novel or novelization when it's clear that no publisher is going to publish a 23-page story as a stand-alone book.

I was going to shut this down at this point, and attack shared worlds and the rest in a future dialogue, but it occurs to me that we haven't discussed one other aspect of this, and that is the franchise novel from the originator's point of view. Now obviously the originator has to be a huge name and have a huge following for the franchise to be worth the powder to blow it to hell. He's got to have written something the stature of a Foundation or a Dune or a Pern or an Amber. Some of these eventually do get franchised, some don't. We won't count the ones where the franchise occurs after the author's death, as in the Foundation or Dune books — but what about the others? Obviously by the time an author achieves the stature and sales that make him and his universe a franchisable commodity, he doesn't need the money ... and the assumption is that even if the books are written by a better writer than the original, as when L. Sprague de Camp continued Robert E. Howard's Conan stories, the readers will still prefer the author that first attracted them.

So other than feeding some serious egomania, can you see any benefit that accrues to the franchiser, as opposed to the franchisee?

—⁕—

BARRY: The benefit that accrues to the franchiser is money. Lots of money. Probably 50 percent of the total advance (this is an informed guess; I know nobody's secrets) as the Asimov Estate share for those three Foundation novels. Probably the same for the old *Thieves World* novelizations. And it is the best kind of money, money-without-having-to-lift-a-finger cash. The temptation for the franchisee would seem to be overwhelming and it is surprising that even more famous properties (Lazarus Long goes By His Bootstraps to The Stranger Land!) have not been exploited. Of course some famous properties are franchised within the family ... the *Dune* novels, for instance.

As far as novelizations of screenplays on films based on the author's own property... Phil Dick was offered $40,000 in the last year of his life to novelize *Blade Runner*. "I already have," he explained, in refusal, "and it is called *Do Androids Dream of Electric Sheep?*" Norman Spinrad said to me that Phil had simply suffered from misguided integrity and a temporary lack of smarts... "What you should do, Phil," he said he had told the author, "is to retype *Do Androids Dream of Electric Sheep?* and turn it into the film company and say 'Hi, here's my novelization.'"

Maybe he would have gotten around to that if he had lived through to the

release of *Total Recall*. In his unobstructive absence, however, the novelization
to that film, based on Phil's short story, was done by Piers Anthony.

—⟨*/*⟩—

MIKE: There's no question that there's money for the creator of the franchise ... but if he's got a viable franchise, he probably has a little less need of
money than most of us. (I don't know about you, but my creditors have expensive tastes.)

I would be thrilled and flattered to someday be the object of a tribute volume, where my friends each contributed a story using my characters or backgrounds. But as for farming those same characters and backgrounds out to a
beginning or low-level writer, and putting my name on a novel I didn't write
for the sole purpose of attracting readers who will be misled into thinking I *did*
write half of it ... well, I'm on Phil Dick's side. Integrity (and I don't think it's
ever misguided, although it can be economically counter-productive) has to
count for a little something every now and then, even for writers, for whom
that particular commodity is not always coin of the realm.

8 Promotion

MIKE: It seems that everyone knows what questions to ask about selling, but most people seem to be totally in the dark about the art of self-promotion (or even whether it's really necessary).

I think we've had some wonderful articles on how to go about it over the years, most notably Fred Pohl's "The Science Fiction Professional" in *The Craft of Science Fiction* and Norman Spinrad's "A Prince from Another Land" in *Fantastic Lives*. I've certainly heard some excellent advice on the topic — what to do and, just as important, what not to waste your time doing — as I'm sure you have.

And yet a lot of writers seem clueless (and some, to be sure, merely seem uninterested) in promoting themselves and their books. I've seen beginners at every convention hold up their latest covers at panels, as if that's going to get anyone to rush to the dealer's room and buy their book, or make the audience forget that they're sitting between two Nebula winners whose accomplishments are known to the audience without the need for flashing covers. I've seen them hit 20 local radio stations, each with a listening audience numbering in the low hundreds, and wonder why sales didn't skyrocket. I've seen them sit in giant Barnes or Borders stores surrounded by their unautographed books and no buyers. I've seen them try to buy their way onto Oprah, Leno or Letterman. (No, it never worked.) I've even known them to pay for ads themselves.

Usually none of it works. And when it does, it's usually a fluke.

So draw upon your four decades as a professional science fiction writer and suggest a few things that will enhance either the author's visibility or his sales, short of shooting the President or dancing naked in Times Square at high noon.

——*ᴥ*——

BARRY: As always— our dialogues have become as formalized, as ritualized as the *commedia dell'arte* and we pair of harlequins as beloved — you perform miracles with the cane and the soft shoe, dazzle the audience with a promise of wonders within the tent ... and then turn to me with a winsome smile. "You're on," you say. "Take them into the tent. Show them the wonders." On a turgid convention panel a decade and a half ago, the audience and panelists sinking beneath spiritlessness toward misery, a desperate Ron Goulart said, "I give you a man! I give you a man who has lived and suffered for his art! A man who has great good news to tell you! I give you a man, I give you..." (long pause, flourish of hand) "*Malzberg!*"

Another long pause. And the subject at hand.

I don't know what conventional publicity works for the science fiction or fantasy novel. If the author is already famous in another field, the celebrity machine goes into effect of course. If the author is not a *People* magazine fixture but merely famous within science fiction or fantasy, a large print order, an author tour, and a little bit of local media (there is no national media) will probably do the job. If the author is neither, there is no clear way.

I can tell you in detail what doesn't work, but you already know that ... your lead-in here is a good précis. Buying space in fan publications, going from convention to convention panel to convention with a proof of the book cover on display doesn't work. Autographing at local bookstores won't work. Autographing at conventions might but only in a limited way. Sales are not really related to author visibility.

If publishers and writers knew what worked, surely it would be done consistently ... and books would sell far better than they do. But William Goldman's famous Hollywood aphorism is as applicable to publishing as to film. *Nobody knows anything. Post facto* it is always possible to explain why the horse won, why there was no other sensible selection. *A priori*: who made up this card? Who can possibly figure this race? (Crooked trainers and jockeys may have, but they sure aren't telling.)

In regard to publicity, self-promotion, sales, almost all of the conventional wisdom is wrong. (I have written "almost all." Not "all." But it is impossible *a priori* to know the difference.) But we fail to understand that. The late Laurence Janifer liked to quote Elbert Hubbard (at least he attributed this to Hubbard): "It isn't what you don't know which destroys you. It's what you think you know which just ain't so.")

In 1970 I thought I knew that published work would find its deserved level in the marketplace on its own terms and without unusual assistance. In 1980 I thought that merciless, brutal, expensive hype could sell anything. In 1985 I thought that it was essentially a lottery; although my career and that of Dean Koontz were polar opposites, those careers had looked interchangeable 15 years earlier and no one could have known with certainty the outcome. Blind, stumbling luck or happenstance.

I was wrong all three times but I cannot at this moment tell you what would have been right.

MIKE: Well, let's examine a few of the more common (or is it more heralded?) methods of bringing yourself, your literature, and your career to the attention of the public in a manner that won't get you arrested.

Signing at your local bookstore might result in three more sales, maybe four on a good day, but it's hardly a career maker. (My own experience is that, for reasons that continue to elude me, I can get a line around the block if I sign at a science fiction shop in the worst slum in town, and I can get a line that will outlast my time period when I sign at a convention — but when I sign at a superstore, even after they've publicized it on television, radio, and/or the print press, I could die of loneliness. I probably sign half a dozen books an hour at such shindigs, and most of the writers I speak to have similar experiences. Got any suggestions as to why?)

Back to signing. As I say, doing it at one or two bookstores doesn't make a dent, and while it's very probable that a 30-city autographing-and-interview tour with all expenses paid by your publisher will yield discernable results, it doesn't happen until you've already shown discernable results without that outlay of cash on his part.

But I remember Ray Feist telling me, years ago, how he went up and down the California coast when his first couple of books came out, signing in every store that would let him in the door. Okay, he's Ray Feist, and his books clearly strike a responsive chord anyway — but he did sell like crazy from the outset. What do you think? Is there a possibility that a self-financed "author tour" might yield meaningful results? (The one thing we know is that once you prove you don't need your publisher's promotion to sell above the average, then — and usually only then — will he be happy to promote the hell out of you.)

I also remember the late Warren Norwood suggesting that there were too many bookstores out there, but there weren't all that many distributors, and he made it his business to befriend most of the distributors in a 6-or-8-state area, drop in on them whenever he had a new book due out, keep in touch, schmooze them whenever he could — and he said his sales increased once he started doing it. No, he never hit the bestseller list, but he stayed in business, and a lot of writers these days are having a hard time doing just that.

In fact, before I turn it over to you and let you overwhelm us with your eons of accumulated wisdom, I think maybe we'd better define, not promotion, but what we want that promotion to achieve. Do I think there's a way to promote yourself from a hanger-on to a bestseller? Hell, no, or we'd be overwhelmed by 50 new bestselling writers every few months. But do I think that some carefully considered promotion will keep a marginal author in business, or turn a decent-selling author into a minimally-to-somewhat-better-than-decent-selling author?

I draw myself up to my full height, look the disbelievers full in the eye, and unhesitatingly answer in the strongest of tones: Possibly.

—◦◦◦◦—

BARRY: Okay, let me try to be practical. This dialogue could easily degenerate into sections by Mike suggesting promotional methods one, two and three and rejoinders from Barry explaining why those methods will not work. Mike would then respond with a grumble and methods four, five and six. Those won't work either, Barry would note. What a depressing exercise this would be. Being the Eeyore of science fiction is not a career plan.

What might work? Let's begin at the point of origin: the book itself. Subject and style do have something to do with sales and visibility, you know. A novelization of the new Superman movie will sell better than, say, the authorized sequels to J.G. Ballard's *Crash* or *The Atrocity Exhibition* assuming that a publisher was misguided enough to take on such a project. The novelization would outsell those proposed sequels by a ratio of at least twenty-to-one unassisted by promotional hype of any kind. One might find this unfortunate, that many more readers are interested in Superman than "The Assassination of John Fitzgerald Kennedy Considered as a Downhill Motor Race" but these are the times in which we live.

In sum and in short: write to the market. Just as the most fundamental censorship is self-censorship, the most fundamental promotion is with the originating material. "Write what is now selling" is perhaps the first advice given to the would-be professional writer. That's laden with traps, of course, but it is as good as advice is likely to get, even better than "Write what you like to read" (unless of course what you like to read are bestsellers).

Promotion and self-promotion cannot sell the promotable any more than an agent, any agent, can sell the unsalable. That finding on agents was part of one of our earliest dialogues and it is just as applicable to this issue. The embracing word for this is "slant," the shaping of material to the presumptive or desired market, and most professional writers learn this early and often to the point of internalization.

So sales and market outcome are situated originally within the manuscript itself. Write material which can be promoted, material to whose promotion you might be able to bring special expertise.

Of course I'd ask this: what if you're reluctant to do self-promotion? What if you're shy or agoraphobic, fearful of crowds or of self-inflation? What if John Updike's recent and already famous speech in June to the Booksellers Convention was right, and the book now must be regarded as little other than a platform to the talk show and the tour? What if conventions, or at least the public part of conventions, make you truly uncomfortable? Is the answer to find another career? Or — Damon Knight's famous short story "The Handler" comes to mind at once — do you hire someone to play yourself in public? Or bringing it all back home: what has worked for you? What would you advise the 30-year younger version of yourself determined to find a career? When you sold

The Branch and the Galactic Midway series and those novels in the 1980s, in what promotional efforts did you engage? What worked? What didn't?

—⌐ɷɷ⌐—

MIKE: I agree that everyone should write to the limit of his ability, and that it helps if one's tastes are the same as the general public's, but I submit that has everything to do with writing and nothing to do with promotion. I rather suspect bemoaning the fact that Superman outsells J. G. Ballard's more impenetrable works really hasn't got much to do with self-promotion either. I think you're confusing the quest for good literature, which is pretty subjective anyway, with the quest for promoting one's self and career.

Further, I would suggest that not every megaseller is cynically crafted to get the author on tours and talk shows, and indeed some come as complete surprises even to the publisher. I offer, in evidence, *Jonathan Livingston Seagull* and *Catch-22*.

And let's be honest: one great cover will do a hell of a lot more for your sales than one great chapter. Or six. Or (probably) fifteen.

The books of mine you mention came out too early in my career for me to do much promotion. I had rather hoped *The Branch*, which is the story of the true Jewish Messiah (not a very nice guy, either) who shows up half a century from now, struck me as being blasphemous and offensive to certain mindsets, so I mailed it to every televangelist and radio preacher whose address I could find, hoping that Jerry Falwell or Jimmy Swaggert might hold it up and exhort twenty million followers not to buy it, which would of course have put it — and me — on the map. Never happened, alas. A few radio preachers screamed enough to get it through, I think, four quick (and small) printings, and that was the end of it.

But that doesn't mean that I — and dozens of other members of this organization — haven't found a number of self-promotion approaches that work.

For example: every time a former Communist country's economy and political freedoms advance to a certain point, they begin developing a legitimate publishing industry. It usually starts with magazines. I'm always first in line to give them award-winning or award-nominated stories at reasonable (i.e., insultingly cheap) rates. I consider this the best self-promotion anyone could do in these emerging economies. You let me put four or five outstanding stories in the first science fiction magazine to appear in a country, and I guarantee you that when the first science fiction book publisher shows up, I'll have enough of a fan following that they'll choose me over just about every writer who *hasn't* sold to the magazine(s).

Is there any empirical evidence that it works? Yeah, there is. Twenty-six book sales in Poland, 20 in Russia, a bunch more in the Czech Republic, Latvia, Lithuania, and on and on, all because I accommodated the initial magazines in those countries with whatever they wanted for whatever they could afford.

I just sold a few more stories to Slovakia. They don't have a science fiction book publisher yet, but I guarantee when one emerges, I'm not going to have any trouble selling to him, because of this self-promotion. (*Three* Hugo winners for $50.00 each? Yeah. What am I going to do—hold out for a better price from their competitor? This is *Slovakia*; they don't have a competitor. Probably never will in my lifetime. But what they do have now is a bunch of Hugo-winning stories to whet their appetites for my books when that end of the industry finally shows its face.)

Another thing you can do is display yourself in markets that don't ordinarily cater to science fiction writers. (No, not *Playgirl*; put your shirt back on.) For example: I just sold a short story to *Nature* magazine. I'm not the first; Nancy Kress and a handful of others have done so too. Did I get rich on it? Of course not. Did someone immediately run out and buy one of my books because of it? I hope so, but I have no proof of it. But if I were to choose the likely place to convert a non-fiction reader to my kind of fiction, I think I'd be a lot better advised to try *Nature* than the aforementioned *Playgirl*, or *Islands*, or any of 200 others I could name. And that, too, is a form of self-promotion. (And if my sales don't go up but a couple of other science magazines ask for stories, then the self-promotion was still effective, just in an unanticipated way.)

Then there's a matter of simply understanding that the world is changing, and learning to adapt to it. Sure, sitting on a panel at a convention is a form of self-promotion, however inadequate. So is talking to a small group of fans in a lobby or a party suite.

But if you do your homework, you'll find chat rooms online where you'll reach a hell of a lot more potential buyers—and your words won't vanish into thin air the moment you utter them. They'll be saved, logged and archived, and while you may only have been speaking to 50 electronic entities when you sent your remarks through the modem, they may wind up getting read, over the next few years, by thousands, some of whom will be impressed or interested enough to risk a few sawbucks on your books.

And here's another: as you know, for the past few years I've spent a couple of hours a day selling elderly computer-challenged fans' and pros' collections on eBay (as well as the estates of some dead fans). And as you know, over the past 6 years, I've sold perhaps 30 novels and 120 stories, including most of my award nominees, to Fictionwise.com. What you won't know until you read this is that, starting about three years ago, I made up a flyer—an advertisement—bragging about all the award-quality Resnick items you could get for reasonable prices on Fictionwise.com, and I put a flyer in every package I send out to eBay clients, since they are clearly computer-literate science fiction readers. That's maybe 80 to 100 flyers a week.

Has it done any good? Well, it made me Fictionwise's Author of the Year—a combination of sales and reader ratings—in head-to-head competition with Dan Brown, Stephen King, Robert A. Heinlein, and that whole crowd, which may have made it easier for me to sell (or sell for more) to a couple of new publishers in the following year.

Also, a number of foreign readers who could never get their hands on the magazines in which my stories appeared were able to purchase the stand-alone stories from Fictionwise.com. A couple of them were translators. One, a gentleman named Luigi who has since become a friend, brought them to the attention of an Italian magazine which bought three of my stories as a result. Another seems to have secured a pair of Finnish sales for me for the same reason: because of my flyer that I included when he bought an item from me on eBay, he was able to find my short stories and convince an editor in his country to buy them. I call that self-promotion; had I not taken the initiative, none of this would have come to pass, and it had nothing to do with *writing*, but rather with *promotion*.

There are more ways, of course; these are just a handful that I've hit upon, and I'll mention some more in my next turn. The guys to ask are people like Kevin J. Anderson, who could write shelves of books on how to bring yourself to the readers' and publishers' attention.

I didn't mean to go on for so long, but I had to make clear that there's a difference between writing and promoting, and to show that even down here in the ghetto, some self-promotion does indeed yield results.

—*ww*—

BARRY: You promise more self-promotional techniques for your next turn and I have to put myself in the position of the reader of these dialogues: Would I rather now read some more Malzberg grumblings or wouldn't it be better to cast them aside and get to the real stuff? Your methods all seem quite workable — I have in fact and from a distance observed them working — and I write the present section sensing that what readers it has will be weary stragglers returning to this section after reading through all of yours ... or those too cynical, discouraged or somnolent to want to move on briskly. This may in fact constitute a precise description of my audience — cynical, discouraged, somnolent readers and let us not forget that useful word "depressed" — and that makes me as uncomfortable as it makes you. But we take our audiences where we can. After all, as the actress said to the donkey and I don't think I want to make this reference more explicit, "At least I'm still working."

But I'll make my remarks this time relatively brief in deference to the polite readers who feel that we should be attended in order, no cutting in line please. All of your self-promotional ideas are quite sensible, all of them work to one degree or another and they all demonstrate what I came to understand long ago ... the originating promotion, it is the obligation of the writer to propound her own work, if she doesn't in early career accept that as a commitment nothing much is going to happen. Publicity departments at most of the major commercial publishers are worthless to most of the list, which means worthless to most science fiction writers.

The genre simply works within too low a set of circulation figures to make any extensive advertising or publicity efforts worthwhile. The publicity department has a pretty good idea how to sell 500,000 hardcover copies of a book which unassisted might sell 100,000 but it has virtually no methodology for or interest in selling 7,500 copies of a book which might otherwise sell 3,500. Or 1,500. It simply doesn't pay and the upper limit, the ceiling, is still so low as to utterly discourage promotional efforts. Same for advertising. In its simplest form: long, long ago Random House bought a half page in *The Magazine of Fantasy & Science Fiction* to advertise my *Beyond Apollo*. The ad cost them $500. It's my presumption that at best it accounted for 50 sales which might otherwise not have been made. What was Random House's profit on 50 copies at $4.95, and was that advertisement justified? The question, as is so often lamentably the case, is itself the answer.

Salvation or at least significant sales for all but the bestselling science fiction and fantasy writers is not to be found within the publisher's division. Publicity, as you have so well indicated, begins at home. Usually ends there as well. But my house as we are reminded, is where the heart is and it takes a heap of living.

—⟰⟰⟰—

MIKE: Apples and oranges again. I talk about promotion; you talk about Riting Gud. I talk about self-promotion, with an emphasis on the *self*; you talk about what publishers' publicity departments will and won't do for you. We'll keep trying; eventually I'm going to drag you, kicking and screaming, into talking about self-promotion.

And believe me, it's important.

Why?

Because you're right about publishers' promotional departments. They're there for the Stephen Kings and Tom Clancys—or if they're science fiction publishers, for the Anne McCaffreys and the Terry Goodkinds. Make your Random House example more favorable—say the ad was so effective that they showed a $400.00 profit above and beyond the cost of it—and you don't have to be a genius to see that the time, effort and money would be better spent elsewhere.

The problem is that very few of us are Anne McCaffrey or Terry Goodkind, just as 30 years ago not an awful lot of us were Robert A. Heinlein or Frank Herbert. And just as you and I have pointed out in a prior dialogue on agents that the reason you read your contracts even after your agent has approved them is that you're maybe 3 percent of your agent's income but you're 100 percent of your own ... so too are you (unless your name is Dean or Nora or something similar) an insignificant flyspeck on your publisher's P-and-L statement, but you alone are ultimately responsible for the only profit and loss you've got.

Self-promotion isn't going to turn you into a bestseller. Not that it can't be done — publishers do it with mediocre books all the time — but if you had the time and (especially) the money required to do it, you wouldn't have to because your publisher would be happily, indeed greedily, doing it for you. I think everyone understands that on the front end.

Science fiction is a marginal field. You'd never know it to read *Locus*, of course, but it is. Romance accounts for more than half the fiction published; we're hovering around 5 percent, for all that we brag about how the field's expanding. Our average advances and print runs are far smaller, and hence our profit margins are far smaller too. That means that not just for beginners, but for midlisters as well, sometimes knowing how to promote yourself will be the difference between getting that next contract and not getting it. Or if it's assured, selling enough copies and getting enough foreign and reprint money to pay your bills.

The state of the market is not good right now. We've got a lot of people, good people and good writers, hanging on by their fingernails. They know their publishers aren't about to send them on a 12-city tour, or buy them full-page ads in the *New York Times Book Review* and *Publishers Weekly*. They want to know if there is anything that they themselves can do to shift the odds a little more in their favor, to help their chances however minimally.

That's why we're discussing self-promotion. Well, that's why one of us is and the other is surely about to start, right?

—◦ɷ◦—

BARRY: You want me to write of self-promotion, what do I know of self-promotion? Or to put it more charitably, what can I possibly add to your own remarks on the subject? You've pretty well got it covered, there's an inclusivity to your remarks.

"Well then," you might say (see? I can do dialogues all by myself), "I've given some examples of what has worked for me, why don't you do the same? What has worked for you?"

Well, nothing much has worked for me. My sales record speaks for itself, doesn't it? I know some of the techniques you outline but I've never been able to practice them with much success or for that matter to practice them at all.

That said, I can suggest that the science fiction convention can be as useful to the promotion of your published work as it can be to the promotion of your sales record. This constitutes after all, the most central audience, what our ever-lovable politicians call "the base." Get to the major regionals, get on panels, talk to the dealers. If you have a new book, arrange for a reading and autographing. Even if there isn't a new book available now, arrange for a reading and autographing and hope for the best.

Beyond that I have no advice other than the obvious. Running for major political office would be nice, a parallel career in the major leagues or the theater would be even nicer but if you don't have it this isn't the kind of thing you can generate quickly enough to assist with the present novel. Janis Ian brought her fame to science fiction five years ago and has had a real impact upon the field but she already had her career of more than three decades; it wasn't something that she dreamed up overnight.

In truth, Mike, I think that self-promotion may be just a little overrated, at least by newer writers. In my many decades I have seen many people come along and do everything apparently right ... wrote the book, went to the conventions, schmoozed, the editors, did the autographing, worked for the SFWA, paneled around the country if not the world ... and it didn't work for them, they disappeared anyway. Doing everything right works some of the time for some of us, for others it doesn't. It's an unpredictable, seemingly accidental business.

To that point: there was a panel at Readercon last year, July 2005, with the interesting premise: "Give us something you know to be true but cannot possibly prove." One of my two suggestions was: "Career outcome is the product of utter randomness."

How grateful our audience, how grateful am I, that you take this to be utter nonsense.

—◄∕∕∕►—

MIKE: Career outcome is the product of utter randomness *unless you do something about it.*

What can do you?

Well, you can write good (and popular) books.

You can sign good contracts—by which I mean, contracts that require your publisher to do the promotion that some of us in this dialogue seem unwilling or unable to do.

You can, by trial and error—or better still, through careful and intelligent observation—see what form of self-promotion works for various of your peers, decide which is most likely to work for you (or which is the least repugnant to you), and practice it.

You can even try a scattershot approach, which is to say: try a bit of everything and see what works, which seems to be the guiding principle of the advertising industry. For example, I don't imagine a newcomer can make much promotional headway at a Worldcon which has maybe one hundred Hugo and Nebula winners walking around, but I could be wrong, at least in some cases, and you'll never know until you try. You can speak at schools, but how many students, even college students, are likely to run out and buy your book because you gave a nice speech? (Still, maybe some will. You won't know without trying.) The reason I don't like the scattershot approach is that your primary business is supposed to be writing, not promoting, and time is your one irreplaceable commodity, so I favor a more calculated approach.

I was going to offer some other proven methods, wasn't I? But we're running out of space, and besides, I have a bunch of awards to prove that I am a professional liar in good standing.

The trick is to remain one, and *effective* self-promotion has a little something to do with that. Not much, but occasionally enough to make a difference.

And for the record, I don't believe that career outcome is the product of utter randomness any more than I believe that all the good things that happen to me are God's doing and all the bad things are Satan's. *I* have a little to do with it, too.

And so does every writer reading this dialogue.

9 e-Publishing Revisited

MIKE: We had a dialogue some years back about e-publishing, at which time I think we both agreed that it was the wave of the future, it would be worth tons of money someday, but at present it was likely, at best, to provide a pretty trivial revenue stream.

I think it's probably time to revisit e-publishing, since e-publishing seems to be revisiting science fiction with a vengeance.

Consider:

1. An electronic editor, Ellen Datlow, has twice won the Best Editor Hugo.
2. Electronically-published stories have won the Nebula.
3. *Omni Online* and *Scifi.com* both paid more than double the rates of the print magazines.
4. *Jim Baen's Universe* is now paying 3½ times more to established authors than any of the print magazines.
5. I've sold some stories to podcasters, for the same rate as I get for print reprints. The most recent one, which appeared on Escape Pod, got 22,000 hits in its first month. That's probably more people than bought the issue of *Asimov's* in which it appeared.
6. Fictionwise.com deals only in reprints of all lengths, not new material. Yet in the few years it's been around, I've made more money in royalties just from reprints that I made from advances and royalties combined from the 13 novels I sold to Signet in the 1980s.

A decade ago a new e-publisher would spring up every week. The usual pitch was that if I'd give them something for free today, they'd make me rich next year. They all died.

These days there's a new e-publisher every week, and the difference is that almost all of them offer coin of the realm.

So is it time to reconsider the place of e-publishing in our little galaxy, and where is it going, step by step, from here? And while I'm thinking of it, what's the life expectancy of the print magazines, and maybe even the print book publishers?

—◦◦◦—

BARRY: E-publishing is difficult to project. It was overhyped, desperately so, in the late 1990s and I can remember one respected literary agent saying on a panel, "In ten years no more books. No more books at all." *Publishers Weekly* was packed with material on the coming New Common Era, every week presented a new start-up. The Rocket Reader ($300 retail price, capacity six novels of average length) was positioned through full-page advertisements in the *New York Times* and elsewhere. "No more books" was the mantra all right. Nicholas Baker's *New Yorker* article on the trashing of the San Francisco Library catalog and index (thrown in dumpsters everywhere) struck terror into all of us electronically disadvantaged.

And then suddenly the wave retreated, leaving the barren shore and most of us on a darkling, shallow plain. No more Rocket Reader. Instead of a start-up a week there was a collapse a week. E-book versions of bestsellers were selling perhaps a thousand copies in toto. My novel, *Underlay*, taken for electronic publication in 1999, sold seven copies according to my last royalty statement which arrived six years ago. Science fiction electronic "bestsellers" became so with sales of 17, 20, 35 copies. The aforementioned literary agent allowed "I had perhaps been a little over-optimistic. Maybe it isn't going to happen all that quickly." The consensus as of a year ago was that the entire electronic concept had been oversold, overanticipated and had collapsed as do so many of the oversold in a society which is dedicated to oversell. Yes, Fictionwise — a well-financed, professional operation — seemed to come through all of this with unswerving, modest profitability ... but the membership does not need me to remind them that both *Omni Online* and the Sci-Fi Channel's fiction department folded. Ellen Datlow made on-line fiction not only respectable but — as she had at *Omni*—cutting-edge, and established a significant presence, published a number of prominent and/or award-winning stories (notably Karen Joy Fowler's Nebula-winning "What I Didn't See"). The Sci-fi Channel showed its appreciation by folding the line in favor of "other means of publicizing the field." Against such planning, Isaac Asimov would write, the Gods themselves would rail in vain. If the electronic concept is making a comeback, it is a halting, stuttering comeback, something like the very recent comeback of your favorite team from your favorite city, the New York Knickerbockers. Your beloved team is doing well only in comparison with its most recent history.

My feeling (and many in the business felt this way during the luxuriantly optimistic late 1990s) was that e-publishing might well have a future, that its time might come ... but it would do so with far less speed and efficacy than its entrepreneurs had projected. The delivery system was awkward and nothing yet had —for efficiency, portability, familiarity, accessibility — replaced the book or the magazine. All of this might change but what was needed would be new generations of readers for whom reading off a screen was as convenient, modal,

I might note the obvious—this dialogue, like the previous 31, is appearing in conventional text, in the *Bulletin* which is typeset and printed and mailed to the membership. It would make much more sense, economically, to make the *Bulletin* an electronic publication, put it on-line at the Science Fiction Writers of America website and offer access to all members ... but to the best of my knowledge this has never been the subject of serious consideration and we are no closer to an electronic *Bulletin* than we were in 1997. Here is a sterling example of ignoring the obvious ... you are welcoming us all to that new electronic era and announcing the death of conventional text in—well, in a conventional text medium. (Larry Janifer once commented on my science fiction that in sum it appeared to be "A man using a megaphone to denounce the use of megaphones.")

If you really want to think Mod, think new, you could consider that the periodic nature of the *Bulletin* itself should be questioned. Why limit the publication to a three-or four-time a year schedule and turn every issue, three months after its nominal date, into an almost unprocurable back item? If a reader—let us be optimistic and say we have a reader—wanted to read the first ten dialogues, say, or wanted to know what we thought of self-promotion, what course could be followed? There's no index to these dialogues and back issues are available on a scattershot basis. Who in any case would want to pay five or six dollars for a back issue? If the organization were truly interested in adopting the electronic model, all issues of the *Bulletin* would be available on-line in perpetuity. But this hasn't happened, not yet, and I would guess that this is the first time the suggestion has ever been made ... and it is made by a writer who, as you rightly infer, is still committed to conventional text as the only true means of "publication."

And indeed, a living anachronism, a genuine, certified Old Guy now (I remember a line from a fee novel I read over 20 years ago, "He was not yet a dirty old man but he lived in mortal fear that any morning now he would awaken and find himself one"), I cannot separate "publication" from print, I find it difficult to see the electronic model as true. I certainly can see that electronic model as a kind of subsidiary right, as a spin-off, an "electronic" edition of the new Danielle Steele bestseller in the same category as an audiobook, but I don't see it constituting publication at the site of origination. And I might suggest that those at the upper levels of the Science Fiction Writers of America hierarchy would agree with me, in terms of the observations I've made above.

Books have a kind of definition and tend to last in the way that electrons don't. That's the way that this organization seems to be voting in relation to the work which itself generates. The door to the future may be far open, we are in essence living in that future ... but just as the automobile, a clearly inefficient transportative means is still the most important product this country has ever produced, just as the automobile still remains to make any conception of national life without the automobile impossible, such may be the case with the print medium. Which means that, as in the year 2001, this neo-electronic revolution may again collapse. It's always time for the automobile to go away, but it doesn't.

—*◠◡◠*—

MIKE: Okay, let's take it objection by objection.

SFWA, you say, isn't on the cutting edge of technology. Of course not. *Entrepreneurs* are on the cutting edge of change; organizations, whether they be SFWA or religions or what-have-you, always lag behind.

But that doesn't mean the individual members of SFWA haven't figured out where the future lies. Even you, paper worshipper that you are, sold a story for electronic publication in 2006 that I know paid almost 4 times what you would have earned from the three digest prozines. A few years ago you sold a batch of electronic reprints to Fictionwise.com for the same amount you'd have gotten from a reprint anthology, maybe even a bit more. You will shortly be writing a regularly-published electronic column for an e-prozine that will pay you about three times what any of the digests would pay — all this in spite of the fact that by your own admission you're an Oldphart and an Unbeliever. Q.E.D.

As for turning these dialogues into phosphors, I don't know about you, but that's how I store them in my computer — and whenever a friend or newcomer has asked to see one or more that are unavailable, I don't print them out, I don't make photocopies, I e-mail them. It's probably getting near time for us to sell the collected dialogues as a book. In all likelihood we'll sell it to a print publisher, this being the first decade of the millennium, — but we'll submit it in electronic form, and proof galleys in .pdf form. And I'll tell you something else — if anyone reads these things twenty years from now, they'll be reading them in electronic form, not on paper.

Does it make me happy? Not especially. I'd rather look at a few shelves of my books than a couple of inches of my disks. But happy or unhappy doesn't matter; true or false does, and as Heinlein pointed out 60 years ago about another set of breakthroughs in "Solution Unsatisfactory," you can't embargo knowledge.

I would certainly agree that the car is *a* major American contribution, for better or worse, to civilization — but there are cities that function just fine without cars. Hell, half the New Yorkers and Londoners I know not only don't own a car, but most of them don't even know how to drive one. And I think that not only the computer industry but certain select individuals such as Jonas Salk might wish to argue with your placing the automobile above all other American contributions to the 20th century.

But to get back to e-publishing, it has also become a marketing tool. More than one romance writer has posted novels that got rejected at one or more houses, and primarily because of reader reaction and word-of-mouth later sold them for top dollar and saw them hit the bestseller lists. (What do I think of it? Personally I'm appalled that self-publishing can produce such results; realistically, I can see that more and more novels are going to be marketed this way, and some of them will sell like wildfire — and, indeed, some of them will deserve to. After all, how many times did *Dune* and *The Forever War* get bounced before they finally found a publisher willing to take a chance on them? How much sooner might they have made their indelible marks had Frank Herbert and Joe Haldeman had this marketing tool available to them?)

Anyway, I think you're barking up the wrong tree as you try to hold back the future. Just look around you: the question is not *whether* electronic publishing will become the dominant publishing medium, but only *when*. My own guess is that books will take a little longer, but magazines are right around the corner. Good or bad, artistic or inartistic makes no difference; all that counts is true or false ... and it's true. And the writer who doesn't begin seeking out the new markets isn't hurting the markets; he's just hurting ... but I think you can guess.

—◦◦◦—

BARRY: For the record: *Dune* did not exactly wallow in obscurity prior to its breakthrough. The novel ran as two long serials in *Analog*, the first four or five parts in 1963, the second three parts in 1965. Many book publishers turned it away feeling that the work was simply too long to be economically feasible, and Chilton's editor Sterling Lanier, a pretty good writer himself, was permitted to take the work for a minimal advance. Its subsequent history is part of the folklore of science fiction (Terry Carr persuaded Don Wollheim to take paperback rights for Ace on the basis that *Stranger in a Strange Land*, a pretty long sf novel, hadn't done badly at all, and had in fact perhaps established an audience for a work of this length). The non-existent Net and its publicity mechanisms would not have been at all relevant, in this instance, to the success of the work. Forty years ago (parodying Arthur Miller) I wrote, "If we cannot understand our history what can we understand?" so I offer you the same plea you have often offered me ... crush me if you will but please do so according to the facts. (*The Forever War* didn't need the Net either ... rejected as a book, it was at Ben Bova's suggestion broken into a series of novelettes which ran in *Analog* in the early 70s, thus persuading St. Martin's Press to take a chance on it and Betty Ballantine to take the paperback rights.)

But this marginalized set of grumbles and they are nothing more dramatic than that, don't of course fully address your point which is that electronic dissemination of prose in the mass market is absolutely inevitable and in less than a couple of decades will be the default mode of publication. This is perhaps true but I do not think that it is indeed inevitable. There may be something about prose, particularly prose fiction in electronic form, which is resistant to a wide audience. Remember the electric car? Clean, practical, cheap energy, perhaps a limited cruising range but most automobile trips are within a 50 mile range and you can recharge the thing in your driveway overnight, perhaps saving the gasoline-powered automobile (on a rental basis) for rare longer trips outside that cruising range.

That Car of the Future isn't happening though. For decades we were promised that cheap electronic vehicle which would become the sole medium of urban automobile transport and for decades the electric car has remained a bizarre novelty, rarely seen and rarely used. This is one Brave New Technological Modification which simply is not happening. I'm not sure why this is the case. That's a level of speculation beyond me, but there may be something in the human psyche which wants an automobile whose range and source of power are at least theoretically unlimited. Similarly, there may be something about the very quality of text and print which is intrinsic to the reading experience.

Isaac Asimov thought so ... he devoted one of his monthly *Fantasy & Science Fiction* essays some 35 years ago to the primacy of print as conveyor of prose ... cheap, convenient, absolutely portable, private, unobtrusive and it can contain pleasing graphics and illustrations as well. Print was not timebound, not a product of the century but, Asimov wrote, an example (like the diatonic scale) of a means of transmission which had reached utter efficiency and maximum effect early. "It's a stirring testimony to the power of the book by a man who loves books," Dean Koontz said to me. "And it is utterly convincing."

Kind of convincing to me as well is the previously noted fact that the technologically oriented and ever so futuristically-inclined Science Fiction Writers of America has failed to abandon the print medium of the *Bulletin* even though 90 percent of the membership (at a minimum) has computer knowledge and access; I don't think that corporately or on the executive level the organization has ever considered phasing out the print *Bulletin*. This seems to me a kind of statement. You might argue that there are a restless group of twenty-somethings and teenagers who will be seizing absolute power in the organization (and everywhere else) in twenty to thirty years and they will kick the print *Bulletin* sniveling down the stairs but I try not to extrapolate without cause and I won't believe this until it happens (and by nature of actuarial tables I probably won't have to believe it at all).

Welcome to 2007, and I have to agree that certain aspects of print, like the science fiction magazines, may soon be leaving the party. But that may be for reasons other than the presumed e-revolution (the magazines have been staggering for decades as I noted at the beginning of this discussion) and the remedy if there is any such may well have nothing to do with those electronic media.

In the meantime and in this era of eternal compromise we hump our way through the imponderable days and, at least in the short run, the electronic media appear less threatening to print than they did ten years ago. This may not by any means signal a trend but it is an observation. Just an observation.

—◦/◦/◦—

MIKE: That sounds remarkably rational and sensible as stated. Problem is, almost every statement either bends reality or ignores it.

Dune was bounced by every science fiction publisher, and wound up being published by Chilton (which dealt primarily in motorcycle books) solely because Sterling Lanier, who dabbled in science fiction, was an editor there. They had so little confidence in it that they printed something like 2,000 copies, and then pulped a few hundred of them, which is why firsts in dust jacket and fine condition go about $5,000 at auction. Were that the situation today, would Terry Carr have been more likely to notice Dune in a hardcover from a motorcycle publisher, or on the internet among other sf items? I submit that every editor, bar none, has to spend considerable time on the internet these days, and that means that in today's publishing world, no editor has time to read books from a house like Chilton unless he's a motorcycle fanatic.

Same thing with The Forever War. Tango all you like on the head of a pin, and it doesn't alter the fact that just about every publishing house turned it down — and that in 2007, a web page can often do you as much good as a truncated appearance in a magazine of diminishing circulation.

Yes, I remember the electric car. Wishful thinking of the past? I don't know. Ask me again when oil is $200 a barrel and gas is $7.50 a gallon. The technology's there — I mean, hell, even today the American ideal is a hybrid SUV — but enormously powerful entrenched interests consider the electric car detrimental to their business. And it always will be — but those interests ain't gonna be so powerful at $7.50 a gallon.

I am second to no one in my admiration for Isaac — but what he said, and what Dean Koontz agreed with, about print technology 35 years ago is simply irrelevant. In 1972 it was almost impossible to look ahead and see the states of print and electronic publishing in 2007, so I certainly don't blame him for being wrong ... but on the other hand I don't credit him with being right just because I love books and I wish he was right. He made a prediction based on the available information ... but today's amount of available information is greater by dozens of levels of magnitude.

As I said, the argument about the Bulletin is meaningless. First, the Bulletin is not required to show a profit, so needn't compete in the marketplace. Second, the Bulletin is run for all SFWA's members, and there are still a few Jurassic holdouts who don't own computers. Third, access to the Bulletin is limited to SFWA's membership and a few subscribers, so there is no need to go electronic and blanket the world (for no more cost, I should add, than blanketing the city block you live on.) And when any of those conditions change, you can bet your asp the Bulletin will go electronic.

You say that the magazines have been staggering for decades, as if science fiction books have not been. Yet it wasn't so long ago that an average midlist sale in paperback was 45,000 copies, and today it's about a third of that. Romance, like it or not, now constitutes more than half of the entire fiction market, and as their book sales and print runs have grown, our have diminished. Oh, not at the top where Isaac lived and Koontz lives, but down here where the bulk of the membership plies its trade. I don't think that even you will question that sales and print runs are down. Therefore, if you acknowledge that the electronic media is in the process of replacing the magazines, and the situation is the same in books (and we have shown over the course of these dialogues that book publishers are not the brightest nor the most adaptable of businessmen), why do you think it won't happen in books too? It'll happen more slowly, because they *aren't* very bright or adaptable, but there's absolutely no question that'll it'll happen.

You doubt it? Walk up to the first hundred kids you see — teens or younger — and ask them whether they'd rather read a printed page or a screen. After they finish looking at you like you're a relic from some other century, which of course you are, I think even you can predict the answer.

10 Collaborations—Theory

MIKE: It occurs to me that there's a subject you and I know about as well as anyone in SFWA, maybe even better (no, Connie, I'm not about to say "writing"), and that subject is collaboration.

I know that you have collaborated on a number of novels with Bill Pronzini. You've collaborated on short fiction with Kathe Koja, Carter Scholz, Jack Dann, me, Pronzini, probably a bunch of others.

As for me, by the year 2002 I had collaborated on short science fiction with 26 different partners, enough to form a nice thick collection—and since it was published I've collaborated with another 15 writers (and am maybe 10 more partners away from a companion piece to the collection). I collaborated on a novel with Jack Chalker and George Alec Effinger. In my starving-writer days I collaborated on some "adult" novels, and this year I'll be collaborating with two more SFWAns on two separate novels.

I've enjoyed some of my collaborating experiences, and I've hated some of them. I've produced some Hugo-nominated work, and I've also had a couple of partners whose work or work habits were so incompatible with my own that we never did produce a finished, saleable story.

I assume your experiences cover the same broad range. So maybe, before we discuss hoped-for triumphs and potential pitfalls, we should start at the beginning. Why *do* you collaborate, and do you like it better or worse than working on your own?

———

BARRY: I'd have to run the figures but I think my number of collaborators is about the same as yours ... certainly more than 20. Some of those collaborations have been quite serious and extended—four novels, about 80 stories with Bill Pronzini over a period of more than 30 years, 25–30 short stories and a never-published novel with Kathe Koja over a much briefer period—and some have been what the British call one-offs: short stories, for instance, with Jeffrey Carpenter (a University of Redlands freshman) in 1978 and Harry Harrison in 1974, both sold to *The Magazine of Fantasy & Science Fiction*. In the aggregate, maybe 140 short stories (about a third of my output in that form) and five novels. That's no record (the cousins who wrote as Ellery Queen certainly published much more than that and never wrote *other* than collaboratively, and Niven & Pournelle have collaborated on very long novels, some of them longer than any of mine with Pronzini) but it's enough —certainly makes me a maven-manqué, anyway.

From all of this have emerged these truisms based on hard experience:

1. Collaboration from a distance looks easier than solo work. Half the time-in-harness and you can always blame your collaborator for the bad parts. In truth, however, collaboration is twice the work and half the money. "Half the money" because it's half the money and "twice the work" because none of this comes from the eyebrow of Zeus; the disparate styles have to be fused into a third voice. If that fusion does not occur the collaboration is little more than a stunt or private joke; it won't work.

2. For these reasons, new writers should be discouraged from collaborating. The Furies sung sweetly for Orestes but then carried the entranced fellow off to Hades. The only good reason for collaboration would be this: both writers are in thrall to a subject, a style, a kind of work of which neither is individually capable. They can — through hard work, through that fusion of style — hope, however, to achieve in collaboration what could not have been done alone and that outcome is urgently desired by both. It is this urgency, this necessity, the radiance if you will, from that goal which will carry the writers through what can often be a rending process, because the joy of the work itself never will.

Like so many who collaborate I fell into the practice sidewise and its true obligation and onerousness were not apparent for a little while. Bill Pronzini and I were good friends already in the early 1970s by correspondence and a couple of meetings. He was selling *Alfred Hitchcock's* with what seemed to be contemptuous ease. I could not sell that magazine at all; my few mystery short stories were either in *Mike Shayne's* magazine or my desk drawer. I sent Pronzini one of the failed efforts, he cleverly rewrote the ending, *Hitchcock* rejected but *Shayne* took it. I tried it again, same outcome. I tried it *again*, same outcome. Three sales anyway of dead manuscripts. He asked for similar diagnosis and office surgery on a couple of science fiction rejects. We sold those too.

Fun, fun, fun. Until Bill came East in 1973 and Daddy took the T-Bird away. He was in New York for the Mystery Writers of America banquet (his Random House Novel, *Panic!*, sold to film for 50K that glorious April) and we went into our bedraggled backyard with bourbon on the rocks. "I have a novel I want to write," he said, "which could be terrific but I know I'm not capable of doing this alone. I want you to come in with me." I pointed out that he had just sold *Panic!* to the movies and delivered an ambitious suspense novel, *Snowbound*, to Clyde Taylor at Putnam's which Taylor expected to make a lot of money. (It did.) "Why would you want to collaborate with an avant-garde science fiction writer on a difficult mystery when you could at the very best make only half the money that you will make on *Snowbound?*

"Because I want to improve as a writer, I want to grow as a writer," Bill said. The Furies sang. Hades' gap yawned.

—⁓—

MIKE: I have a feeling we're not going to be in accord about almost any aspect of collaborating. (Big surprise, right?)

I know the official reason to collaborate is so that each author can bring one or more areas of expertise to a story that the other lacks, and that the finished product will therefore be a richer story than either could have produced alone.

I've done two collaborations, both novellas, for that reason. Once Susan Shwartz lacked the knowledge/experience of East Africa to give her story the proper verisimilitude. That particular subject was one of my strengths, we collaborated, and we got a Hugo/Nebula nominee and minor award winner out of it.

And once you and I pooled our ignorance. As you'll recall, we'd each been invited to a shared world anthology. Neither of us had read the books that created the world we were supposed to be sharing, so we each read *some* of the books, gave each other incredibly condensed versions of what we'd assimilated, and we each wrote half the story. It's since resold a few times, so I guess we fooled the world.

But there are a lot of other, equally valid reasons for collaborating. Let me count the ways—or, rather, the justifications:

1. It's a form of bonding. I have many friends in this field. I only see most of them a few days a year, sometimes less. One way of cementing that friendship is to collaborate on a story, to have a creative project that we can share. I have enjoyed some collaborations more than others, but I can honestly say that it's never cost me a friend.

2. Writing is a lonely business. You sit in your office (or attic, or garret) and spent endless hours working alone. Thanks to the internet, you can now collaborate with writers who are out of your immediate vicinity without waiting days or weeks for your pages to reach each other by snail mail, and it makes it a little less lonely.

3. I get an average of maybe eight anthology assignments a year, sometimes more — and since I write novels for a living and short fiction for pleasure (and a very small percentage of my living), I occasionally have to conclude that I simply cannot take the time to create a story for a particular anthology, given the required length and deadline. But I can always find time to polish a collaborator's story, and it means that I don't disappoint an editor who sought me

out and asked me to contribute to the project, I make *something* (or, from your viewpoint, half of something), I add to my bibliography, and I get to genuflect to #1 and/or #2 above.

4. I believe I'm one of the luckiest guys in the world. I have been able to make my living doing exactly what I most love to do—writing science fiction, and it has been a mostly joyful experience for well over a third of a century. I can't pay back; everyone who helped me 35 and 40 years ago is rich or dead or both. So I try to pay forward, and one of the ways I do it is to help talented newcomers get in print by collaborating with them. I've collaborated with a bunch of the people I taught at Clarion, with a couple of wannabees who impressed me at a Calgary workshop, with other beginners and near-beginners who were having some difficulty breaking into print despite their talent. That's why I started collaborating with Nick DiChario; he was clearly an extremely gifted newcomer, and clearly I saw it before some of the magazine editors did. (He's since been nominated for some Hugos and other awards, and we have collaborated so often that we actually sold a book of our collaborative short stories a few years ago ... but in the beginning, it was because I didn't want the field to lose that rare talent because he was getting discouraged trying to break into print on a regular basis.)

5. I tend to approach a story in a certain way, both conceptually and in the writing of it. Collaborating can be extremely educational, even after as many millions of words as I've sold. Jim Kelly doesn't see or approach a story quite the way Kristine Kathryn Rusch does, and she doesn't see or approach it quite the way Nancy Kress does, and she doesn't see or approach it quite the way Bob Sheckley did, and he didn't see or approach it quite the way Catherine Asaro does, and she doesn't see or approach it quite the way Harry Turtledove does, and he doesn't see or approach it quite the way you do.... Well, you get the point—and since I've worked with all of you, and maybe 40 others, and have seen first-hand how you all think and how you attack a story, I've expanded my own approaches and methodology, and that has to be a Good Thing.

Okay, tell me why I'm wrong, and then maybe we'll get down to the nitty-gritty of *how* we collaborate.

—⁊⁊⁊—

BARRY: You're not wrong. You're absolutely right. Your reasons for collaboration are valid, they overlap with many of my own and I have in the aggregate little to regret in my collaborative experiences. Three of the four novels with Bill Pronzini were extremely difficult, some of the hardest work I've ever had: endless drafts, scene rewrite, plot restructuring, attempts to get the voice right—but those three novels worked very well to our literary (if not financial) satisfaction and one of them, *The Running of Beasts* (Putnam 1976) may be close to the best we've ever done individually. The short stories with Kathe

Koja were — whatever their commercial outcome — miraculous in their speed and ease of composition; we were in such accord that the drafts seemed interchangeable. She could have written my draft, I could have written hers. "This doesn't feel like collaboration," she wrote me early, "but *conspiracy*."

And for all of its difficulties (difficulties which become manifest when it's not game-playing or chatter, when a serious attempt is being made to produce work of qualities) collaboration is *companionable*, there is someone else in the room and in the script with you. The damnable loneliness of writing, something understood by all of us (even the ebullient types such as you and Isaac Asimov) can be alleviated when there is another presence and the work becomes an exchange of interchange rather than a monolith.

So, agreeing for once with all you say, let me move on to your question: How do you collaborate? And the answer here has always been "It all depends." I have used ten or a hundred means of collaboration. In the Pronzini collaborations alone almost all of those means have been employed. Alternate sections. Rewriting of a first draft. Writing an audacious first sentence with an implied dare for the other to pick up on it. Composing a story to answer a question. (In "Prose Bowl" that question was, "What if writers competed in composition as if it were a series of football-type playoffs leading to a football-type Super Bowl?") Composing a story to pose a question. (That question in "A Clone at Last" was "What if a man who couldn't get laid in a whorehouse cloned an opposite sex version of himself?" Tributes/pastiches of writers we admired ("What Kind of Person Are You?" for Jack Ritchie). Demolitions of writing or writers we did not admire. (A long scene in *The Running of Beasts* was covertly a vicious put-on of a then-recent pretentious short story with a line about the enormity of the sexual act.) We collaborated, Bill Pronzini and I, in every conceivable literary fashion, up, down, backward and forward and that multiplicity of method was enacted through my many other collaborations.

Jeffrey Carpenter, that University of Redlands freshman, had a wild take on *Mork and Mindy* played without laughs, but couldn't after three directed rewrites find an ending. I wrote the ending. Valerie King had an ending implicit within her short-short story but didn't know it; I made it explicit. Harry Harrison wrote a stunt opening paragraph depicting me in the throes of a heart attack; I wrote a second paragraph giving him the heart attack back and we sold the mangled remains to Ed Ferman. The day Lillian Hellman died I wrote the Hammett-Chandler story which had haunted me for years (and with the holder of the Estate dead I was now freed from her specter) but my short story was amorphous; Carter Scholz doubled the length, found some brilliant scenes involving Nathanael West and a farmhouse upstate and "The High Purpose" in the 11/85 issue of Ed Ferman's magazine may be the single story of which I am proudest. Each of these methods worked because each was best for the work under consideration.

I remember well that novella in which we exploited our mutual ignorance of the source series. Do you think we dare give its name? A friend in the Rutgers University dormitory which was Erika's residence for her freshman year told her that it was the best science fiction story he had ever read. (He was not the same guy-in-the-dormitory who told her that *Phase IV* which I had novelized for Pocket Books, was his all-time favorite film which he watched three times a year. Rutgers, now home of championship football and basketball, had to settle for other distinctions in the athletically impoverished 90s.)

As a generalization on collaboration: whatever works *works* and needs no further justification.

—*∿∿∿*—

MIKE: Do I think we dare give its name? Not until the creator of the particular world we shared has passed onto the next plane of existence. He'd never sue, but why hurt his feelings or enrage him admitting we hadn't read the source? Might have to duck pretty fast—and what's a duck without source? (Sorry about that.)

My first dozen or so collaborations were with Paul Neimark, back in the late 1960s and early 1970s when we were both trudging through the "adult" field on our way to becoming Real Writers. (He later wrote the bestselling *She Lives*.) I was as fast a writer as you back then, and Paul was perhaps even a shade faster, and we decided to see how fast we could knock off one of these masterpieces. We lived a couple of miles apart in Highland Park, Illinois, at the time, and we had our daughters riding their bikes back and forth between the houses all day carrying chapters and partial chapters to each of us. We started at 10:00 in the morning—I occasionally got up before noon back then; horrible habit, and I've since learned better—and we finished the book at 9:00 at night. Okay, so they were only 50,000-worders back then, but that's *still* a lot of saleable words to grind out in a day (with time off to watch the Preakness in the afternoon). We didn't collaborate to produce a work neither of us could have produced alone. We didn't collaborate to cement a friendship. We didn't collaborate to overcome the loneliness of the long-distance writer. We collaborated because we *loathed* writing softcore sex books, and were happy to take half the money if we only had to do half the work. We couldn't afford to take none of the money and do none of the work, but that was the goal. (Another perfectly valid reason for collaborations, now that I think of it.)

Even then, I didn't mind the collaborating, only the limitations of the subject matter.

But there *is* one form of collaboration I hate. Problem is, it's not officially a collaboration—and that, of course, is screenwriting. The problem is that they pay you so much that you find ways of justifying it to yourself.

You don't have an official collaborator—at least, not at the beginning. But you have a producer going over every scene, first with an accountant who will tell you which scenes they can afford to do and which ones have to be jettisoned or rewritten for purely financial reasons; and when the accountant is gone, the producer — a few are highly literate, but most are barely sophisticated enough to write their names in the dirt with a stick — will tell you what changes *he* wants made. (Or his wife, or his kid, or his niece's hairdresser.) And I've never met a non-writer, including (especially) producers, who truly comprehends that if you make this major change on page 67, it's going to effect everything else from page 22 to page 103, and his one "little" change has just required you to completely rewrite the screenplay.

The special effects wizard will tell you what he can and can't do (these days, thanks to CGI, which often substitutes for both plot and character, he can do damned near anything — for a price), and then the producer will tell you whether the budget can handle that price. The director will tell you that you are somehow not managing to get his vision on paper, and you'd better take another run at it. And if you explain that you are adapting your own book or writing an original screenplay and this is *your* vision you're capturing, you've just bought a one-way ticket to the unemployment line. Directors are Gods; writers are infinitely interchangeable pieces.

Then, for reasons I explained the last time we talked about Hollywood, the odds are about 20-to-1 you're going to be rewritten anyway, so you've got still more collaborators. (I still remember the two writers who shared the Academy Award for *The Rain Man*. The first time they'd ever met was when they went up on stage to accept their Oscars.)

Okay, so there's one kind of collaboration that I don't enjoy.

While I was venting about Hollywood, I thought of one that may not exactly qualify as a collaboration, but I truly don't know what else it could possibly be, since it is a pooling of talents — yours as a writer, and your cover artist's as an interpreter of that writing. From time to time I've had artists who had been assigned to do my covers phone or e-mail me to ask what some person or alien or planet looked like, and when it's done with care, it's a very satisfying collaboration. Sometimes the writer and artist almost become a team, contemporarily or posthumously. You need look no farther than Edgar Rice Burroughs and J. Allen St. John, A. Merritt and Virgil Finlay, or Robert E. Howard and both Frank Frazetta and Roy G. Krenkel.

And now I've thought of still another type of collaboration, but since I've been running off at the keyboard here, I'll pose it to you. Not all editors are merely purchasing agents, though I'm sure we frequently wish they were. Have you had any interesting collaborations with any editors — which I suppose means, have they given you any input that made a story or a book different and/or better?

———*୨/୨/୨*———

BARRY: Haven't had that much help from editors in regard to work completed and delivered. Yes, Maurice Girodias gave me the premise and progression of the novel *Screen* entire in 1968 and his Olympia Press published it soon enough. Four years later George Ernsberger described the perimeter and the nature of the two leading characters in that *Lone Wolf* series he wanted me to write and that's what he got. But I can think of only a couple of instances in which editorial advice on a completed work was helpful: Ellen Datlow took in hand the rather fuzzy "Folly for Three," submitted to her second vampire anthology, found the real theme and progression, and directed me through a revision which enormously improved the story because it had at last been properly realized.

And in 1972 Robert Hoskins (1933–1993), my editor at Lancer, looked at the completed manuscript of a science fiction novel I had delivered two weeks earlier on a virtually open contract (an outline in one paragraph of about 60 words) which sat rather uneasily on his desk, and raised his head to show me an expression of utter disgust. "Barry," he said, "Why did you do this? Would you please go home and write me a novel?" This constituted the entire text of his editorial input, but he must have found Sheckley's Laxian Key because, in a flare of rage, I took the manuscript home, put it in a corner and in an angry fortnight wrote *The Men Inside*, which Hoskins took wordlessly and published in 1973. It didn't make much money (five or six overseas sales, though) and it wasn't on the Hugo or Nebula ballot, but I still think it's my best or second best science fiction novel and it wouldn't have existed without that one forceful piece of editorial advice. Hoskins knew what he was doing there.

(I did sell the novel which incited his disgust to Ace and it was published in 1974, that was *The Day of the Burning* and I don't think it was *that* bad, but its replacement was much better.)

Of course my experience with editorial input and collaboration was not typical ... most science fiction writers of my generation and the generation just earlier often published stories with Horace Gold, John W. Campbell and Frederik Pohl which could have been defined as true collaborations. I think it's fair to speculate that more than half the contents of *Galaxy* from 1950 to 1959 would not have existed without Gold's instigation and editorial intervention ... little as writers like Theodore Sturgeon might have celebrated that. Gold never saw a manuscript he felt he couldn't improve, at least in terms of his magazine, and these unsought, unwitting collaborations infuriated many of his contributors.

Collaboration between writers should, of course, never infuriate; writing is difficult enough on its own terms. Occasionally it does and the obvious course is for the collaborators to part at the earliest opportunity. (In all my decades I've had only one such experience; my prospective collaborator lectured me on the weaknesses of a story opening *which I had not yet delivered*. This way to the egress.) Sometimes this is not possible; Gilbert and Sullivan loathed one another, as history has made clear, but they were entirely too successful; neither they nor D'Oyly Carte, their producer, could afford to quit. (Sullivan tried several times but he had an expensive gambling habit and loved his social life, and these could not be properly sustained by grand opera, operettas with lesser collaborators, conducting or instrumental composition, as he learned bitterly over and again.) Success can be as painful as failure but the quality of that pain can be addictive.

But collaboration should be an act of friendship ... just like buying a story (as R.A. Lafferty wrote Damon Knight). I've found it so and *je ne regrette rien*, from that tiny story "Geraniums" with Valerie King to the sprawling catalogue with Bill Pronzini which for many writers would itself be a career entire.

———✐———

MIKE: Every time I've done a shared-world story I've had collaborative input from the editor; ditto for my novelizations of a terrible TV show and an interesting computer game. (Never had any input back in the starving-writer days when I novelized some nudie movies, but then, the scripts were only about eight pages long to begin with, and all the screenwriter, producer, director and actors cared about was that their real names never appeared in print, a consideration which they had in common with the novelizer.)

Yes, there are certainly some collaborations in science fiction that draw major money — the Kevin Anderson–Brian Herbert *Dune* books, all the Larry Niven–Jerry Pournelle novels, and the endlessly collaborating Baen crew of David Drake, David Weber, Eric Flint, Mercedes Lackey and John Ringo. But unlike Sullivan, I think it's apparent that most or all of these collaborators have done and can do just fine on their own. Still, it's one more reason to consider collaborating: very occasionally the advance pulled down by a team is greater than the sum of the advances pulled down by the individual members of that team.

I think that pretty much covers the theory behind collaborating. (Well, one more: two good friends can collaborate for the *SFWA Bulletin* if they almost never agree on anything.) Next issue we'll get down to the nitty-gritty, the how-to, the *practice* of collaboration.

11 Collaborations — Practice

MIKE: Last issue we discussed the theory of collaboration, the justification for sitting down and sharing the creative process with someone else.

Now it's time to get down to the actual nuts and bolts of collaborating. I've had more than 40 collaborative partners, you've had close to 20, so we can certainly address the subject with some authority.

I suspect the only kind we haven't done is the Kuttner/Moore type, where he would write a few pages, pop off to the bathroom or to answer a phone call, and come back to find out that she'd picked up in the middle of his unfinished sentence and written four more pages in the identical style. But then, they were a married couple who worked together every day for almost two decades. Most of our collaborations are long distance, by mail in the past, by e-mail today.

So (says your collaborator on this dialogue, neatly avoiding the first examples), I won't ask how you collaborate, because you've had enough partners that I suspect that you've collaborated in every way possible ... but perhaps you'd like to suggest the way or ways that you feel most comfortable (and does the fact that you find it comfortable make the stories demonstrably better?)

—⁓—

BARRY: As noted in the previous dialogue, I've collaborated in every imaginable (and I'd add a "few unimaginable" if that wasn't perhaps a bit suggestive) fashion: alternate sections, completely rewritten drafts, tightly structured, no structure whatsoever. I don't think that any is necessarily and abstractly "better" than any other. The method that best suits the work is the method best adopted.

Kathleen Koja and I wrote moody, atmospheric short stories, highly dependent upon an attempted linguistic virtuosity and often (deliberately) sliding into obscurity and murk. For such stories, alternating sections seemed best. We were working at keeping the voice consistent and holding in place work which if completely drafted and rewritten might have lost spontaneity or (with one writer having utter control of the draft) disappeared into obscurity.

99

Conversely, three of the novels written with Bill Pronzini were aimed at the commercial suspense market, were highly plot-dependent and hung upon the foreshadowing, the planting of clues and the continuing implication of character. Working in alternating first drafts would surely have taken these works off track. What we did — and this necessitated at least one face-to-face session of about a week's duration, usually at the starting point — was to lay out what we called a "progression" ... a carefully-detailed chapter-by-chapter accounting of the plot after which, working to that outline, we would write alternating chapters. I would then write a third draft of that extant second draft, and Bill would do a final-and-polish. If this sounds tortuous I note that I am here making it simply because the progression often had to be reshaped after the original draft and frequently the second-draft chapters were not successful. There are pages in *The Running of Beasts* which were rewritten 20–25 times and *still* don't seem quite right. ("Let's do another polish, boss, before we let it go.") There was a long scene in that novel in which one of the characters mourned over the corpse of his girlfriend at the funeral home, powerful and depressing, maybe the most powerful writing in the book, but it had no plot function, skewed the focus and was pitilessly dumped, all 5000 words of it. I think that at base we still feel that this book needs another draft or ten, that if we could only just get it right, well then everything would have been different. Just as the short stories with Kathleen were effortless to write and easy to relinquish (we wanted someone else to see how well we could do this) the Pronzini novels were let go only grudgingly.

So it is the nature of the work which determines the method. Of course sometimes — but rarely with intense or "serious" work — it is the method which determines the work. Harry Harrison, as I've noted, gave me a heart attack to open "The Everything I Type Is True Machine" in 1974; what the heck, I gave him a heart attack of his own on the second page. (He enacted something equally regrettable upon me in his second go-round.) A careful progression, an outline, even some real sense of where the story might want to go, would have cut off what was essentially a joke and written in that spirit. (We sold it to *Fantasy & Science Fiction* so it couldn't have been that bad.)

The work shapes the method. That is an insight I would put in the Common Book of Prayer right below what the very wise Gerald F. Reidenbaugh, Drama Department Chairman at Syracuse, said to the Shubert Fellow in September 1964 on the heart of playwriting: "The structure *is* the vision.")

I don't think I worked on anything — collaboratively, individually — as hard as I worked on those progressions for *The Running of Beasts*, *Acts of Mercy* and *Night Screams*. Collaboration, seriously approached, is extraordinarily difficult. (And approached not so seriously it can be fun but "fun" and "writing" are oxymoronic and meant to be so.)

MIKE: I take enormous issue with your throwaway line here. Why in the world would you write if it *wasn't* fun? Lord knows there are easier ways to make a living.

(I would also question why any writer would want a story to deliberately slide into obscurity and murk, but I suppose that's fodder for a whole different dialogue. Or mudder, if you're a race track *aficionado*.)

Anyway, let me get to the subject at hand, and try to lay out some ground rules for collaborators.

Rule #1 (and by far the most important): Determine before a word is written who has the final say. I would imagine more teams (and friendships) break up over that than for any other reason. You are (presumably) professionals, and you put your professional reputations on the line every time you submit a story. If one partner is pleased with what you've done and one isn't, if one wants to submit *now* and one wants to keep polishing and rewriting, you'd better know on the front end which partner's opinion is going to rule the day.

(How two journeyman pros of equal stature decide that on a contribution to a magazine is up to them. If it will provide a bit of a guideline, my own rule of thumb has always been that if the story is an assignment rather than a speculative job, whoever was given the assignment gets the final say, which seems only fair. Writer A and Writer B may be equal in ability, and may put in equal efforts on the story, but if Editor X specifically requested the story of Writer A, then it seems reasonable that Writer A, by virtue of getting a pre-sold assignment, should have the final word.)

Rule #2: Determine, before a word is written, how the byline will appear — which is to say, whose name will be first. Again, if it's an assignment, clearly the editor will want the author he solicited to be the first name on the byline, but sensitive (read: petulant, childish, selfish, pigheaded) egos can get a little out of hand when the story turns out even better than anticipated (or worse), and it's best to have this settled on the front end.

Rule #3: Determine, before a word is written, how the collaborators are going to split the money. It's very easy to say "half-and-half," and that's the way it usually works ... but there are always extenuating circumstances.

You think not?

Circumstance #1: Writer A has sold a highly-acclaimed 30,000-word novella at some point in the past. He is offered a book contract. For whatever reason — deadlines, laziness, lust for his potential opposite-sex collaborator — he seeks a partner. Since he wrote the original 30,000 words, most of which will remain, and since it was his concept and his handling of the original that got him the contract, and since an equal division of labors on the new section implies that he'll probably have written 60% to 65% of the finished product, is a 50–50 split fair?

Circumstance #2: Writer A has a nice idea but a totally unsalable story. In fact, he has a *lot* of unsalable stories. In truth, he's not a very good writer or a very frequent seller. But his friend Writer B is both, and agrees to take one of Writer A's horribly-mishandled concepts, rewrite it from scratch, and sell it to one of his regular markets. He may call it a collaboration out of friendship, but clearly he did almost all of the final draft, and indeed it sold only because of his literary skills, so is a 50–50 split the only conceivable one?

There are other circumstances, of course, but you get the idea.

So here are three considerations—or, if you prefer, three potential conflicts—that *must* be solved before the collaborators sit down to write, or there may be huge problems up the road.

Time for me to go collaborate with the coffee maker. You want to give them a few rules for *after* the writing begins?

—ɷɷɷ—

BARRY: Agree with your first principle. One writer has to be the Captain of the little cruiser and must be so designated at the outset. Someone must be permitted the final call. It doesn't matter who—it can in close cases be settled by a coin flip or in fact the identity of the Captain might be determined anew with every collaboration—but one of you must have the right to unchallenged declare the draft at an end, or one particular market to be off-limits or one more draft necessary. If there isn't a clear line of authority *outside* the perimeter of the story itself, there can be a good deal of trouble and it's possible to get mired (speaking of mud and murk) in a process without definable end.

In my two most important collaborations, with Pronzini and Kathleen Koja, the other writer was the Captain. This was understood from the start, it never varied through the duration of the collaboration and all its produce and I never wanted it any other way. (It was contributory to the decision that in both cases I felt the other to be the stronger writer.) In my collaborative short stories with two young writers, Valerie King and Jeffrey Carpenter, who were unpublished at the time, there was never any question that I would have control of the final script (I would not have offered collaboration without that control). Valerie King's little vignette had a neat idea but no ending; Jeffrey Carpenter's savage account of how returned astronauts would be integrated into the population was closely observed and had some brutal comic dialogue but its ending was fatuous, a silly joke which sold out a disturbing story for a cheap laugh. Neither fix was particularly difficult, both — in my opinion — were obvious and in one case early and in the other late I made the fix and sold the story to the first editor who saw it. (And in both cases the market had been my determination.)

As a generality, I'd rather be the crew than the Captain. It suits my deferential and ever-accommodating personality and also (passive-aggressive fashion) removes from me the ultimate responsibility. As another generality, and to avert any argument, I've always asked that my collaborator's name precede mine on the script and in the published version. There have been a few cases (as with Carpenter) where the editor went against that instruction, used my name in precedence but I was never happy with that.

Does precedence of name matter other than as the servant of ego? I would not think so and yet "Sullivan and Gilbert" seems, somehow, deeply wrong. Hart and Kaufman? Hammerstein and Rodgers? May and Nichols? Great collaborations make for euphonious collaborative names (just as great horses, except for Smarty Jones, always have great names) and yet "Sullivan and Gilbert" makes me twitch.

Next entry, I'll go into the particulars of one major and one minor collaborative work; a brief documentary of the technique applied. Meanwhile, why don't you tell us—no names necessary of course—of your easiest collaboration and your most difficult. Did you ever have a collaboration so unhappy that you resolved to have as little as possible to do in future with the person?

—*ooo*—

MIKE: Where to start? With great horses' names, of course. I take it you've never heard of Swaps, Tim Tam, or Seattle Slew?

The easiest collaboration? My first inclination is to say Nick DiChario, because we did eleven of them, enough for a hardcover collection a few years back, and we're still good friends. But actually, just about every collaboration I've done with a top writer has been easy and pleasant. Of them all, *you* have been the most difficult to collaborate with, because your authorial voice is so distinctive; I can't match it—I doubt that anyone can, though Dick Lupoff came close in a parody he did of your work years ago—so I have to rewrite every sentence of yours to give the story a consistent tone. Pain in the ass, but of course, the end results were fine, and they all sold to major markets. If I had to name one writer beside Nick who was most in tune with me, at least on the story we were writing, it'd probably be either Bob Sheckley or Harry Turtledove.

Is there anyone I will never work with again? Yes, a few. Is there anyone I will have nothing to do with because of the collaborative experience? No, of course not; I'm not that petty. You can't blame someone because his approach and methodology is so different from yours that the collaboration becomes an unsatisfactory experience.

Is there anyone I'll never collaborate with? Yes. My award-winning daughter. I keep asking her, and she keeps refusing, saying I'm too grumpy and bossy. Can you imagine that? Sweet, innocent, soft-spoken me? (She did write the intro to my collection of collaborations a few years back—and spent most of it explaining why she won't collaborate with me. She's still in the will, but just barely.)

Okay, so how do I collaborate?

With a pro of equal stature, no problem. We discuss the story, sometimes in person or on the phone, more often via e-mail. Usually they'll do either the first half and I'll finish it (Rusch, Asaro, Burstein, Kelly, Kress, Gerrold) or we'll do alternating sections (you — at least on our novella — Ian, Sheckley, Shwartz), or they'll do the draft and I'll do the polish (Turtledove, Kenyon, Sherman, Marston).

With newcomers, they *always* do the first draft, and I always do the polish. Which makes sense. But usually I have to restrain them a bit. Since they *are* newcomers, and I'm essentially offering them a guaranteed sale, most of the time they want to impress me, and instead of doing it with their writing, they do it by tossing out 75 ideas, of which maybe 72 are not viable. If they come up with an acceptable plot, or one I can make acceptable, I prefer that, because it gives them a story they're interested in writing for reasons above and beyond getting into print. If they can't come up with one, I'll give them the plot, and usually an outline of a couple of pages (maybe 500 words) for a short story. I don't like them to write without first discussing it with me, because there's usually a reason they haven't sold, or sold much, and I don't want them to write a complete story that I can't save but have to dump. It's a waste of both our time, and it doesn't do much for their self-confidence.

For a short story, I'd prefer to see the whole draft; I mean, how the hell much is there to a 5,000-worder anyway? If I need to see something before they're done, it'll be the first 400 words. If a newcomer's going to make a catastrophic mistake, that's usually where it'll be — or where it'll begin. (And that's why, when I edited a trio of men's magazines back in my starving-editor days, it was company policy to fire any first reader who couldn't reject 30 stories an hour. You've *got* to grab the reader on page 1, especially if you're a beginner and the reader hasn't learned to trust you yet.)

Typical mistakes I'd have to fix? Use of name brands in something less than glowing circumstances. Use of plots and concepts that were new to the beginner but old hat to the editor who assigned the stories. And (especially) excess wordage. (I never had to prune a story written by any of the names I mentioned above. I invariably had to cut 25 to 40 percent of the beginners' stories.)

You'll notice I'm speaking solely of short fiction here. I have thus far collaborated on only one science fiction novel — and that was a gimmick book, a round-robin novel with Jack Chalker and George Alec Effinger where each of us tried to stick the next guy in line with an insoluble problem. I'll be collaborating on novels with a couple of journeyman SFWA writers in the next year, and I'm sure we won't run into any problems, but I can't discuss the process until I undergo it. I collaborated with Paul Neimark, as I've mentioned, on a couple of dozen adult novels, back in the late 1960s and early 1970s, but we were only after money, not quality, and were writing for publishers who cared less about quality than page count and deadlines, so I don't think it's a meaningful experience for this topic.

Okay, I can see you're dying to tell me about your collaborations, and also why Swaps wasn't a great horse, so I shall gracefully and cordially step aside (see Laura? *Cordially*, and with a friendly smile and non-threatening manner) and let you take over.

———◦∿∿∿◦———

BARRY: Swaps was not a great horse. Swaps did not campaign out of California, never came to the New York tracks (the center of the racing universe just as New York City is the center of Western Civilization) and, correct me here if necessary, never won a race outside of California other than the Kentucky Derby. Nashua destroyed him in the famous 1954 match race, not that (post–Ruffian) I am any fan of match races. And Paul di Filippo's first published story in *Unearth* in 1977, a parody of my astronaut fictions, was even deadlier than Richard Lupoff's "Grebzlam's Game" in *Fantastic* a few years earlier. (The Lupoff was good, you understand. It made me want to go to a bunker and hide for a few years. Instead I settled for a statement of general renunciation. Note how well that worked.)

The minor collaboration: Jeffrey Carpenter, an 18-year-old freshman at the University of Redlands in 1978 when I was Writer in Residence for the first time, had a cute short-short about returning astronauts; after communal months in orbit they had become so attuned to the common good and chaste brotherly love that they were unable to re-integrate into the vicious society to which the Project had returned them. Gentle, loving, vulnerable, the first returnees were helpless victims. In its wisdom and after that disaster, the Project elected to return to the halfway houses of families who would treat them as unkindly, contemptuously, brutally as they treated one another. Carpenter tracked that process.

Neatly if somewhat clumsily written, but it had no ending; the astronaut who centered the story had a lot of mean things done to him and was humiliated. I told Carpenter that the story with a polish might be salable if he could manage some conclusion. He tried, but the polish was not successful — he was young, and this was his first completed story — and the only ending he could find was the astronaut being murdered; that was melodramatic and also predictable. Simply repeated the point. Two rewrites didn't help (he had no better idea for an ending) so with a sigh I took the story and his permission, final drafted toward a conclusion where the astronaut, goaded to fury, screamed and cursed at his hosts who smiled and welcomed him back to Earth. Ed Ferman took it quickly. I assumed a reluctant domination here, but don't think the story could have otherwise sold and it *should* have sold; it was a *Mork and Mindy* spinoff with some real savagery.

The Running of Beasts was, as I've noted severally, a very difficult novel to write. The premise upon which it rested was as close to original as any which crossed my line of sight: a serial murderer in an Adirondacks community committed his crimes in a fugue state and the "normal" personality had no idea that he was the killer. The novel used several points of view (a reporter, a washed-up alcoholic actor, a television commentator, a local constable, the area's sheriff and the killer himself in italicized scenes detailing murder) to stagger through the crimes and the solution; any of the viewpoint characters could have been the assailant. To bring this off in some social context, to make all the viewpoint characters sympathetic, credible and capable of being the killer, and to manage this in a way which would fairly clue without being predictable or fatuous was difficult. Extremely difficult. The foreshadowing was careful, and as good as was our work, we never thought the novel had been managed to its fullest potential. The actual ending — the revelation of the killer's identity *after* the case had been apparently "solved" — occurred to us only in the final draft and it was a shocker, but also demanded keying and we had to rework some of the foreshadowing.

Endless drafts here, endless exchanging of manuscripts in that ancient era of 1976 before e-mail. There are, as I have noted, pages of that novel whose published version represents 25 previous drafts. Everybody wrote everything, and 31 years later I know that Bill Pronzini feels as I do, that if we could get just *one* more draft, well, sir, the work would have been adapted for your local movie palace decades ago. But this was one of those maddeningly elusive works which will always need one more draft and, losing a promised 250K deal, we received finally a tenth of that from David Susskind's Talent Associates. Film was never made (or again maybe it was, maybe it opened in four theatres in 1980 or was made in France. How would we know? In situations like this the author is the last to learn or never learns or is dead or is all three.)

We learned a lot writing that novel and are probably the better for it but there is no way I would go through that process again. Pronzini won't ever come off the California circuit again and I, like Kelso, am New York based.

———❧———

MIKE: 1. Swaps set a world record in Florida. 2. Swaps set 2 American records in Chicago. 3. The match race was held in 1955, not 1954, and the only reason it was held at all — Swaps had an infected foot and his principals wanted to scratch — is because Washington Park and NBC had spent tens of millions of dollars promoting the race and wouldn't allow him to scratch. 4. New York is the center of Western Civilization only to thoroughly provincial New Yorkers. (Well, you *did* say to correct you if necessary. It was.)

Any method that produces a good story is a viable method, but some are a hell of a lot more difficult than others. Janis Ian and I tossed it back and forth almost literally a paragraph at a time, which produced a very nice story but was wildly counter-productive in terms of time spent. Every once in a while, with a journeyman pro I trust, I simply get half the story, with no prior knowledge of what it's going to be about, and if it's well-written (and it almost always is) it becomes a truly interesting challenge. Of course, the biggest challenge when going half-and-half rather than polishing a partner's entire draft, is matching that authorial voice. Yours, as I say, is so unique as to be unreproducible except as the parodies you mentioned ... but most of my partners' voices have been reasonably close to mine. Usually it's a matter of deciding which of two correct means of expression to use. For example, Kris Rusch is a "Barry said" advocate while I am a "said Barry" devotee. They're both fine; the trick is to hit upon one mode of expression, whether formal or colloquial, and remain consistent.

It occurs to me that there's one other major mechanical point we haven't addressed, and that is that both parties had better be using compatible word processing programs. That was more important in the old days, when there was Word and Word Perfect and Easywriter II and Volkswriter and a dozen others; these days almost everyone uses some form of Word. (Though I should point out that you, unique individual that you are, do not, so everything you send me must get converted into .txt files, worked on, returned as e-mail, and so forth, and only when we're all done do I convert the finished product to a Word file so the nice people at the *SFWA Bulletin* can read it.)

Okay, got any last words of wisdom — about collaborating, not about Swaps — before we close this thing? Maybe a couple of general guidelines we haven't touched upon yet?

—*◊◊◊*—

BARRY: If I were as much of an authority on horse racing as I claim to be on the art and craft of science fiction I would have lived a simpler life. Or, as the epigraph to my *Underlay* would have it, "I would have been wearing diamonds ... except that I ran out of money too soon." Nashua *was* a better horse than Swaps though, just as Native Dancer was a better horse than Dark Star.

Bad things happen to good horses in the Kentucky Derby. Bad things can happen to good writers in collaboration too ... some writers (like Fredric Brown and Randall Garrett, say) should never have collaborated. That is because collaboration can sometime bring out the worst rather than the better parts of those writers; the mechanics or play of collaboration can sometimes occlude vision, get between the writers and the material itself. Overall, however, and handled respectfully and with a sense of proportion (this is *not* the answer to all of your individual problems) collaboration can be a pretty good thing and I recommend it. Literary writers and quality lit editors tend not to understand collaboration as well as do we in the genres by the way: the editor of the *Georgia Review* confessed in a letter responding to my story with Batya Swift Yasgur that he simply had no idea how or why writers could collaborate on a story and he was at a loss to suggest revision because he could not imagine how it would be done. (We persuaded him that it could be done and sold the story.)

Once again, showing that we are more adaptable and professional than those quality lit people, we fare onward. But one final advisement: unless you and your collaborator are Ellery Queen, don't quit writing's day job. And writing's day job is your own work.

MIKE: Fortunately, most racing writers and experts are not provincial New Yorkers, which is why Swaps was voted Horse of the Year.

As for the rest of it, I don't know that examples of how either of us collaborated in particular cases have any meaning outside of those cases, so it might be best to sum up with some reasonable general principles:

1. Determine on the front end who has the final say.

2. Determine the byline.

3. Determine the way you will split the money.

4. Make sure you can read each other's files (that's technically, not artistically).

5. If it's an assignment and you decide to get a collaborator, clear it with your editor first.

6. Have an understanding up front regarding resales (i.e., what if one of you is desperate for the money four years up the road, and the other, who is less desperate, insists on holding out for a higher price?)

7. Have an understanding up front regarding individual collections, and how the pay breaks down, since a collection will be paid for with one advance, not broken down by stories.

8. Don't come to me when your partner wants to kill you.

SECTION 2

The Business

12 Agents

MIKE: There are a lot of misconceptions about agents.

One is that you can't sell without one. This is demonstrably false; I think most of us sold our first novels without an agent.

Another is that an agent can sell an inferior book. Also false. An agent can get your manuscript read faster, and can probably negotiate a better advance (though you should remember that if it's only 10 or 15 percent better, it's going right into the agent's pocket), but no agent can make an editor buy an inferior novel.

(Well, yes, they can — but only if it's "You buy Joe Phan's first novel or you don't get the new Stephen King/Tom Clancy/Danielle Steele book." But while it's theoretically possible, consider the reaction of King/Clancy/Steele when this gets out — and it *always* gets out — and ask yourself just how long Mr. or Mrs. Eight-Figure Advance would stay with such an agent.)

Still, an agent's a handy thing to have. They usually know who's buying what, they *can* get you a faster read, the good ones can spot little killer clauses in contracts that slip by a lot of writers, they act as a buffer between the author and the editor, they harass the publisher and his accountant for your money, they make your foreign sales, some of them make your movie/tv sales, some of them make your short fiction sales. The good ones are worth their weight in gold; the bad ones can destroy a writer's career so fast you wouldn't believe it.

And *I'm* on the outside looking in. *You* have worked for a literary agency for the past couple of decades. What particular insights can you bring to the subject of agents that most writers don't know but really *should* know?

———

BARRY: It's more than a couple of decades, Mike. With some time off for good behavior (i.e., the fiction of "full-time" freelancing), I've been affiliated with the Scott Meredith Literary Agency, man and boy, for 33 years. I walked into the place on 6/2/65 and with distraction and interruptions, presidential impeachment and resignations, the excitement surrounding the Gulf of Tonkin resolution and the American flight from Saigon, I've been here since. It has been interesting, as you know. It is my theory that the arc of the Scott Meredith Literary Agency, open for business on 6/29/46 and continuously under Scott Meredith's aegis until his death on 2/11/93, is an arc which has become a paradigm for the course of publishing in this country from the end of World War II through the end of the century. That course has involved every aspect of how the delivery system has changed, and it's a remarkable story, still misunderstood or (in the main) not understood at all. Someday I am going to attempt the True History of the Scott Meredith Literary Agency, and it will amaze and divert the multitudes (or so I would like to believe).

In the meantime, pending that guided tour of the cemetery of so many possibilities, you ask for "particular insights ... that most writers don't know but really should know." That's a large question whose generality somewhat terrifies. These past years, when I'm asked "How you doing?" or "What's going on?" or "What's the big problem in your life as you see it?," I've been responding, "These questions are too large for me. I cannot deal with them. Ask me if Bruckner or Mahler is the better composer and I can say some interesting things; ask me why Walter Tevis's *Mockingbird*, although better written, sardonic, and altogether a more mature work than *The Man Who Fell to Earth*, is not a better novel and I'll suggest why that is the case." But what writers "don't know but really should know" makes me kind of shudder. What's your opinion of dogs? What's the real significance of pari-mutuel horse racing? You get the idea.

But here are a couple of facts that most writers should know if they don't:

1. Agents are like divorce lawyers or medical practitioners. There are good lawyers (I hope) and not-so-good lawyers, but all of them in the State of New Jersey have to deal with the rules and statutes of divorce in the State. Lawyer A can't find a whole new set of statutes or conditions unknown to Lawyer B; Lawyer C can't change the custody or division-of-property laws. Some lawyers are better than others at working around the system or making the system less onerous; none of them, however, can shift the system itself.

And whether I'm represented by the Virginia Kidd Agency, Curtis Brown, Robert Gottlieb of William Morris, your own Eleanor Wood, or the Scott Meredith Literary Agency, my agent is confronted by the same editors, the same publishers, the same marketing conditions. No agent can create a new editor or series of markets. Once in a great while, a new agent might market a science fiction novel out of genre and obtain a better outcome (placement or advance or both) than might have been the case in genre, but this is rare. You can't sneak science fiction into mainstream markets under a disguise and you cannot, as an agent, turn a $5,000 deal into a $100,000 sale to someone who doesn't know what's going on. Not any more.

This occasionally happened decades ago. John Cristopher's *No Blade of Grass* was rejected in the mid–1950s by many science fiction markets who found this post–nuclear novel familiar, predictable, the same old stuff. Scott Meredith's inspiration was to market it to *The Saturday Evening Post* as a "controversial Cold War novel." The *Post* fell upon the work as if it were a true tour of the Kremlin's plans. The magazine paid $80,000 and ran it serially; there was a movie sale for more than that. Then a *Reader's Digest* condensed book. The novel rejected by Ballantine and Ace became a best seller.

So this kind of thing could happen in the old days, but these are newer days and the *Post* doesn't exist anymore. If your agent can't sell your novel, it's not likely that a new agent can find a different outcome, and a prospective new agent would be inclined to reject the novel unread anyway and ask for something new; agents hate to take on work which has already been through its logical range of markets.

2) Agents are something like symphonic conductors; it's a profession which is open to fraudulence and incompetence because the audience cannot really tell a good one from a bad one or (Orpheus Chamber Orchestra) from no conductor at all. Many agents appear "better" than others because they represent more successful writers; success goes to success. It was easy for Joe Torre to look intelligent managing the New York Yankees but he's the same guy who, when managing the Mets and Cardinals, was thought of as being pretty dumb. Give me Stephen King and I'll do better than Stephen King's agent would do with me. In fact, you or I could do just about as well with the King account as any of the agents I've named above. And King's agent — as you suggest — can't sell a bad novel by an unknown writer. You rise or sink to your material.

But, as with symphonic conductors, when a great one does come along, the audience (not to say every musician in the orchestra) can tell the difference. Bernstein could gets sounds out of Mahler than Mitropoulos or Mehta (good conductors both, you understand) couldn't. There are writers who owe their very careers to brilliant agenting. I just know of no systematic way in which a writer in early or even mid-career can find such an agent. And of course — this is a cliché — one agent may be terrible for X and very good for Y. There is no agent about whom disgruntled ex-clients cannot tell unhappy stories; there is none among these agents who cannot elicit testimonials. It all depends. It is a highly subjective business.

But I wouldn't look for an agent to get a career started, and I wouldn't have undue expectation of any agent; a writer's career rests largely on her own efforts. Agents are ancillary. They can make it easier, and they can also make it a lot worse. (You're quite right in saying there are agents who "can destroy a writer's career so fast you wouldn't believe it.")

All that being said, it's still worth trying to get a good agent, just as the orchestra board, cynical as it may be, knows that it's worth making a real effort to get a good conductor. How would you recommend that writers conduct such a search?

—◁◈▷—

MIKE: Let me begin by reiterating that I think an agent can make an enormous difference. The one I got rid of in 1983 had sold maybe a dozen novels for me — but always to the same publisher; it was easy for her to do, much easier than shopping around for better offers, and of course I had no idea that any other publisher had any interest in me — so as long as *my* publisher was buying I was happy. I didn't know much about the foreign market, so I didn't object to not making any foreign sales until 1983, when I made my first two — and came away with twice the money I'd been paid in America ($1,000 more from Japan, $1,000 less from Germany), which made me realize what I'd been missing. And when she tried to sell a sequel to *Birthright: The Book of Man*, a novel in which I had killed off the entire human race, without first asking me if I would or could write it, I decided it was a good time to part company.

My new agent put my next novel up for auction, which scared the hell out of me. After all, my previous agent had convinced me that no one else wanted me, and I was sure this was bound to offend my current publisher, possibly to the point I would be cut loose. (I was very naive.) Within weeks *three* different publishers were bidding, and all had offered me at least 300 percent more than I'd been getting. My new agent also made 31 foreign sales in the first 18 months we were together (and 16 years later, we're still together). And she's never tried to sell a sequel that couldn't possibly be written without invalidating the original novel.

So yeah, an agent can make a difference.

A good agent also knows that clients are not interchangeable, that each requires special handling. You can't market an Anne McCaffrey, who lives on the *New York Times* bestseller list, the way you market Nancy Kress or Connie Willis, who don't show up on the *New York Times* list (no shame there; hardly any of us do) but win more than their share of Hugos and Nebulas. And you can't market Nancy and Connie the same way, because while both are brilliant they don't write the same kind of stories. And neither of them can be marketed like Gene Wolfe, who can't be marketed like Michael Bishop, who can't be marketed like Lois McMaster Bujold, who can't be marketed like me. The agent who doesn't realize this, who assumes that because it's all called science fiction it must all be sold and promoted in the same way, is doing her entire stable a disservice.

Okay, so how do you find the agent who's right for you?

Step one: get your hands on a SFWA Directory and turn to the back, where every agent and his/her stable of SFWA writers is listed. See where you think you'd be most comfortable. Are you happier with a new agent, who lacks experience and some clout, but who doesn't have 27 writers who out-earn you? Are you happier with an established agent, who will perhaps have less time for you, but may bring more expertise to the table?

Step two: contact some of the writers in the stable and ask them for pros and cons about the agent. And since most of them will have nothing but favorable comments—those who don't will have left—try to find some writers who *did* leave and find out why.

Then it's a matter of deciding what's important to you, personally.

For example: Does the agent have a good foreign desk? They're not all interchangeable, you know.

For example: Does the agent return phone calls promptly? And is this important to you?

For example: Does the agent charge 10 percent or 15 percent? And if it's 15 percent, what do you get that other writers don't get for 10 percent?

For example: What incidental expenses will he bill you for? (This can run the gamut from postage and phone calls to copying and use of personal couriers for in-city delivery of manuscripts.)

For example: Does the agent deal with Hollywood (including TV) himself, or does he have a media specialist agent? And if so, is the media agent any good? Who does the media agent handle and what has he sold?

For example: Can the agent receive e-mail? (If not, and if you like to keep in constant touch, you're probably looking at some hefty phone bills.)

For example: Does the agent attend Worldcon, World Fantasy Con, and/or the Nebula Banquet? (If not, it means every time you want a face-to-face with the agent, you're going to have to fly to New York, with its attendant plane-fares, hotel and restaurant prices.)

For example: Does the agent pay you the instant the check arrives, or does he wait until his bank clears it? (This can be a couple of weeks on some foreign checks. Will this make a difference in your ability to pay your bills on time?)

For example: Does the agent handle short fiction, or does he want you to do it yourself? (And do you *want* an agent to handle short fiction? Most agents prefer not to, and most writers are perfectly happy that way—but a few agents insist upon it.)

For example: Will the agent handle your career personally, or is his stable so large that you'll be given to some skilled (or perhaps unskilled) assistant?

For example: Does the agent's expertise extend beyond science fiction and fantasy, and if so, does it cover areas in which you might wish to write in the future?

All of the above are valid considerations, but they're not necessarily *equal* considerations. You have to decide which are more important to you, and which are less so.

Do you want an agent who molds your career, tells you what to write, and acts as a first reader—or do you want one who will take what you offer without question and send it out immediately? Do you want one who reports every rejection, or do you want to use your agent as a buffer *from* rejection and only be told the good news?

Another consideration: is your agent solvent? I don't mean, do his checks bounce ... but is he making a decent living? Not only does it show some competence on his part, but it avoids a pitfall that has hamstrung more than one writer. Which is to say, when you get a call that a publisher has just offered $6,000 for your masterpiece and you'd better take it because it's been turned down everywhere else, can you trust what your agent says—or could it be that this is only the first or second publisher to see it but your agent has got to get his hands on a quick $600 for rent or child support or whatever? As everyone says, your relationship with your agent is very much like a marriage—and marriages built on trust tend to last the longest.

Now Barry, since you've spent 33 years, more or less, in a literary agency—and how you sold 90+ books and 300+ stories during just the first decade of that time remains a mystery to me—perhaps you'd care to tell us how different sales strategies are developed, and how they work? And you might even address fee reading.

—◈◈◈—

BARRY: "You might address fee reading," the man says as an afterthought. Ever so shyly. "You might want to address those remarks on Jews we heard on the tape transcripts, Mr. President." "Mr. President, one little question about that female intern." Something like that. Talk about backing into the horned beast.

Anyway, and all right, let's address the issue of fee reading. As you and most of the membership know, the Scott Meredith Agency, since its inception, has offered to read the work of unpublished or unestablished writers for money, with the understanding that saleable work would be represented by the agency, potentially saleable work would be directed through revision by the agency, and that unsaleable work would—well, it would be kindly declined. Over this very long period of time—the Agency opened its doors on 6/29/46 and fee reading was always a constituent—the program has had its successes and its problems. Many prominent or not-so-prominent one-time clients of the agency originally came through the fee department, including several present SFWA members; I won't mention their names but will note that Richard S. Prather, John Farris, Bruce Douglas Reeves (who he?), Bill Pronzini, and Jeffrey M. Wallman are all important novelists who showed up at the beginning with $25 or $35 in hand, a hopeful expression, and a manuscript.

What's even more interesting than a list of fee-paying writers who became agency clients is a list of fee-paying writers who did *not* become clients—whose works were declined by the agency or unsuccessfully marketed. Here are just a few, and in no particular order: Stephen King, Evan S. Connell, Jr., Robert Parker, Raymond Carver, John Barth. The novel on which Gus Van Sant's first screenplay and film were based was rejected by the agency. This all goes to prove something, although what that something might be is not entirely clear.

Another interesting list would be those who have worked for the fee department — writing responses in Scott Meredith's name. Here are a few (and again, in no particular order): myself. Donald E. Westlake. Lawrence Block. Lester del Rey. Lawrence M. Janifer. Damon Knight. Allen Ginsberg. Donald A. Fine. Phil Klass (better known as "William Tenn"). Talk about the true unwritten history!

My own position on fee reading is that like almost everything else in this world — marriage, love, happiness, the effects of wealth or poverty — is that it's all contextual, it all depends. Depends upon the acuity of the person reading the manuscript, depends upon the ability or potential of the author. (Hopeless is almost always hopeless.) I've never endorsed the system, I've never condemned it. (Would be hypocrisy certainly to condemn.) There are better ways to get an agent and a publisher but unconnected writers have always had a problem with access and most publishers won't even screen unsolicited materials any more. So if you're out there in the provinces (and for an unpublished writer West 29th Street can be a province) you've got to try something.

At the least, most fee correspondence from at least this agency has been competent, lucid and to the point, and over the years the agency readers have passed on little work which has subsequently proven to be saleable. The record isn't terrific but it's probably been acceptable. I can't talk to the practices of any other agencies.

Sales strategies? "How are different sales strategies developed?" If it's Dean Koontz or Stephen King you don't need a sales strategy, you just need an open phone line. If it's a Mike Resnick at this point in his career you don't need much of a sales strategy either; the agent and the publishers have a pretty good assessment of the writer's audience, ability and potential and it's just a question of how much a publisher wants to risk and whether the publisher wants to try to change the equation. Sales strategy comes more into play in the case of a writer at the very beginning of a career or perhaps coming off a hot first book which has sold or been reviewed beyond all expectations and which makes possible a leap in advance and possibilities. But is the largest advance necessarily the best offer in its totality? Is the largest publisher the best publisher? These are questions which can only be answered on an ad hoc basis and I suppose that it is here — and here more than in any other area — where the differential abilities of the agents and their sympatico with the client can make a real difference.

I think, overall, the role of an agent is overrated. John Updike has never had one. Neither did John O'Hara. Nabokov had representation for some foreign language rights but, after he left Cornell to write full-time in 1958, had no agent for his manuscripts. Dean R. Koontz has had four agents, each of which did better for him than the last, but this was because Koontz was doing better and Agent #1 might have done as well for the present-day Koontz as is Agent #4. You or I could do pretty well for Stephen King, I suspect, while the William Morris Agency would have a hard time promoting ancillary and subsidiary rights to the work of Ray Cummings. No agent can be better than the work represented (some can be worse), no agent can, as I've said, find a new set of markets.

But tell me how and through whose efforts you've made your movie sales (did Eleanor Wood or a cooperating agent manage those as well?) and I will be content and fully informed.

—*∿∿*—

MIKE: My first couple of movie options came through a cooperating Hollywood-based agent. But, possibly because he represented literally hundreds of category writers, he never followed up on them. He seemed content to make option money and let it go at that, so finally I let *him* go.

Now, over the years, we saw one talented writer after another go out to Hollywood to conquer the movie world ... and we saw one talented writer after another vanish from sight or wind up writing Saturday morning cartoon shows for television. We spent the better part of 25 years observing them and trying to learn from their mistakes, and when we thought we'd figured most of it out, we decided it was time to take a fling at Hollywood ourselves. (I say "we" because Carol, my wife and screenplay collaborator, is a far better and more visual screenwriter than I am. One of the things I discovered is that you have to chuck almost everything you learned as a prose writer before you can become even a mildly competent screenwriter, and since she hadn't been writing prose professionally for a quarter of a century she had a lot less to unlearn.)

The first thing we realized was that you can't market a script the way you market a manuscript. Studio script departments are just enormous slush buildings.

The second thing was that the easiest way to sell a script was not to market it yourself—writers are pretty unimportant cogs in the movie machine—but to package it with a hot director and a hungry producer. (How you find them is another story, and has almost nothing to do with agents.)

The third thing was that this is a business of personal contact and cachet, far more than the prose writing business, and you use your contacts to make more contacts. In the past three years we've sold two screenplays and optioned seven books and two stories—and every single deal, every contact we've made, can all be traced back to the first producer and director who optioned *Santiago* years ago. They introduced us to their friends, who introduced us to *their* friends, and it became a geometric progression.

Now, one of the interesting things we learned along the way is that, unless you're planning to make Hollywood a full-time career, you don't actually need an agent.

That's right. Unlike literary agents, what Hollywood agents primarily do is put you together with people who might be interested in buying your services. They set up meetings. They arrange lunches. But once an offer is actually on the table, your Hollywood agent steps aside and your Hollywood *lawyer* takes over the negotiation — and Hollywood lawyers eat Hollywood agents for breakfast.

(Yeah, I know: you have a friend who sells screenplays and doesn't have a lawyer, just an agent. Right. But if that's the case, then his *agency* has one or more lawyers to handle the negotiations.)

Now, if you want full-time work, as I said, you want an agent. And full-time work entails getting rewrite jobs (80 percent of all the contract writing in Hollywood, maybe a little more, is rewriting). It entails hawking scripts that you've written on whim or on spec. It entails endless business lunches and meetings, and in most of them you'll know three minutes into them that you're not getting hired today.

Hollywood is so eccentric, so alien to Carol's and my values and lifestyle, that we're willing to give them only ten weeks a year. And since we've reached the point where they call us with offers at least once a year, frequently two and three times, we have more work than we can handle, and hence have never hired a Hollywood agent. (We *do* have Quentin Tarantino's lawyer. And no, we didn't just walk in off the street to get her. Again, it was a matter of contacts.)

Most prose writers look upon Hollywood with some contempt. It shows in their attitudes, and it shows in their writing, and that's why Hollywood is so loath to hire prose writers. Screenwriting is a totally different discipline from prose writing, but it's every bit as demanding and precise, and until one masters the art — and you can't go into it saying, "Hell, what's so hard about writing *Porky's #8* or *Halloween #17*?" — I wouldn't advise anyone to quit their day job or back out of their book contracts ... and if you're *not* going into it full-time, I also wouldn't advise getting a Hollywood agent.

Another thing to consider: Hollywood rewrites *everything*. There are a lot of reasons for this. One is that they're trying to create art by committee, and hence a lot of people have input into the script. Another is that sometimes scripts, like books, need revising. There are other reasons, dozens of them. But there are two primary reasons, neither of them known to the general public: first, it gives executives cover (if the movie flops, they can blame it on the half-dozen writers, whereas if they go with the first script, it's their fault for showing such poor judgment); and second, while most Hollywood execs are brilliant men in their fields, their fields are marketing and making deals, and since they do not know the intricacies of screenplay construction, all they can do is voice a vague dissatisfaction when a screenplay doesn't meet their expectations. They are not writers, and hence cannot tell a writer how to fix or change it; so they flit from one writer or writing team to another until finally someone intuits what they want and delivers it to them.

And since rewriting is part of the culture, what this means — and I've talked to a number of SFWAns who have experienced this — is that if you do get an agent, he'll almost certainly have you rewrite your treatment or your screenplay endlessly, *without pay*, until he thinks he can sell it. But he has no more knowledge about what will sell than you do; if he did, he'd have one of his better-paid and better-credentialed journeyman writers script it.

If, after all this, you still feel you *must* get a Hollywood agent, then there are two ways to go: you can join a major agency that handles actors, directors, writers, the whole nine yards. (The advantage is that such agencies often package entire movies, and you certainly have a better chance of selling your screenplay if Mel Gibson and Meg Ryan and Ivan Reitman are attached to it. The disadvantage is that such an agency probably has 50 or more writers who make more money than you, have been with the agency longer than you, and would also like to be packaged with the agency's name actors and directors.) The other way is to join what is called a boutique agency, a small house dealing (in this case) exclusively with writers; your screenplay will be given more respect, more time, more attention — and will be far more difficult to sell since it won't come packaged with anything else.

The one other thing I can tell you about Hollywood agents and agencies is that they invariably try to steer their clients into television, where one makes smaller but far more regular paychecks. The loyalty of most agents is to their agencies first and their clients second — and their agencies need cash flow. The problem is that there is a very definite social and economic ladder in Hollywood, and movies are at the top of it; if you write enough television, you'll be tagged as someone who couldn't make it in movies, and you'll have a much harder time getting off the small screen and onto the big one. Now, if you're Joe Straczynski you're making zillions and doing just what you want and you needn't give a damn about that, but most people aren't Joe Straczynski, and it bears mentioning.

Why do we put up with it? Because once you get your foot in the door, you'll find that your check for each draft of your screenplay dwarfs anything you ever saw from your novels.

In sum, this is an incredibly idiosyncratic field. Everything I've said is true, based on our experience — but if there's a successful SFWA screenwriter whose experience is diametrically opposed to ours, I wouldn't be surprised.

So much for what I know about Hollywood. Now, very briefly, how do you know when a literary agent is about to become a major force in the field, and how do you know when a literary agent is over the hill?

—∿∿∿—

BARRY: Well, that's another of those questions. "How long should a novel be? How much money is good money for a novel? What defines a 'professional writing career'?"

But addressing this one I think of the collected sayings of the sainted or soon-to-be-sainted Yogi Berra discussing a restaurant: "It's become too popular. No one goes there anymore."

Thus with agents. By the time an agent acquires a reputation as a hot, talked-about, promising agent-on-the-rise who has done some really good things on behalf of writers at a relatively early career stage, well, it's already too late. At least for similarly unestablished writers. The agent has made deals, found larger quarters, been besieged by potential clients, has hired or expanded a staff and has focused her attention on the present client list. You might be able to sign on but it's already too late, at least for an unestablished writer. Unless you're a real acquisition for the agent, you're going to be passed onto a new assistant or sloughed off altogether.

In sum, it is the same problem with agents as with, say, romance novels ... by the time the word gets out to the provinces that romances are what is selling now, by the time you read it in *Writer's Digest* or even *Publishers Weekly*, publishers are stocked five years ahead. You can't follow a trend, you have to *be* a trend, at least if you're trying to get something started outside of New York, away from fast access,

And, not so ironically (because it can be powerfully damaging to those caught in the trap), the signs of an agent or agency in decline are very similar to those of a "hot agent" addressed a little too late ... disdain, assistants, long gaps in response, a clear inattentiveness, a willingness to take a lower offer for the work of an unestablished writer "because it's not important enough" (or, the other face of the syndrome, an unwillingness to even represent work not seen as "breakthrough" or "crossover" or "major market"). If your agent won't return or have someone return your phone calls within two days, or if your editor or an editor you query says that she has not been able to connect with the agent ... these are, as they say, signs that you've got a problem.

Not all agents are on the rise or in decline, of course; there are many who have been at a stable and reliable level of function for a long time and will continue to be. But it's a business no less volatile than publishing, and I can think of four agents or agencies, very important 10–20 years ago, which are obliterated or might as well be. No substitute for vigilance, and ultimately the career of a writer is in her own hands. An agent can't take that responsibility and shouldn't be asked. Depend first and last on your own resources; anything beyond that is a blessing.

Unestablished writers tend to overvalue the role of agents the way high school students overvalue the role of sex in a relationship. Important, yes; to die for, yes— but ancillary, Mike, and the earlier this is understood, the better.

———

MIKE: The only thing I can add to that is that it's harder to pinpoint an agent's tastes than you think. Virginia Kidd, for example, handles Gene Wolfe, Anne McCaffrey, Alan Dean Foster, and the estate of James Tiptree, Jr. It would be hard to find four more different writers. Which does she prefer? I've no idea, and since she's an ethical agent, I'm sure she'll never tell you.

Ralph Vicinanza handles James Patrick Kelly, Julian May, Jerry Pournelle, and Connie Willis. Again, what does that tell you about his taste? Zip.

So I suggest that when selecting an agent, you don't try to determine what he or she likes, because that's really not very important (beyond the fact that they don't out-and-out loathe your work). Look at their accomplishments, and if their accomplishments meet with your approval, the rest will take care of itself.

13 Money

MIKE: We keep skirting and tiptoeing around the issue of money, so maybe it's time we addressed it.

I'm writing this during the Republican debates in early December, and one of the interesting things is that every single one of their tax-cut plans—and each of them has one — exempts a family of four that makes $36,000 a year, so it's pretty fair to say that's the new poverty level in this heated-up economy.

Now, it seems to me that if you choose to enter the field, it's realistic to assume that you want to make at least double the poverty level in a reasonable period of time. Otherwise, why bother? There are lots of easier ways to make a buck.

So ... how do you go about it, barring a bestseller or a movie sale?

I'd say that within four or five books you should have your advances up past $15,000 if you expect to have any kind of career at all. So let's say you've been in the field four years, long enough to establish whether or not you can sell, and you're able to turn out two novels a year.

And let's say you get $17,500 apiece for them. Do you pack it in and go dig ditches?

No.

You remember that for every dollar you make in America, you'll make at least one overseas. England, France, Germany, Japan, Italy, and Poland are the most likely markets, but there are dozens of others. Some will only pay $500 for a book; some will pay $7,500; most pay somewhere in between ... but when the dust clears, your foreign money should come to at least $17,500. OK, it won't be $17,500 on the same book in the same year that you get your U.S. advance; it takes a few years. But it'll be money from your first or third or fifth novel. All that matters is that you keep producing regularly, so you can keep selling overseas regularly.

So now you've got a pair of $17,500 advances — that's $35,000 — and you've got another $35,000 coming from overseas. Now, just to keep your name in front of the public, you sell two shorts, a novelette and a novella (or the equivalent) each year. That's another $2,500.

So your advances aren't up to $20,000, and you only write two books a year ... but yeah, after you pay your dues for a few years, you can double that $36,000 we mentioned. Without being a superstar, or a Hugo/Nebula winner, or grinding out Trekbooks or Wookiebooks.

Is there a flaw there somewhere?

——◦/◦/◦——

BARRY: Well, as is your wont (or your will as one of your characters might assert) you take the cheerful, positive, forward-looking position. Get your advances to $17,500 in four years, write two books a year, double your income per book on the foreign and subsidiary sales, and live happily ever after, even if the movie option money is somewhat delayed.

Me, I have an, ah, somewhat bleaker perspective on all of this. For several reasons. Here they are:

1. It's no certainty that our hypothetical writer will be able to get the advance to $17,500 in four years or forty. The going rate for first novels in the genre markets— unless you're a *Star Trek* actor fronting for a SFWA member actually writing the book — is maybe $5,000–6,000, and about the best the first novelist can expect is a two-book contract with little likelihood that a third novel will be contracted before the first is published. If the novels sell poorly — and most do, Mike, most first novels sell somewhat under 10,000 copies in mass market paperback now — there's a substantial likelihood that the writer will be dropped right there. A funny thing has happened on the way to those $17,500 advances; the writer has no advance at all and will have to scramble for another contract.

This of course is not an extreme case, a case which represents only a kind of more likely scenario. The first novel could have sold to Harcourt Brace, could have sold to Spectra or del Rey on a hard-soft deal, might be a Tor hardcover with advances of $15,000–20,000 and the substantial possibility (as there is not in paperback original) of significant royalty income. But these are less likely instances; the reality for most first novelists is as I've noted above and more than half of them face the likelihood of having to seek a new publisher — and thus in effect restart a career — with that third or fourth novel. It can be done, of course — maybe a pseudonym, maybe a different kind of novel, maybe the editor at the first house turns up in a new job and is able to bring over parts of her list — but it's not routine and in any case it takes time. Time is a relative concept, of course, a part-timer writing novels as an adjunct to full-time employment, a neo–Hal Clement, say, can take a long view, but a writer who has on the basis of a couple of sales leapt into full-time freelancing has either a short view or nothing at all. What I'm trying to say is that it's an exceptional — not impossible, just exceptional — instance to move to an advance level of your $17,500 without hindrance or difficulty and many writers (perhaps even most) can find themselves scrambling along at the four-figure level if at all for many, many years.

2. And can a $17,500 level of advance be taken for granted, seen as a kind of financial floor? The problem with making this kind of money if you're not a Niven or Benford or Resnick — which means most of us— is that sales level is not likely to sustain that advance; the unearned advance can in fact be substantial and the publisher may be inclined to say, "I can find someone who sells this badly at one-third of the price," and that's a blow to yet another hypothetical career. Unless you're at a high sales or prestige level and $17,500 is the kind of anomalous figure which is really too low to indicate this (while being high enough to be really exposed), you — our hypothetical writer — is at precisely that level which is most vulnerable. In fact, this represents the kind of writer — been around a while, obviously has some talent, can write but hasn't cultivated enough of an audience or halo for the really big money — who is most likely to be cut. I can think of two writers right away — there are, alas, many, many more — who are well-respected novelists, have been around for quite a while, have sold somewhere between 10–20 novels, are sterling members of the SFWA who got their advances to the $10,000–15,000 level who were let go by their publishers and have been told to find another outlet. Their sales figures are locked and predictable, their range is well-known and it's below the level of their advances, they can't be paid more and it's pointless to offer them less, and they have been in the words of a mystery writer I know "depublished." Yes, they can find a pseudonym and start again or maybe they can do franchise work, but it's going to be for a third or less of their previous advances and these two writers have probably elected not even to try.

As so many writers have discovered, while there is indeed no ceiling to a writer's income, there is also no floor, no fail-safe mechanism for all but well-established writers. "Kill the body and the head will die" is a well-known trainers' aphorism for boxers; for freelance writing (and publishers for that matter) it translates, "Kill the frontlist and the backlist will die." Without a steady flow of new work, the backlist shrivels, decays, becomes ultimately impractical. Everything is hedged about continued production and sales; take that away and everything can collapse.

Which brings around Hemingway's advice: "Writing is not a full-time occupation"; I think he had something else in mind (Big Ernie made Big Statement in Big Ketchum) but it certainly applies here. If you're not moving forward constantly, you're regressing. General managers in pro sports understand this very well. So keep the day job.

All that being said, I'd note that doubling advances in foreign and royalty income isn't exactly an automatic process. It's certainly possible, but one has to struggle here as in almost every other place. Bad contracts can make subsidiary income disappear. I leave it to you to explain this.

MIKE: Ah, Barry, you make me feel old and tired. We see a glass that's filled halfway to the rim. I say it's half full; you want to know who pissed in it.

I'm not holding the figure of $17,500 a book as a Holy Grail. Hell, it's a *minimum*. If you want to make double what Al Gore, Bill Bradley, George W. Bush, and that whole crowd considers the top of the poverty level, then that's the *least* you can get away with.

Can everyone make it? Of course not. But if they can't reach that minimal level after 8 or 10 books, then they'd better cling to their day jobs and their working spouses. On the other hand, I can rattle off the names of 40 to 60 SFWA members who make at least $30,000 a book.

What has happened is what we used to pray would happen: computers have taken over the field, there are no more secrets, and for perhaps the first time in history, advances are based on performance and not on hype. We all used to sit around and bitch about it: we pretty much knew who sold and who didn't, and it didn't have a hell of a lot to do with how much they earned. We watched writers bludgeon publishers with hype, and we watched them deftly change houses in order to stay a step or two ahead of their returns.

Well, that's all changed, with one or two exceptions. Computer returns have made it impossible to lie about sales, to use hype rather than figures. The money's still there — just look at some of the deals that are reported in *Locus* and *Science Fiction Chronicle* — but it's going to different people. We have a new generation of stars, accepted by the public if not their peers, and they're accomplishing that stardom at the newsstands and the book racks, not on the convention circuit and the publisher's lunches. There's probably more money in science fiction and fantasy today than there's ever been — but it's no longer going to (generic) you just because it went to you last year and four and seven years ago. Now it's truly a matter, from the publisher's point of view, of: What have you done for me lately?

And they've done a little bit for us lately, too — or at least the economics of publishing has. I'm not a new writer, but I'm not an old-timer in the sense that Jack Williamson and Fred Pohl, or even Algis Budrys and Robert Sheckley are. My first hardcover advance was $800. My first paperback advance — my first three, in fact — were $1,500 apiece. My first paperback books carried cover prices of 50 cents and paid 4 percent royalties. That means I made a whopping 2 cents a book, once I'd earned out my advance (and at 2 cents a book you didn't earn it out very fast, take my word for it).

Today your typical paperback seems to go for about $7.00, and your average royalty rate — not your best, not your worst, just your average — is 8 percent. That means you make 56 cents every time you sell a book.

Ten thousand sales back when I broke in meant you made $200 to apply against your advance. Today it means you make $5,600 to apply against your advance.

That's important to remember, because with 1,200 or so titles a year compared to the 150 or so when I broke in, the average number of copies sold is less. But believe me, it's not 28 times less, and we're making 28 times more money per sale.

Do you see what I'm driving at? If not, let me spell it out. There was a time when 22,000 sales of a paperback was death to a beginning writer who hoped to make more on his next book. But if you're making a 10 percent royalty, you will actually earn money over and above amortizing a $15,000 advance with 22,000 sales. And of course, the publisher's break-even point is always lower, usually much lower, than the figure the writer needs to earn out his advance.

Can bad contracts wipe out your subsidiary earnings? Sure. They can wipe you out domestically, too. If there's room after your response, I'll give you my favorite example of such. But I'd also point out that when I say your foreign earnings will equal your domestic earnings, that's a *minimum* for a journeyman writer. Most will testify that they make between 150 and 200 percent as much overseas as here.

And of course there are other sources. We won't count book club income, since that goes directly to the publisher, who will be reluctant to part with it until (and sometimes after) you earn out. But there are specialty editions, where you keep 100 percent of the money; there's Easton Press, where again you won't see the advance, but you'll make between $3,000 and $5,000 autographing signature pages; there's Hollywood, which is becoming more and more active in optioning science fiction and which you don't share with your publisher; there's computer games; there's role-playing games; there's a legitimate market in comic books, now that DC and Marvel no longer own all of that world. I won't even mention electronic rights, since no one knows what they're worth, but the day will come when they're probably worth as much as all the others, bar Hollywood, put together.

So, Barry, how about admitting that the glass is maybe 60 percent full, and suggesting how else to make the most of it?

——*◊◊◊*——

BARRY: Okay, the glass is half full. With sparkling water. All the winds are mild and every prospect pleases.

And here is how to make the most of it: write in series, link the novels and extend the series as much as feasible. Publishers love series because readers do. The first novel of a series is no more difficult to launch than a standalone work and subsequent volumes are easier; if the series has any success at all, the audience will build from book to book and the material is pre-sold.

Of course some series launches fail; in many cases series even with a successful launch begin to fade after the second or sixth or sixteenth novel. Nothing is predictable in this business. But there is far more predictability in the series for reader and publishers than in the stand-alone; the series deals in assured expectation and nothing is more important in genre publishing. Science fiction is in marketing terms a genre, has been termed such by the book publishers for more than half a century, will continue to be so. A genre involves a kind of prepackaging and the series is the more definitive.

Campbell, a reflective descendant of the pulp editors and a loyal employee of Street & Smith, the great pulp chain, certainly knew this and urged his writers to produce in a series format. His magazine published them in profusion: Bullard of the Space Patrol, Baldy, Weapon Shops, Ole Doc Methuselah, Mixed Men, Foundation, Robotics, Gallegher, City, Lensman, Okie, Nicholas Von Rijn, Paratime Police, Bureau of Slick Tricks, on and on. Campbell would urge writers to consider series even when a story seemed a stand-alone; surely Wilmar Shiras' *Children of the Atom* developed this way. Harry Harrison thought that *Deathworld* was a novella, but it turned out to be a considerable series, three novels of which appeared in *Astounding*. Series were the staple of pulp fiction.

In fact, series are a staple of any kind of fiction. Literary fiction? Leslie Epstein has written several novellas about his Steinway Quintet, Roth's Zuckerman has been the patron of four novels, John Updike's Bech has been gathered into three volumes of short stories, and they are still, from the standpoint of market and career, the way to go in genre today. Raymond Chandler's six canonic Marlowe novels are a series; Sherlock Holmes is self-evident. Hammett never wrote series or sequels but film did it for him in *The Thin Man* property and he was happy to take the money. Beyond this refractory advice, my suggestion would be: if you can't or won't write series, then at least use a common background. Niven's Known Space, Heinlein's Future History, James Schmitz's Tales of the Hub, and so on. Try to make the work as coherent, as unified, as connected as possible. It is true that the greatest science fiction novels are stand-alone (this is not true of fantasy: Tolkien, Narnia, Darkover), but most successful works in the genre have been connected by plot or background or both. Branding is what it is now called in advertising and circulation.

It would be interesting to make a list of prominent or successful science fiction writers (not quite the same thing, of course) who never worked in series format or at least in common background. Norman Spinrad and Alfred Bester come to mind. Walter Miller, Jr.? No, not a chance: a sequel to *A Canticle for Leibowitz* occupied Miller for close to 40 years (he published nothing during that period), and of course was finished for him by Terry Bisson and published posthumously.

So much for subject matter, this for technique: be reasonably prolific. At least a novel a year; two would be better (two series, or a series and a stand-alone or, as was more often the case ten or twenty years ago, a pseudonym for half the work). Try to hold onto all foreign and subsidiary rights; if some foreign rights must be given as a concession, try to make sure that the author has sole and exclusive right to negotiate. If that sole and exclusive right remains with the publisher then at least — I speak from unpleasant and, I fear, widely-shared experience — demand that the foreign monies be paid out upon publisher receipt, that they not be held until the next royalty period or — worst of all and a deal-breaker — be applied to the unearned portion of the advance. In that case, there's a reasonable expectation that the author will never see any foreign income. (I did not. Granted the publisher only 10 percent of the foreign money but didn't notice that the stupid agent gave applicability to the publisher. I lost the full amount of the German advance, about $1,000 ... heady money in the early 1970s, at least for me, and fully half of the advance Avon had paid.) Learn from my experience as I did not, and do this.

Otherwise? Otherwise, three precepts, presented by Damon Knight as the last words of *In Search of Wonder*: Read your contracts. Love your work. Make friends where you can.

And if you haven't closed it out, keep the day job. Larry McMurtry has. Louis Auchincloss has. T.S. Eliot was an editor at Faber & Faber almost to the end. Joseph Heller was still at *Time* more than a decade after the publication of *Catch-22*. This is a problematic business and never more dangerous than at the point the problems seem resolved.

———*∿∿∿*———

MIKE: Actually, Norman wrote a sequel, too: *Child of Fortune* was a sequel to *The Void Captain's Tale*.

Interesting that you should mention unearned advance. It's not a term we see much in contracts these days, but it can lead to such heinous practices that perhaps it deserves some brief discussion.

Let's take the classic case, which is when you sell your novel to a hardcover publisher and then sell or auction the paperback rights to another publisher. It's been industry standard ever since the invention of the paperback that under these conditions, the hardcover publisher gets half the paperback advance. (After all, the argument goes — and yes, of course it's the hardcover publisher's argument — he's the one who invested in your book initially; the paperback publisher is coming around after your novel has already been shown to command some respect and attention in the marketplace.)

So let's give the author a hypothetical advance of $50,000 for the hardcover. It gets great reviews, and a week or two later he gets an offer of $70,000 for the paperback. (Or, if we're living in a Malzbergian universe, divide all sums by ten; I promise it'll work the same.)

So how much money does the author realize from the paperback resale? Well, your first inclination is (or should be) to say $35,000, which is half of the $70,000 offer, the hardcover publisher keeping the other half.

It's possible, of course. The math is right.

But it's just as possible, and far more likely, that the answer is Zero.

How can this be?

Easy.

The author gets a letter from the hardcover house which says, in essence,

"Dear Author: We are in receipt of a check for $70,000 for the paperback rights to your wonderful novel. Now, as you know, $35,000 of this is ours. As for the other $35,000, theoretically it's yours—but your book has only earned $11,000 of its advance, which means the unearned advance is $39,000 ... so we'll just hold this check for $35,000 until you earn out."

And the next day, since the hardcover publisher has made his profit, the novel is remaindered—after all, his road men have dozens of books to push that *haven't* yet shown a profit—and shucks and darn if the contract doesn't also state that any book selling for less than 50 percent of the listed cover price pays no royalties at all.

Sure it's a scam, albeit a legal one once you sign a contract agreeing to it. Thing is, there wouldn't be scams like this if authors weren't worth scamming.

Not everyone can make a living in this field. Nowhere is it written in stone that just wanting to be a writer, just trying your best day in and day out, guarantees you an audience. But the fact remains that in the mid–1960s, those science fiction writers who made a full-time living from the field numbered in single digits, and today they come close to (or perhaps even reach) triple digits.

Sure, series books make it easier, but there are authors who have made it without them. And even with this television-raised generation, eventually they get tired of the same unchanging characters and situations in every book (unless one of the characters has pointy ears, anyway.)

I submit that one (no, not every last one) can make a living from this field by writing at the peak of one's abilities. It's certainly easier if one panders to the whims of the marketplace, but (granting a certain degree of ability and accessibility, and an occasional push by one's publisher) it's not essential.

They come from out of nowhere, some with series, some without—Cherryh, Bujold, Gibson, Robinson, Kress, Willis, a few dozen others—and if they tell stories people want to read, they stick around and pay their bills.

It's really as simple as that.

14 Pseudonyms

MIKE: There have always been fads and trends in writing, and especially in science fiction. The current trend — and it's one I find very disturbing — is to use a pseudonym at the drop of a hat.

Changing from horror to sf? Change your name.

Changing from hard sf to soft sf? Change your name.

Want to write a mystery novel? Change your name.

Did your last book tank? Change your name.

Now, I'll be the first to admit that sometimes it works. Megan Lindholm (everybody's favorite example) has to be very happy that she became Robin Hobb. Piers Anthony Jacob has been living on the various bestseller lists as Piers Anthony for more than a quarter of a century.

But I would submit that Lindholm/Hobb is an exception, and Anthony/Jacob doesn't really qualify since he has *always* written as Piers Anthony.

This is not to say there aren't valid reasons to write under a pseudonym. I've done it hundreds of times for what I consider the most valid reason of all.

In my starving writer days, I wrote and sold a couple of hundred anonymous novels which we shall euphemistically define as "the kind men like." I was not proud of them. They were written for editors who didn't want it good, they wanted it Thursday. (A *lot* of aging SFWAns—far more than you might think—labored in those fields 30 to 40 years ago.) I never spent more than 4 days to turn out one of these 55,000-word masterpieces; I felt that after 96 hours my brain would turn to putty and run out my ears. I never wanted to meet anyone who bought and read one. And since I viewed these books as "Product" rather than Art — and to me, that disqualifies them from any claim to literature — I didn't wish to be identified with them by anyone except the person who made out the checks, so I used a pseudonym. I also used one on the seven monthly tabloids (like *The National Inquirer*, only worse) that I packaged.

To me, that is the single most valid reason for using a pseudonym — because the author has no wish to be associated with the product.

There's another one, almost equally valid, and one over which writers usu-

131

ally have no choice. It began in the hero pulp magazines almost 70 years ago. Walter Gibson hired on to write a monthly novel for *The Shadow*, a new magazine that had been created solely to keep the copyright on a mysterious radio show host of that name. Street & Smith, the publishers, decided to use the house name of Maxwell Grant for the Shadow novels, ostensibly to lend continuity on those months that Gibson couldn't make his deadline.

A little time goes by, and suddenly *The Shadow* is selling a million copies an issue and is moved up to semi-monthly publication. Gibson walks into the Street & Smith offices and says, "*I* did that for you. Now *you* do something for me. I want a thousand a novel, twice a month." They said No. He said, "You give me a raise or I'll leave and take my million readers with me." Leave if you want, said Street & Smith, but next week there will be a new Maxwell Grant churning out Shadow novels and who will know the difference?

So when Street & Smith began *Doc Savage*, which was primarily written by Lester Dent, all the novels were credited to "Kenneth Robeson." Rivals saw the beauty in this, and thus *The Spider* novels, written mostly by Norvell Page, bore the pseudonym of "Grant Stockbridge." Soon almost all the other hero pulps fell into step.

Fortunately they never insisted on this practice anywhere but the continuing hero magazines— until 40 years later. Harlequin had not yet bought Silhouette, and when 37-year-old Janet Dailey, whose books had sold 110,000,000 (that's right: 110 *million*) copies during the previous six years, signed a 60-book contract with Silhouette (and, unlike Gibson's false threat, *did* take her readers with her), some exec at Harlequin remembered the good old days and declared that all future novels must be written under house names— a practice that spread to Silhouette when Harlequin bought it a few years later. (My understanding is that the practice has finally been overturned in court.)

Okay, those are the two reasons for using a pseudonym that I would never challenge. But you've spent a third of a century, on and off, working for a literary agency ... and you've also used pseudonyms yourself, so maybe your take on it is a little different?

—◦◦◦—

BARRY: Plenty more examples, Mike. Plenty more.

John Benyon Harris was a British writer of indifferent reputation and few sales; in the early 1950s, as Alexei Panshin said, "He broke a bottle of champagne over the bow and sailed forth as John Wyndham." Changed everything. Henry Kuttner became famous but only by virtue of the work he published (collaboratively with his wife Catherine Moore for the most part) as "Lewis Padgett" and "Lawrence O'Donnell." Phil Klass decided that he would save his real name for the non-apprentice work, put the byline "William Tenn" on "Alexander The Bait" (*Astounding*, 2/46), his first sale, and you know the rest. Benyon Harris didn't really get going until he fled his previous byline and Kuttner, who was regarded as a debased *Marvel Science Fiction* bottom-of-the-market hack in the 40s had to become Padgett and O'Donnell because his own name was close to anathemic. (He published only one story under his own name in *Astounding*, the top market.)

Taking a new name in early (or mid-) career or assuming a false name from the outset are tactics which can be seen as quite explicable and defensible. Michael Crichton's first novel, a mystery, was published as "John Lange," creating endless consternation for bibliographers because, of course, "John Lange" is the real name of a writer known better under his pseudonym — John Norman. Crichton, like Klass, wanted to reserve his own name for non-apprentice work; his apprentice work was good enough to win an Edgar but it was *The Andromeda Strain* by Crichton with which, of course, he broke his own bottle over the sales. I was told in 1979 by my then literary agent that if I wanted any kind of continuing career, I would be best advised to take a pseudonym, my "real" name, such as it is, already having little other than negative commercial value. (My reluctance to take this advice, in fact the very existence of this advice by a sensitive and intelligent agent, was an important factor in my decision to look for something in my future other than ostensibly "full-time" writing.)

There's that and there's also the issue of house names which have a long and scandalous history having converted authors of some of the most successful novels into work-for-hire, interchangeable, contemptuously treated hacks. Pinnacle Books, in fact, sued Don Pendleton when, in 1972 he attempted to take his enormously successful Executioner series on the open market; Pinnacle had paid him $2,500 advances for the eight to ten extant novels and no royalties, and when Pendleton attempted to leave claimed that his name as well as the series were theirs. (This was settled, ultimately. Pendleton was forced to walk away from a 4-book $250,000 offer from NAL but Pinnacle did disgorge an enormous amount of royalties and matched the NAL offer.) That case set some kind of informal precedent; a writer's "real" name cannot be used as a house name, regardless of the nature of the contract signed.

As a generalization, a writer is best advised to publish everything under her own name unless there is reason of the most compelling sort not to. That was the dictum of the late Scott Meredith and it appears to be yours as well. But there are a whole forest of exemptions and exceptions, many of them in the last decade intimately tied to the sales force and their computers. The generalization could for many writers be dangerous.

—⁓—

MIKE: OK, so much for the valid reasons. The problem I see is that (some) writers are changing names with the frequency that they change, well, not clothes, but let's say automobiles. It seems to be this year's fashion.

I'm on a few professional listservs, and one in particular is adamant that

second volume slide 97 percent from the first. It commands me to remind you
of what has become an editorial truism: "It is easier to sell a first novel now
than a second." A first novel represents—in however illusory fashion—a field
of possibility; it is a new romance. The second novel, like life together after the
decision to become roommates, can be sourly possessed of history. First novelists with poor sale figures stand to remain first novelists. The all-powerful
computer, the tutor of the sales force, remembers and records everything. If
the new writer has a passionate or very strong editor or is so brilliantly accomplished as to make initial sales figures of lesser interest, she may be able to
elude inevitability. Most new writers however, faced with 75 percent returns
and mass-market sales in the 8,000 copy range (not unusual figures by any
means) are unable to overcome such obstacles.

So, the authority of failure commands me to remind you, the adoption of
a pen-name may not (as you suggest) come from false vanity, artistic timidity
or poor judgment. It may well be a necessity and, at that, an imposed necessity. Agents and editors may demand this. I have already noted that Clyde Taylor, my agent for a few years in the late 1970s, recommended in all sincerity
and helpfulness that I adopt a pseudonym and start my career anew. My refusal
to do so—my unwillingness to even consider this although I respected his
advice and knew that the man was right—was part of a number of decisions I
was compelled to make at about that time which have led me at this moment
to the trembling verge of my Golden Years. (Which for all I know may be well
embarked, perhaps even sere and yellow as I speak.)

We are talking, Mike, of what are often compelled decisions. Also, apart
from this, it is often a good idea to use another name when writing in another
genre. Isaac Asimov didn't but when he published his first mystery in 1956 he
was already ISAAC ASIMOV (and that Avon paperback original was nonetheless a complete failure, sunk out of print for twenty years). John D. MacDonald didn't. But Kristine Kathryn Rusch—who is embarked upon a brilliant
career—has and there are strong reasons for this.

One can be proud of one's work and yet unable to sell it. Artistic "integrity"
does not have to lead, necessarily, to the trap of silence but it can do so and
used in a misguided fashion it can do so very quickly.

———⟡———

MIKE: Flattery will get you almost anywhere with me—but it stops short
of getting me to agree when I think you're wrong.

Let's take an example. Author X had sold some science fiction, has even
built a bit of a following. He sells a fantasy novel as Y, so as not to give his loyal
readers something they're not anticipating. Then he sells a mystery short story
as Z. And a Western novel as Q. And now he's considering selling a mystery
novel as M. (Why M? It's a "cozy" mystery, and his short story, written as Z,
was colder and bleaker than James Ellroy.)

Brilliant planning? I think not.

Let's remember: he has a bit of a following as X. Enough so they might buy a few thousand copies of the fantasy he wrote as Y — but they don't know he wrote it, and they're disinclined to spend $6.95 on a paperback by a new author.

Let's say his sf and his fantasy both get great reviews. There's absolutely no carryover to his mysteries or his Western. Even within the mystery field, the people who liked his Z story have no reason to look at his M novel, and vice versa.

In other words, what begins as a (usually) futile attempt to fool the distributor frequently ends in a (usually) successful attempt, however inadvertent, to trick the reader — almost always to the writer's detriment.

And let's be honest: there are a lot of reasons for changing names in midcareer, but 90 percent of the time it is an attempt to trick the distributor who is aware of your poor sales (and not coincidentally to fool the reader who has sampled your work and decided not to buy it again.)

As far as I am concerned, there is only one inarguably valid reason for changing your name in mid-career, and that is when your agent comes up to you and tells you that she cannot sell you anywhere if you *don't* change it. All the other reasons seem to be career strategies based on current fads and a few incredibly fortunate examples, and I happen to think that the most valid career strategy is Write Good, and if that's not working, Write Better. Certainly putting the effort into improving your writing rather than your strategy, especially when it depends to some extent on duplicity, has to be more productive.

That's the bottom line, I suppose. I am not convinced that subterfuge — and when all is said and done, that's the purpose of name-changing nine times out of ten — helps you to become a better writer.

(As for writers who changed genres without changing names, let me just name a few who didn't starve to death: John D. MacDonald, Brian Garfield, Fredric Brown, Lee Hoffman, Joe Haldeman, Isaac Asimov, Tom Disch, John Sladek ... need I go on?)

—◦◦◦—

BARRY: Sladek is not a good example, Mike. (Nor for that matter is Lee Hoffman; famous fan and fanzine editor but a very narrow profile in science fiction. Won the Spur Award from the Western Writers of America in the 1970s for best novel as, interestingly, did the science fiction writer Chad Oliver, but her Westerns never had to compete with her science fiction.) Sladek, a wonderful writer with great ambition, faded out of print due to collapsing sales and was pretty well undone by the 1970s. He published little in the last two decades of his sadly abbreviated life (1937–1999).

Sladek wrote mysteries, he wrote science fiction, he wrote mainstream novels, he stubbornly or bravely maintained his name through all of this and his audience, such as it was, utterly fractured. He was certainly unable to carry over the audience for his science fiction to the mysteries and after several mysteries failed commercially, he found himself virtually unable to re-enter science fiction. If he had used a pseudonym for the mysteries the situation might have been different but he refused to do so. (He and Tom Disch did use a pseudonym for some Gothic novels on which they collaborated in the late 1960s.) All of this is very sad because Sladek was a wonderful writer and his early career showed enormous promise; he sold *Playboy* a couple of stories in the 1960s and his collaborative mainstream novel with Tom Disch, *Black Alice*, sold better than Doubleday expected and has become both a cult and collector's edition. But ultimately, at least in his lifetime, Sladek's career came to nothing.

But as we turn from Sladek, Lee Hoffman and the reproductive system, we get to the heart of the issue: we are not talking of aesthetics, of pride in one's work, of artistic achievement, of artistic integrity. We are talking in the case of the struggling writer with a sheer issue of survival. You say that "As far as I am concerned there is only one inarguably valid reason for changing your name and that is when your agent ... tells you that she cannot sell you anywhere if you don't change it." And this, Mike, is precisely the case with many writers. (You could have noted that the word "editor" can be substituted for "agent" in that sentence with equal validity. The problem is that when your editor tells you to get another life, your editor is rarely in a position to smuggle you into the house under another identity ... it's an act of subterfuge which could cost an editor her job.) It's a Hobson's Choice which is to say — remember Isaac Asimov's essay on the subject — no choice at all.

Or look at it like so: for most of us in or once in what F. Scott Fitzgerald (in his authority of failure) called the freelance racket, it's mostly been an issue of staying ahead of the sheriff; that's what freelancers do, those who aren't named Grisham or Steele or King or Resnick; they try to stay ahead of their sales figures. In the pre-computer days this could be done; you could buy off the sheriff (sheriffs were for sale like everyone else) or make an arrangement with the boys in the back room who knew where the sheriff's body was buried. That's what freelancing was; it was an exercise of cunning.

But that's no longer possible. Computerization has drained the mystery from the distribution and sales process; now they know how many copies you are selling a week and exactly where they are being sold and how those raw numbers compare to last week's. Those numbers are available to everyone with a computer and they tend to be fixed and inalterable.

Cunning can still prevail in this subjective business but it must take different forms and one of its most important forms is in the election of a penname. Let me note again: this is not an aesthetic, philosophical or emotional matter, it is often beyond choice. It is a way — an important and in some cases the only way — to deal with an onerous situation.

I wouldn't deal with it. We know what happened. I wouldn't overgeneralize from my situation, certainly. But I wouldn't ignore it.

———*ᴕᴕᴕ*———

MIKE: Okay, let's take Sladek since a) he's dead, and b) you didn't argue with Garfield, MacDonald, Disch, or the others.

Let's grant that, from a monetary point of view, he didn't have much of a career, brilliant as he was. Let's further grant that he sold equally poorly whether writing science fiction, mysteries, or mainstream.

Are you seriously suggesting that he would have broken out and made piles of money just by writing his mysteries as John Smith or his mainstreams as John Jones?

Come on, Barry — here's a guy who, even though I personally loved his writing, proved he couldn't find an appreciative audience of any size no matter in what field he labored. Are you saying all the readers who gave Sladek one chance in mysteries or science fiction before abandoning him would have picked up a disguised Sladek book and decided that *this* guy was worth buying every time he had a new book on the stands?

Leave Art aside. I'm suggesting that in a best case scenario, you'll pull some of your readers with you when you move to another category, and in a worst case scenario you won't. But if it is your writing that has put them off, be it because of plotting, characterization, or simply the way you push a noun up against a verb, I can't see that a change of name is going to make them love what they were predisposed to hate or ignore.

Exceptions? Sure. There are exceptions to everything. I already mentioned a major one. Here's another: you're a starving writer who has to pay his bills and put food on the table, so you do some TV novelizations, or some sharecrop books. Yes, your sales will be far better than if you'd written your own books — but you are also expected to write in a certain style which is probably not your own, and you are writing for an audience which may very well not appreciate the kind of stories you want to tell when you're free to do so. (How many Star Trek fans really want to read, say, *Hyperion* or *A Deepness in the Sky* or *Herovit's World*?) Under those circumstances, you might consider a pseudonym — but simply from an economic point of view, that may be counter-productive, in that you may start all over with a beginner's print run under your own name after selling six digits' worth of books in someone else's universe with your true name hidden behind a house name or a pseudonym.

It's not an easy decision, but it's one that I think is being made far too easily and far too often these days.

15 Print-on-Demand

Mike: I've been writing a bi-monthly column for beginners for more than seven years now, and every now and then I deliver up a truth that has them screaming like stuck pigs. I recently did it again, so I thought maybe you and I might discuss the subject rationally, like two undistressed professionals.

The subject is Print-on-Demand books, and there are a lot of perfectly valid reasons to make use of them and those who publish them — but there is one area, the area that seems most attractive to beginners, that I consider professional poison, and that area is selling your original novel to a POD publisher.

Most of the beginners have explained to me, at hysterical length, that at least their books will see print in a field that is stacked against newcomers, and they have come up with bold and unique new ways of publicizing the novels once they're published, and the main thing is to get it out on the stands.

The beginners also point out that even though they're getting almost no advance (and in many cases, not a single penny up front), why, look at *Catch-22, Jonathan Livingston Seagull,* and *The Hunt for Red October,* to name just three megasellers that were bought for rock-bottom advances.

The answer, of course, is threefold:

First, they got minimal professional advances, but those advances were still many multiples beyond what POD publishers pay for original science fiction novels.

Second, those three books roll off the tongue because they are among the very few megahits that surprised even the publishers.

Third, and finally, the rule that those titles are the exception to is that sales are made in the contract, not in the writing.

For example, if a publisher pays $3,500 for a first novel — about what they've been paying for better than a quarter of a century now — and gives the book a piece of cheap generic cover art, and budgets minimal (or no) advertising, the only possible way he can get hurt is to pay for printing and shipping 150,000 copies and gobbling 138,735 returns of a heavily advertised flop a few months later ... so of course he doesn't do that. He prints what the contract suggests will be the proper number: maybe 16,000 paperbacks. And with precious few exceptions, the author will sell under 10,000 copies and never see a penny's worth of royalties.

Go to the other extreme. The publisher pays $500,000 for a mediocre novel. Good, bad, or mediocre, he stands to take a serious red-ink bath if the book doesn't sell enough copies, so he'll print maybe 800,000 copies, he'll give it the best cover art he can obtain, it'll get raised metallic type or cut-outs or whatever (it varies from year to year) so the distributor will know that this is the major opus the publisher is pushing this month, there will be dump displays and full-color posters in every bookstore, full-page ads in a dozen major publications, a 20-city author tour, maybe even TV ads in New York and Los Angeles, and the road men will be told that *this* is the title they've got to sell. And, of course, because of this effort, the book sells 500,000 copies in 10 weeks and quickly goes back to press for another quarter million.

Like I say, the sales are determined by the contract. Minimal variations in sales will occasionally be determined by the quality of the book and the number of favorable or unfavorable reviews, but, also like I say, they're minimal.

Now let's consider the typical POD novel. The publisher pays little or, more often, no advance, so he has no money to recoup other than paying for a tiny print run. Being a small press, he will do almost no advertising. Since it's print on demand, you can figure a first printing of maybe 200 to 250 copies if the book's a trade paperback, maybe 100 if it's a hardcover. Hard to get rich on even a 75 percent sell-through.

Ah, say the beginners, but we're sending out all kinds of promotional material to the chains—and it may well be that the chains will order copies. After all, it doesn't cost *them* anything to order 55,000 copies and return 53,000 a couple of months later. The publisher pays the printing bill and shipping costs both ways—and while a New York mass market house with deep pockets and its own sales force might take that kind of chance, no small press will. If the publisher wants to stay in business, he'll place a few copies with Amazon.com and Barnesandnoble.com and let it go at that. He can't afford a multi-thousand-copy print run; that's why he's POD.

So what does all this mean?

First, that the newcomer who places his novel with a POD small press will earn *far* less than a substandard first novel advance from any mass market publisher.

Second, most people, seeing the novel, will assume, rightly or wrongly, that it wasn't good enough to sell to mass market, since even the casual reader can figure out that a small press can't match advances with Tor, Ace, Bantam, del Rey, Eos, Baen, Roc, DAW, and that whole crowd. (In fact, the casual reader will have a hard time finding any of those 200 copies; they're certainly not going to be in his local bookstore.)

Third, when the newcomer wises up and goes to a mass market publisher with Novel #2, the very best thing that can happen is for the editor to be totally ignorant of Novel #1. Because if the editor asks how much the first novel sold, the answer, no matter how it's sugar-coated, is not likely to encourage the purchase of #2.

Before we get onto what I consider the legitimate and beneficial uses of POD publishers, let me know: am I missing something here? Is it possible for the next major career to begin with a POD novel?

—⁓⁓⁓—

BARRY: No, I don't think that the next "major career," whatever that is, or the major career after that will be launched by POD. It is possible that a writer who comes later to success will have an earlier POD publication (to be revived by trade publishing). William Gibson, for instance, published his first story in *Unearth*, a small-circulation semi-prozine, in 1977. Did that publication inaugurate his career? Five years later, his second story was published in *Omni*, and *that* was where the career began.

Cordwainer Smith's first story, "Scanners Live in Vain," was published in 1950 in *Fantasy Book*, a (very) small-circulation semi-prozine published in California; but Smith was invisible until that story, reprinted by Fred Pohl, ghost-editing for Robert A. Heinlein, was placed in the 1954 anthology *Assignment in Tomorrow* where it created in a small way astonishment, and the next year, Smith's "The Game of Rat and Dragon" in *Galaxy*, capitalizing on the anthology, started Smith's career. Somebody's POD book may be reprinted after its author becomes otherwise established and may in fact become quite valuable, but POD is no launching pad.

POD is a dumping ground.

POD is where books go to die; where literary corpses go to be embalmed. It is a suitable place for the end of a career or perhaps a place of interregnum for a writer trying something else or unable to sell the trade publishers; it is not a place where a career can be born. I don't think that it's a place where a career can be sustained, either.

This is a drastic statement and I do not mean to give offense to the readers of this publication, honorable persons all, who are POD publishers; they mean very well and they have become a useful market for reprints if the author (note Barry Longyear's essay in a recent issue) is willing to assume the responsibility for publicity and knows how to work the Internet. POD is certainly a step or two above outright self-publishing or the unspeakable vanity press on the hierarchy of publishing. But saying that and giving due credit to the good will of the POD publishers (I have no reason to think that any of them are dishonorable), they are no place to begin a career or to continue one. They are, arguably, a place for out-of-print work and of course POD can be a market for a kind of book which would be of little interest to the contemporary trade publishers. (You've placed a few such titles, Mike, in the nature of offbeat collections or compilations of themed essays.) An established writer could do worse than bring her laundry list to POD (assuming that she had a pretty good idea of the kind of people who would like to read her laundry list and an equally good idea of how to reach them).

But a new novel or collection? No. I cannot make any argument for POD here.

———*∿∿∿*———

MIKE: Before we get onto the beneficial uses of POD — and there are a few, trust me for the moment — let's dwell just a bit longer on using POD for original novels.

The examples you gave above are all perfectly true, but I'm not sure they're valid, because the Gibson and the Cordwainer Smith pieces were *stories*, not novels. I wonder where Gibson's career would be had he given *Neuromancer* to a POD publisher and kept his fingers crossed that someone would notice it.

And while we're at it, you're the half of the team that has worked for a literary agent. I assume that at one time or another you've seen a typical POD novel contract. If we haven't scared people off yet, what can you say about the contract that might drive the final nail into the coffin?

———*∿∿∿*———

BARRY: Take a look at the contract offered by one of the largest POD publishers — perhaps *the* largest. It gives the publisher "sole and exclusive right to license" the property in all editions throughout the world and a 50 percent share of the proceeds of all such licenses ... in practical terms, and I know no other such, the publisher, for the minimum effort of printing perhaps ten or twenty copies of a book (a couple of complimentaries to the author and all the rest paid), shares equally in all proceeds of the work from all other editions. Putting it another way, the POD publisher has become an agent taking a 50 percent commission, a rate which exceeds all ethical boundaries. Furthermore, during the period of the license — seven years in most cases— the author may engage in no other contracts for the work: the "exclusivity" clause granted to the publisher means that the author has utterly lost control of her work. If a German agent forwards a publisher an offer of 8000 Euros to reprint an old title which has been licensed to the POD publisher, the author must stand aside in favor of the POD making the contract and taking 4000 Euros for no expenditure and no effort. This is beyond confiscatory.

Or take a look at the contract of another very large POD publisher. Here the author is charged "production costs," which will be deducted from any proceeds and the proceeds are split equally between the publisher and the author. Once again, the POD publisher has become an agent taking 50 percent commission ... and the assumption by the author of complete production costs means that this POD publisher is offering absolutely nothing whatsoever but the opportunity for the writer to give away half of her property for a very long time, if not in perpetuity.

Say, in this latter case, that "production costs"—graphics, setting, scanning, printing—are a thousand dollars; say that the book sells over a two-year period 400 copies (a generous estimate) at, say, $12.00 apiece for trade paperback format. That's a gross of $4800, an author's share of $1400 less $1000 "production costs" ... the author has realized $400 from the sale of those 400 copies. And yielded 50 percent of all subsidiary rights.

You may call this "publication," Mike ... or at least your *Ask Bwana* correspondents may call it that. I have another word or words for it but we're writing a gentlemanly column of gentle advice and we will let our equally gentle readers use their extrapolative imagination, okay?

—◦◊◦—

Mike: No, I don't think I've ever called that "publication," and yes, a lot of beginners have. Hopefully enough of them are reading this dialogue so that they'll not only learn a little something about the contract but also tell their friends.

(Of course, all contracts are negotiable—but if you are new enough and naive enough to place your novel with a POD publisher, you probably don't have very much bargaining power.)

OK, so much for new novels. What *do* you use a POD house for? I mean, hell, I can read a contract, I can count, and I use them. So it's a fair and valid question.

The most obvious answer is that I give them books that I cannot sell to mass market.

But that's too simplistic an answer. After all, I'm not an egomaniac—or at least, I'm not an exceptionally stupid one—and only a stupid egomaniac would go to the trouble of preparing a manuscript, *any* manuscript, for a POD publisher without some reason beyond merely wanting to see a few copies of it in print.

Let me break it down by the types of manuscripts I've given them.

The first is what I consider my charity work. In this field, as has been said so many times, you can't pay back, so you pay forward. So, starting a couple of years ago, I've been doing one book a year of "how-to" advice, either artistic, technical, or financial, for new writers. These are not new books, or rather the material isn't new. One was a study of first and final drafts of award-winning and award-nominated stories, which showed beginners how you edit and polish your own work. One was a collection of successful outlines and synopses, edited by me but contributed by about 20 SFWA members, each of which resulted in a major book sale, so beginners could see exactly how it's done. One is a collection of 40 of those *Ask Bwana* columns you mentioned. And so on. Eventually these dialogues will become one. Charity work. (Though I have to point out that even after taking my editorial fee, I was distributing pro rata royalties to those 20 SFWA members only four months after that book of outlines was published. So sometimes even charity work sells.)

The second is collections. If your name isn't Bradbury, Silverberg, or Willis, it's harder than you think to sell a collection to mass market. Oh, I've done it, you've done it, we've all done it —*occasionally*. But I don't write occasional short stories; I write frequent short stories. Enough for a collection almost every year. But my mass market publishers don't want a Resnick collection every year, and I suspect my mass market readers probably don't either, since they've been conditioned to reading short stories in the magazines and novels in book form. But while I may place most of my collections with small press or POD publishers in America, the rest of the world doesn't view collections the same way American publishers do, and once I get my hands on a new collection, it goes off to a couple of dozen countries, and invariably sells to one or more of them. So in this case, POD is a marketing tool — and of course, if you have any clout at all, you make sure that the contract is not the type you listed above. You share no subsidiary, electronic, or foreign rights, you lease the collection for only three or four years, never more than five, you demand enough author's copies to send to all your potential foreign markets, and so on.

The third — and the only difference here is content — is reprint novels. Again, most of us have resold some of our work to mass market, but when you've been around as long as you and I have, we've got too damned many books to constantly resell to mass market. I wouldn't want to anyway; if there are 40 Resnick novels to choose from, invariably too many buyers will choose the reprints that have already earned out rather than the new ones that *have* to earn out if I am to keep my creditors in mink.

An added benefit from new editions of old novels is that many foreign editors, presented with a 1982 or 1991 paperback with a $2.25 or $3.50 cover price on it, will feel that your agent has been hawking this novel unsuccessfully for over a decade (and they might well be right) ... but show them a new trade paperback or hardcover of the same book, with new cover art, and a 2002-type pricetag, and they're much more likely to buy it — or at least, that's been my experience.

All right, those are my three best reasons. What's your take on it?

—◦◦◦—

BARRY: Well, they're good reasons. And remember one of the truisms of the business: Any contract is negotiable. No contract is written in stone. You can ask for better terms. You can demand better terms as the price of taking the contract. You can fight for special privileges. In all of my years signing contracts and agenting them I have found that there is only one clause which is absolutely non-negotiable ... publication of the manuscript. It is possible to extract a delivery advance for a novel which a publisher finds unacceptable, it is possible to negotiate a kill fee equal to the full fee for an article ... but no publisher will guarantee publication of a work. That gives the writer a kind of leverage which no publisher will ever yield and of course can expose the publisher (in the case of extremely controversial or undocumented nonfiction) to heavy legal penalties. Publishers will never agree to that clause. But I know of no other — zero percent of all subsidiary rights, a 50 percent royalty rate and so on and on — which in one case or another has not been granted.

That said, it might be possible to work a POD contract into acceptability ... the two publishers whose contracts I have described might be willing for a writer or property of significant weight to make the kind of changes which would result in an equitable contract. But any writer with that kind of clout, any property with that kind of potential doesn't need a POD publisher, will never get near POD. Heinlein's and Asimov's ancient backlist are happily published mass-market by the conglomerates. I'm sure that POD would offer them equivalent or better terms ... but why would they need POD? And how could POD possibly meet the expected demand for their backlist?

It couldn't and in the real world which I — not the Heinlein or Asimov backlists, just your humble servant — occupy, sales of POD books are almost always terrible. You seem to have done well with a couple of yours but they are the exception; I have seen royalty statements, I know these figures and a 20-copy sale of a novel in the first month of publication is regarded as a bestseller by the POD publishers. Writers whose names would be recognizable to three-quarters of those reading this dialogue are receiving semi-annual statements indicating sales of five copies. (And for those five sales they are yielding half of any money they might receive for a foreign edition.) Even if one could adjust the terms of a contract, the parameters of POD publishing remain essentially unchanged. A sale of 200 copies of a new novel, 40 copies of a reprint over a six-month period would be exceptional. (The figures are equally dismal for electronic editions but that is another column.)

Everything's negotiable, sure. But what if there's nothing to negotiate?

MIKE: My experiences are a bit different. Not much. I mean, hell, you don't go on safari with 1,200 POD sales any more than with 120 or 12.

But, as I said, I do find them useful for non–mass-market works (I prefer that term to "non-commercial," though there's not all that much wriggle room between the two) that I wish to sell overseas — and I should add that some of my POD collections have also brought dozens of my less well-known short stories to the attention of Fictionwise.com and others, and hence made me a few hundred dollars here and a few thousand there that I assume I wouldn't have made otherwise.

So, leaving original novels and hideous unnegotiated contracts behind, can you in summary find no use whatsoever for POD?

—◦◦◦—

BARRY: I find (almost) no use for POD. I'm no longer a fan of generalities in the first place, and in the second place I'm aware that a POD publisher or three may be subscribers to this *Bulletin* and may be reading this exchange and I certainly do not want to cause offense. The SFWA can use all the friends it can get, probably because a good number of its enemies are enrolled members.

But really: what is the point of POD? You've made a case for some of your own books, for the kind of projects in which a conventional publisher would have no interest and it is a convincing case ... for you. You're an established writer, beyond established, you're one of the ten or twenty most successful living writers of science fiction; you can engage, like the Pope, in indulgences, and that's what I take your POD projects to be. Because of your success you're able to undertake projects and anthologies which won't really pay but which perhaps deserve to be done for their own sake, would not otherwise be done, and give exposure to a few people. This is laudable but none of it has to do—does it, Mike?—with professional publishing. It has to do, as I've said, with indulgences. If you were struggling to build a career—let's take a look at the Mike Resnick of 1984—would you have the time or interest to go this far afield, put in this much time for this kind of compensation?

That is why POD—if I were going to countenance it at all—would only be, paradoxically enough, for those who don't need it ... for writers who are economically or professionally free (by achievement or by grim choice) from the rigors of the marketplace. In that sense, I could condone POD publishing in the same way that the professional writers' journals (I almost want to put quote marks around that one, let's try it: "professional writers' journals") will condone subsidy publishing ... if you have lots of money, if you're dying to see your work in print and pass it on to your friends and relatives, if you're *really* dying and just want to pass it on to yourself and you don't mind the expense then go ahead and do it but understand the probable outcome. Similarly, if you're an eager but unsuccessful aspirant who simply wants some evidence of "publication" no matter how tenuous, and you don't mind essentially burying your work ... then POD may be the place for you. And, at the other end, if you're an aging or aged science fiction writer with a significant body of work but no longer able to sell new books, let alone find reprint offers for the backlist (a situation faced by more than 85 percent of us now), then POD for a few novels published in the 1960s or 1970s may not be such a bad deal ... there are a couple of fresh copies of the book for (as you say) foreign submission and if standards of production of most POD are fairly low, such books can still look better on the shelf than Ace Doubles, copyright 1957, or Berkley novels, circa 1967.

But be warned—if you're that hypothetical out-of-print, aging writer, your semi-annual sales will be somewhere in the range of a dozen copies; over

10 years you might sell a hundred and — am I being somewhat perseverant about this? — you've given half of the money and the sole and exclusive right to sub-license to the POD publisher. If an Italian or French publisher swaddles an overaged fan of your work who wants to bring that 1954 Ace Double to a new audience, you're not only compelled to give half of the advance to the POD pub-lisher ... you're compelled to send your eager, overaged fan to negotiate with your POD publisher. You have lost any effective control of your own work; that part of your backlist published POD no longer belongs to you.

As I told writers again and again when acting for the SFWA Grievance so many years ago and as my distinguished predecessor in that post, Joe Halde-man, had even more eloquently told some complainants ... there are worse things than being not published. Many worse things. And I don't even think of POD as "publication."

You obviously disagree but it is this disagreement — hi there, Mr. Ebert — which renders these dialogues so lovable.

— ✺ —

MIKE: Hi right back at you, Mr. Siskel. No, I don't disagree with anything you've said, provided the conditions are those you've laid out. But as I've pointed out here and in so many other forums, the most useful word in pub-lishing is "No." Say it and you'd be surprised at the concessions that are made. No established writer — and by "established," let's hypothesize a writer whose name is not totally unknown to the non–sf-fandom reader — has to give away 50 percent of *anything*. All he has to do is say "No!," and you'd be surprised how quickly a POD publisher will decide that selling a couple of hundred extra copies of his reprint novel is more desirable than earning 50 percent of noth-ing, which is what he's likely to get hawking reprint/foreign rights of a first nov-elist who came to him because he couldn't crack the mass market.

And, whether it's charity work, or a desire to make a few hundred copies of an old non-bestseller available to his current fans, or a need to have a cur-rent edition to show to foreign editors, once that "No!" is firmly said and prop-erly responded to, there *are* some reasons to consider POD.

But, I fully agree, never as a primary source of income.

16 Professionalism

MIKE: Since I've been writing a column (elsewhere) for beginning writers, I've been asked, from time to time, exactly what a writer owes his editor and publisher, and what they in turn owe the writer.

First and foremost, of course, each of them owes a certain adherence to the terms of the contract. The writer owes his editor a manuscript of X number of words that bears at least a passing resemblance to the synopsis that was used to make the sale. The editor owes the writer his support and his best editorial judgment. The publisher owes the writer Z dollars upon acceptance, and whatever the contract calls for in terms of promotion.

But what *else* do they owe one another? What other obligations has a writer got — if any? How about an editor? A publisher? Are the terms of the contract the end-all be-all, other that a certain degree of civility, or are there certain general obligations of professionalism that accrue to every writer and editor and publisher, whether spelled out in terms of the contract or not?

—ᴥᴥᴥ—

BARRY: Here are the obligations of professionalism: you deliver contracted or promised manuscripts on time, you answer your mail, return phone calls promptly and treat editors and colleagues with civility unless severely provoked, and then you treat them with somewhat less civility. Simple, huh? No mystery to any of this. And yet —

And yet I am reminded of my essay many years ago reminiscing none too warmly about my brief tenure (4/68–10/68) as editor of Sol Cohen's *Amazing/Fantastic*: "I could tell the difference between a good story and a bad story. At the time I thought that this represented the base level of how an editor should function. I learned that it was instead the most that could be expected of an editor." I would have expected that my first paragraph articulated the minimum level of professional conduct when as you and I know it represents perhaps the outer limit. Not to berate the members of SFWA and by inference the reader of these columns. We all have our problems and me too; somewhere in my dark history is a contracted but undelivered novel (terms were altered

149

so that I did not have to return the advance) and several of our household names, writers whom I will not dishonor by identifying here, made pocket-careers in their failing decades by signing contracts and taking advances for work that they not only did not deliver but knew they would not deliver ... proposals which in many cases were sold in identical format to multiple publishers. Didn't keep any of them out of the Science Fiction Hall of Fame and I don't think it should. Many writers carry so much resentment, a burning, aching recrimination which deepens with the years, that they find a lack of civility the only way that they can strike at the system. (Of course in so doing they hurt their friends, not their enemies; the SMOFs (Secret Master[s] of Fandom) are always fully sequestered from retaliation.)

I see that I am making a series of excuses; that what my first paragraph has given I am in the procedure of taking away. Without excusing unprofessional behavior (at least unprofessional behavior by the members of the Science Fiction Hall of Fame) I do note that it can be explained, if not necessarily justified. Well, justified by most standards anyway. It sure can be justified by me: get to know any writer well enough, someone (not me!) wrote somewhere, "and you will inevitably find that unsolaced bitterness, that feeling of entitlement which comes from what is felt to be great injury."

—◢◢◢—

MIKE: I think I'm going to start with the minimal professionalism a writer owes his editor and publisher:

1. He owes them the best writing of which he is capable, whether he likes the assignment or not.

2. He owes them a professional manuscript, which is to say, one that has been proofread and corrected. After all, if a writer shows contempt for his work by not going over it and correcting it before handing it in, why should an editor treat it with any greater respect?

3. He owes them an honest effort to meet his deadline.

4. In this day and age, he owes them a computer copy in a common, readable format, especially with shorter-than-booklength works. Since most business correspondence is now carried on through e-mail, he owes it to them to check his e-mailbox frequently, respond promptly, and to have a computer and system that is compatible with most other systems.

5. He owes them civil behavior.

6. He owes them a fast, competent turnaround when proofreading galleys.

7. He owes them whatever small extras are requested to promote the book or story, from having an autograph session at a convention to supplying a photo or brief bio for the dust jacket or introductory material.

And what is the minimum owed the writer by his editor and publisher?

1. An honest appraisal of his work when it is delivered. (That would seem to be an absolute given, but we've all seen what happens to orphaned books after inter-office wars.)

2. A prompt reading and a prompt decision.

3. Prompt pay.

4. Prompt and honest royalty statements on books.

5. A honest effort to promote the book or story to the best of the editor's and publisher's ability.

6. A caring handling of the material, by which I mean a good and competent copy editor (they're hard to find and always to be cherished when found), an artist who will do justice to the work, ample amounts of time to read the copy-edited manuscript and the galleys.

7. Prompt delivery of the author's copies.

8. A willingness to share, if not all reviews (some books get hundreds), at least all major ones.

9. Civil behavior.

Those lists came out shorter than I thought they would. What am I missing?

———*♦♦♦*———

BARRY: What you're missing — what we have been intermittently missing through the course of these exchanges although I try to be alert — is a sense of history, is an awareness that new campaigns are simply old campaigns with a few labels changed and of course a different set of characters. The opposite of repertory theatre — same play, same masks, different actors. In 1966 Damon Knight had an article in this very *SFWA Bulletin* on the subject of editorial courtesy and ranked the markets in those terms ... from hardcover publishers (nice and thoughtful) all the way down to men's magazines ("unbelievably rude"). Knight felt that editorial courtesy should be contractual, that the obligations of the publisher should be explicit and part of the terms of the agreement, if they weren't then such courtesies could not be expected. "A verbal contract isn't worth the paper it is written on" and so forth.

And here we are, 37 years later, still worrying the same issue: writers should do this, editors should do that and why the hell so often do they do neither? I think that Damon was on to something: unless we can get it codified in contracts — all of it, the writer's obligations, the editor's necessity — the situation will never change, there will be a range of response, some will exhibit apropos behavior and some will not. But how willing would the membership be (let alone publishers) to make this part of the model contract? Isn't lying to one's publisher, for so many ("Just polishing it up, boss") part of Standard Operating Procedure? Didn't Avram Davidson, may his soul rest in peace, have an essay in the *SFWA Forum* decades ago bragging on the various and ingenious

ways he had found to defraud his publishers, obtain and keep advances for
books he had no intention of ever writing? What was that essay doing in an
official publication, come to think of it?

—◦◦◦—

MIKE: Actually, the most honest *and* courteous guys I ever dealt with were
in the sex field during my starving-writer days 35 years ago. If they said they
were going to buy something from you, it was written in stone. If they said they
were going to pay you, you got the money within 48 hours and their checks
were good as gold. (If they said they were going to kill you, they did that pretty
promptly and efficiently, too—but no one ever said it to me.)

If Avram wrote that essay—and if he did, I missed it—then he was in
opposition to pretty much everything I believe about professionalism. I think
when you make a commitment, either verbal or contractual, to anyone for any
reason, you keep it. Period.

As for lying to editors, I don't think it's necessary. A *lot* of novels come in
late; they get published. The only time I can remember a publisher going to
court to cancel a contract on a late book was in 1975, when a journalist was
two years late handing in a book on the Nixon White House, which of course
had been the Ford White House for over a year. For what it's worth, I think the
publisher was justified.

But I'm not aware of any publisher suing to reject a late novel. Oh, a few
years back a couple of our more venal mass market houses used it as an excuse
to get rid of writers they no longer wanted—but I noticed that they never pulled
that shit on a leader, just on writers they wanted to dump.

Anyway, that's why major novels are hardly ever scheduled until they come
in. Otherwise, the publisher explains away a lot of ads and eats a lot of crow,
like Scholastic recently did for the fifth Harry Potter book.

Well, you've told me that our founder, Damon Knight, felt that editorial
courtesy should be written into a contract. Since I knew Damon, I have to ask:
what did he say about authorial courtesy?

—◦◦◦—

BARRY: Damon, to my recollection, had nothing to say about authorial
courtesy. Damon proceeded under a series of assumptions which still govern
the reflexes of much of the SFWA membership and for that matter most of the
membership of the Author's Guild: a) Writers are special, b) because they are
special their suffering is special, c) writers are victims, d) publishers are
intractably venal, e) given a chance to treat a writer inequitably publishers will
always take it, f) because of the inequity of power held by publishers and writers, writers breaching contracts or otherwise trying to find their way through
a situation by delay, lying, deliberately incompetent work (to break an option)
should be understood and forgiven.

Perhaps these assumptions are defensible. Damon, after all, founded a writers' organization and he did so believing that such an organization was needed because writers needed to be defended in an overall situation where they had very little protection. If publishers or editors felt abused, Damon might have said (I do not wish to appropriate his voice or to speak for him; this is speculation) then they were free to form their own organizations or craft guilds ... their problems were really not our problems. There was, at least in the earlier years of SFWA, little concern for mutuality of interest and any collegiality was on the basis of individual relationships, it was not organizational.

As with so much else in these 37 years there have been changes and there is perhaps a somewhat greater perception of common interest than there was at that time. But Avram's essay in that Cogswell-edited *Forum* could be viewed as something very close to bragging about the way in which he had circumvented contracts and could also be seen as a covert instruction to other writers ... here's a shopping list, here's how to do it. (I should note that there were a couple of letters to the *Forum*, one of them mine, raising questions about that essay and that in a sequel in the next issue Davidson claimed to have delivered an overdue contract and was now calmly awaiting the riches that would descend upon him.) This was not a helpful point of view for what had to be perceived as the covert sanction of an organization whose official publication would print that essay and in fact — but hardly for that one reason — Cogswell departed as editor of the *Forum* shortly thereafter.

I know that writers are by no means special and it is very hard — I have come to know a lot of writers — to see them as victims but I'll say this: there is an imbalance in power and it is an imbalance which publishers have always been willing to exploit. There are a relatively few writers whose names are known and which make a difference in sales, but publishers perceive most writers as interchangeable or (in the case of those who have published several books to flat or declining sales figures) absolutely disposable. We might raise the issue of what, in light of all this, members of this organization might expect of it in terms of practical assistance: I did Grievance work for half a decade some time ago and I know that the organization does see some kind of obligation ... but how much in those practical terms should SFWA attempt? Or should there be any obligation at all? Doesn't a Grievance function, if it is going to be at all effective, have to be ascribed to a union rather than the anomalous organization which we have today?

———✍———

MIKE: I might believe writers were special if I hadn't been rubbing shoulders with them for 40 years. I'm not aware that their suffering is any more special than anyone else's. If they are victims, it is because they choose to be; no one holds a gun to their heads and insists that they write for a living until the day they die. I won't argue about publishers being venal; they certainly are —

but I'll argue that that's no excuse or justification for venality in a writer. And, finally, I have a difficult time believing that there is ever a reason for purposely, almost by design, breaching a contract that no one forced the writer to sign.

Because I've been a writer, and many of my friends are writers, I've heard all these arguments (I'm inclined to say: all this pap) for decades. I didn't believe it then; I don't believe it now.

But I've also been an editor (weekly tabloids and monthly men's magazines in my starving-writer days, and science fiction anthologies more recently) and a publisher (racy mass market paperbacks, back in the earlies), and I have to say that almost every writer's ruse is not only venal but totally transparent. Science fiction conventions don't reinvent the wheel anywhere near as often as new writers reinvent every tired lie and scam. It didn't make me mad as an editor; it just made me feel *tired*, and maybe a bit old before my time.

I think what it comes down to is this: you either have a sense of personal honor or you don't. And if you do, you stick to it whether the publisher and editor behave with equal honor or not. It's easy to think of them as the enemy, but they really aren't. They want a bestseller as much as you do—and depending on how much they've invested in you, maybe more. They do not sign a contract with the hope that you will be late, that you'll deliver a deliberate turkey to bust an option clause, that you'll use wide margins and tons of brief dialog in order to deliver a 400-page, 100,000-word manuscript that actually measures out at 64,000 words.

A publisher puts his money on the line when you sell him a book. He pays you, and if he's lucky, he sees a finished manuscript a year or two later. I think you'd have to be awfully foolish, perhaps even unbalanced, to truly believe that he hopes it will bomb and that he'll do his best to sabotage it.

What SFWA should do, in terms of Grievance or any other function, is a fascinating question, and we'll deal with it in another essay, one devoted to SFWA—but this one's devoted to professionalism, and (let me duck behind this rock here) if Avram actually wrote what you said and SFWA actually published it, I'm suddenly not so sure that SFWA and professionalism have all that much in common.

—◦◦◦—

BARRY: Oh, Avram wrote it and Cogswell published and shortly thereafter Cogswell and the *Forum* went speedily in different directions. It was not only the Davidson instruction booklet on how to shaft publishers which got Cogswell canned but his vicious attack on Keith Laumer's *Analog* story, "The Plague," his photos of underdressed ladies on the cheap pulp paper, his printing of a photograph of a five-year-old child over the caption, "Don Pfeihl, editor of *Vertex* enjoys socializing at the annual SFWA cocktail party." Cogswell got away with this stuff in the late fifties working out of the Department of English offices at Ball State University, but the Administration of the SFWA in the mid-seventies found this intolerable and one can well suspect why. I realize that this is a low blow to a man already dead ... but I always felt that Keith Laumer's nearly fatal stroke two months after Cogswell's mockery of "The Plague" in the *Forum* might have been triggered by that article. Certainly the explosion of rage a man with high blood pressure must have felt could not have done him any good.

But Cogswell is gone and the *Forum* is but a shadow of its once ever-industrious self, now devoted — 40 percent of its pagination — to long lists of Nebula nominations and near-nominations and almost-nominations and non-nominations— and we can focus upon the somewhat more conterminous issue of the SFWA as a professional organization, one which we agree deserves a column of its own and which we should for the moment defer but certainly one to be pondered. I have pondered and reached some tentative conclusions (which will surprise few) and which I will in course Discuss, Compare and Contrast.

Meanwhile: do writers as a class— as you suggest — reinvent the scams, duplicity, deceits of previous generations of writers? Well, they would be atypical examples of humanity if they failed to do so and one thing writers are not (consider your earlier remark) is atypical. Writers are very much like people except that in understanding less they find themselves driven to extremes of articulacy to first explore, then explain, their ignorance. Every generation of writers approaches the scams as if they were new, of course. I am reminded of Platoon Sergeant Wheeler who gathered the Third Platoon of I Company around him at Fort Dix in the barracks at first nightfall of the first day of Basic Training to say, "All of you guys at this moment are trying to figure out a way to beat the system. Forget it. Hundreds of thousands of the finest and the worst minds have passed through this system over these hundred years and there is nothing you can try that hasn't been tried, nothing you can do that hasn't already failed. You can fight the system and start on your way to the Stockade or you can give it up and go along and have a relatively easy time. It's up to you."

This masterful speech applied to the circumstances of numb or terrified recruits; it wouldn't work so well in Writing Basic Training. Writers are not put through the obstacle course, writers don't face 4:00 A.M. Reveille, writers do not do 20-mile forced marches with full field pack. If they were subject to this they would not be writing articles for the house publication bragging about how they had made fools of the system.

On the other hand, a few recruits made it to OCS and a scattering went further than that; there are some majors, light colonels, maybe even a general who came from that mix. Where did Avram go?

———*o/o/o*———

MIKE: Correct me if I'm wrong, but you seem to be saying that it's all right for a writer to lie, to cheat, to mislead his editor in any way whatsoever because of the way (generic) editors treat (generic) writers, and that the only reason not to do so is because editors have seen it all and it won't work. Is that essentially your position? Because if it is, then I imagine you would also toss out all the points of professionalism I listed early on.

Anyway, my question is not *do* writers as a class reinvent all the scams? You've made it clear that at least a sizeable minority of them do. What I want to know is: do you think they *should*?

Or, to put it as simply as I can: do you owe the previously-defined professionalism to yourself, or to your editor and publisher? If you owe it to them, then perhaps— and only perhaps— there are extenuating circumstances in individual cases that would allow you to ignore it. But if you owe it to yourself, as I believe, then who you're dealing with and how they treat you personally (and how they treat writers as a group) makes no difference; you must behave honorably and professionally for the simple reason that you are trying your best to be an honorable man who takes pride in his behavior and his profession.

So which is it?

———*◊/◊/◊*———

BARRY: No, I am not recommending that writers should cheat, steal, lie or vote a straight ticket. Writers are quite capable of finding misalliance on their own without advice from me. To the contrary I believe that writers should be honest, ethical, prompt on delivery dates, courteous to publishers and should split their ballot judiciously when the best candidates for governor and senator come from opposite party affiliation. You seem to have missed the point of my paragraphs and of First Sergeant Wheeler's advice to the troops.

Wheeler was saying, "Don't try this, everyone has tried everything and there's nothing new you can do to beat the system, you might as well go along." For practical if not ideological reasons. Third Platoon India Company did go along with the system — most of them — and went on to lead decent civilian post-military lives in that pre–Vietnam, Cuban Missile Crisis pre–Reserve call-up in 1962 time. Wheeler's point was that it could only be easier that way. That was my point too, although newer writers, looking at the often horrid examples presented by some older writers might think that if these practices worked for them they might still be working. Sometimes they do.

Writers and publishers are not in fundamental concord; I wish that such were the case but it is not. Publishers are often unfair to writers, writers to publishers, would that this were not the case. We should all work in mutuality toward a better outcome. I have been looking for this through my own many decades in the business and perhaps matters are getting better although they may be getting worse. This is, as we have agreed, a subjective business.

What Theodore Cogswell (1918–1987) did which was very wrong (let me pick up on this for a moment) was to use an organization publication —funded by the dues of members— as a medium to attack a member, to hold up that writer before his peers as a fool. Cogswell did not do this as a correspondent to the *SFWA Forum*, he did not do it as the contributor of an article. Both would have been questionable ... but Cogswell did this in his capacity as editor of the publication and this, speaking of professionalism, decency, and courtesy among writers, should not have been done.

But in fact I don't think that his attack on "The Plague" was the reason that he was fired. I don't think that he was fired for his questionable taste in pictures. No, I think that it was the photograph whose caption identified Don Pfeihl as a little boy which got the old Brigadier The Axe. Make a fool of a fellow writer, sure ... but don't offend an editor, even the editor of a minor and soon-to-be-departed magazine. Courage!

—*∽∿∿*—

MIKE: You think it was wrong to attack a member — I've only seen it done about every other issue of the *Forum* for a third of a century — but it *wasn't* wrong to run a piece by a respected writer telling other writers how to lie and cheat on their contracts? I find that ... ah ... interesting.

(I think it's wrong to attack members under any circumstance — in print or in person. That's why I skip most SFWA meetings and spend so little time in the SFWA Suite or its online equivalent.)

This, incidentally, was nothing new in Cogswell-edited publications. The most fascinating reading in the last few years was the huge (and expensive) volume of the near-complete PITFCS (*The Proceedings of the Institute for Twenty-First Century Studies*), the forerunner to the *Forum* that Cogswell edited before there *was* a SFWA. (For the curious: Advent published it; it's being distributed by NESFA.)

Well, the initial question was what do a writer and an editor/publisher owe each other beyond the terms of the contract — and there would seem to be considerable doubt, currently and historically.

So maybe I should conclude by saying that what they owe each other isn't really all that important. If they break the contract, the lawyers will step in and see that it's fulfilled or that the side that breached it suffers some consequence.

But that doesn't let them off the hook. I think what each owes *himself*, in terms of personal integrity and honor, remains vitally important and probably comes to the same thing in the end. If you have it, you'll exercise it; and if you don't have it, no contract or consequence can force it upon you.

17 Myths

MIKE: I suppose it's not surprising in a field that spends so much time creating and transmogrifying myths that a number of myths still exist about the nature of the business itself. Some of them exist because of a simple misunderstanding of the rules of the game, some exist due to willful ignorance on the part of people who don't want to know better, some exist because nobody's taken the time to puncture them.

That's where we come in, needles at the ready.

And since I'm writing the opening section here, I suppose I might as well address the first myth, which is that everyone who signs a book contract fully intends to honor it to the letter, and that indeed there are dire punishments in store for those who don't.

Let's take the writer's end first. He promises to deliver his novel by a certain date. No novel has ever been rejected for being a week late. Or a month. Or a year. Some have been delivered as much as a eight years late, in this field, during the tenure of 80 percent of the current SFWA membership, and have been accepted and published. It's just not a very meaningful clause, though everyone negotiates it as if it was. (I'll allow this caveat: it's probably meaningful on media tie-ins, since the life of a movie or television show is limited, and the interest of a fan of said movie or show even more so.)

The writer promises to deliver a minimum number of words. Meaningless. Some old-time writers like myself figure 10 words a line, 25 lines to a page, 1,000 words every 4 pages—the rule of thumb for those of us who learned on typewriters. Nowadays your computer can do a word count ... but even here not all computers count the same: some count non-trivial spaces, some count all the characters and divide by 5, some do the same but divide by 6. Makes no difference. If you promise 100,000 words, no one's going to reject your manuscript for coming in at 91,500 words. Or 125,000 words, for that matter. And everyone knows that going in.

Now, at the publisher's end, he promises to pay you a signature advance, which is to say, a certain amount of money, usually half the entire advance, the day he receives your signed contract. Anyone you know ever get it that fast? Or within a week? Or within two weeks? Ditto for the acceptance fee, which is usually the other half of the advance. The day the editor says, "I accept this manuscript for publication," that check is supposed to be cut and in the mail to you. Know anyone who ever got it three days later? A week? Three weeks?

(About three years ago I got the delivery check five weeks after handing in a manuscript. This was so incredibly fast and unexpected that when I ran into the publisher at Worldcon I thanked him for the prompt payment. When I told him I'd only waited a little over a month for my payment, he was clearly distressed and mentioned, quite seriously, that he was going to give his accounting department hell for paying me that quickly.)

Then there's the royalty statement. Most contracts call for two statements a year — February 1 (for the second half of the prior year) and August 1 (for the first half of the current year). I don't think any writer seriously expects to see that statement, and any check that accompanies it, before early May and early November, frequently later. A few editors, years ago, explained to me that publishers knew that you couldn't get a suit into court for four to five months, so it became an industry standard for mass market houses. If they hang onto your money for 14 weeks or so, and both sides know up front that they're going to do it, you won't waste the money on a lawyer since the cause of your legal complaint will evaporate before you get to court — and in the meantime, the publisher gets an average of seven months' float on the writers' overdue royalties every year.

I know it, you know it, every writer who's been around the block knows it, yet we continue to negotiate contracts as if both sides intend to honor the letter of the law.

Have you got a particular myth you'd like to hold up to the light?

———✴✴✴———

BARRY: Oh, there are so many myths sustaining (and in other cases destroying) writers. Like Willie Loman we live on a smile and a shoeshine, most of us. Let me synoptically and only partially count the ways:

1. Deliver before the due date on the contract, in fact deliver way early. The editor will be awed by your professionalism, your speed, your virtuosity and will take you ever more seriously.

No she won't. Deliver early and you must be some kind of contemptuous hack, deliver very early and you must be some magnified kind of contemptuous hack. Also, the material — because of the speed of delivery — must be inferior. Delivering exactly on time represents a kind of professionalism admired in the 1950s and 1960s, tolerated now, delivering late means that the work has been carefully tuned and agonizingly perfected, deliver very late and the work must be of the highest quality.

2. Your book publisher and you are on the same side; you both want to sell as many copies as possible.

Although the absolute opposite may not be true, the interests of the publisher and writer of a genre science fiction or fantasy novel are certainly not
confluent. The author wants to sell as many copies as possible, the publisher
is more interested in controlling losses and eliminating risk. That means for
most genre novels a ceiling on the number of copies printed, and of course a
ceiling on the expenditure for advertising (which for most books is regarded
as a waste of money). The writer wants to win, the publisher wants not to risk
and sometimes—in the case of a book which comes in far below editorial expectation—wants to publish, if at all, as minimally as possible.

3. A contract with a guaranteed advertising budget is a wonderful docu-
ment to which every writer should aspire and for which every writer and agent
should fight.

"Advertising guarantees" are unenforceable and in most cases are never
met, sometimes completely ignored. What is the writer going to do, sue the publisher who holds the writer's work hostage? Something like matrimonial law;
maybe you *do* want to go to court to prove your ex-spouse-to-be is a monster
or an idiot or both, but what precisely will this gain for you? The lawyers win.

4. Option clauses are meaningful.

No, option clauses are not meaningful. Publishers—in the case of writers
whose work has failed or whom they wish to send away—pay them no heed.
And writers—well, as Hunter Thompson pointed out almost 40 years ago in a
letter to Scott Meredith explaining how much he hated the publisher of his
Hell's Angels and how badly he wanted to get away, "Any writer with any brains
at all can figure out a way to break an option clause." (Hint: submit 100 blank
or obscenity-laden pages and announce that this is your next novel.)

I could go on. And on and on. But let us talk of myths—wasn't it Vonnegut who called them Foma?—in a more embracing sense. How lush did you
imagine, at 14, the sex life of your favorite writers to be or have been?

—◆◆◆—

MIKE: I've noticed over the past third of a century a certain fascination on
your part with the sex lives of science fiction writers. I personally think watching grass grow and listening to plaster dry both have more to recommend them,
and there's probably a lot more frenetic activity in snail races.

Before I take on the next myth, I do want to address the last one — option
clauses—for a moment. In most cases they're totally meaningless, but a bad one
can be a real pain in the ass. Give the publisher an option on your next book,
to be exercised 60 days after publication of your current one ... and suddenly
you've just given away your right to sell anything, even a serious scientific study
of the sex lives of writers, until two months after the book you are working on
comes out, which with slog times for writers and lag times for publishers, may
effectively keep you out of the marketplace for three years or more.

(What you want to do, of course, is give the publisher an option on your next science fiction book, or limiting it still farther, on your next science fiction book in that particular series, to be exercised within 30 or 60 days not of publication but of delivery of your current manuscript. A publisher will want the broadest option he can get; a writer will want to sign the narrowest one he can get away with.)

OK, another myth. I am a new writer. I am having a difficult time breaking in (or breaking in again). I try to figure out what will make me more acceptable to all those newcomer-hating publishers, and I say: Aha! I have it! I will sell my book for *less* than the publisher regularly offers to new writers, but in exchange I will demand a higher royalty rate. This will make me more affordable than all the other future Willises and Silverbergs trying to sell to the same house, and they will be so happy to get me for that price that they'll take the savings and use it to promote me, and in the long run my greater sales and higher royalty rate will make me more money that I'd have gotten with a standard contract.

Now, believe it or not, that's not a straw dog I set up just to knock down. I can't tell you how many times I've heard that very same strategy voiced by newcomers, each of whom is convinced that it can't fail.

So much for the myth. Out here in the real world, just the opposite is true. You let a publisher get you for a tiny advance and the one thing he knows up front is that he can't lose money unless he buys you a Frank Frazetta cover, promotes you with full-page ads in all the prozines, and prints 300,000 copies of your book. So, being a reasonable corporate entity, he does none of those things: he pays you the $1,750 or whatever you asked for, gives you cheap generic cover art, prints 8,300 paperbacks, and is happy to offer you a 12 percent royalty rate with the comforting knowledge that he'll never have to shell out a single cent in royalties.

The trick, contrary to the myth, is not to make yourself so cheap that a publisher will jump at the chance to publish you, but to make yourself and/or your package expensive enough that your publisher stands to take a loss if he *doesn't* get out there and promote the hell out of the book.

As for selling yourself cheap, I have to point out that you're not unique. Writing has this much in common with acting and prostitution: there are always talented amateurs willing to give away for free the very same commodity that you're trying to sell.

My eyes are mythting up (sorry about that), so I guess it's your turn.

—⟨ν⟩⟨ν⟩—

BARRY: The only science fiction writer whose sex life interests me is my own; I was trying to make another point in that query (most male writers, as the eponymous Norman Mailer pointed out in an interview decades ago, are originally drawn to the pursuit in hope of getting laid) but obviously did not make it too well. Writing as a means of getting laid is another myth, by the way, a little less pernicious than some of the others and — just occasionally — a little less liable to disillusionment but there must be over a thousand less circuitous ways of attaining the act of generation (Elvis managed it all the time, so did Warren G. Harding) and I recommend them all in preference.

Selling cheaply as a means of exciting interest is not so much a myth as a misunderstanding to which newer writers are prey; give it away cheap, undersell the competition, live 120 years. Except that it doesn't work that way, just as with delivering the novel six months early proves that you must be an awful hack writing yard goods, so selling yourself cheaply means that the work is cheap. Publishers are already contemptuous enough of most of the genre work they publish, they tend to get nervous though if the writers suggest that they are even more contemptuous. This is not the way to go.

That there *is* a definite way to go, a clear career path is another myth, one of the most dangerous; newer writers think that a writing career can be compared to a medical or legal career or perhaps one in business ... go to school, get a degree, get in at the entering level, work your way through the corporation or the patient list, get into a partnership, etc., etc. It doesn't work that way of course; as my friend Carter Scholz noted years ago, "There is no career path for writers" and that cannot be uttered strongly or repetitively enough, *There is no career path for writers*. Most writers, as Nelson Algren said, kind of fail into it, come to writing as a means of not having been successful (or not feeling successful) somewhere else and even then they just kind of wander around. Careers begin, advance, go into inexplicable retrograde, collapse, soar, seemingly out of the writers' control. They are unpredictable most of all to those having them, and yesterday provides little clue to tomorrow in career terms (maybe a little more so in terms of fulfilling contracts). That dense and tangled wood in which Dante's protagonist found himself distinctly resembles the world of the writer. In *Zuckerman Unbound*, Roth's eponymous protagonist thinks about Samuel Beckett's play *Waiting for Godot* and thinks, "What is all the fuss about? You can find the same thing going on in Zuckerman's study at 11 A.M. every morning." Dr. Angst makes home visits. Of course you will deny this circumstance in your own life but, as I wrote a long time ago (dialogue 7 or 8?) you write from the authority of success, I from the authority of failure, and failure, old pal and comrade, can teach you a few goddamned things that success never will.

Give us more of the benefits of success, please.

———⟨⟨⟨⟩⟩⟩———

MIKE: The greatest benefit of success is that you know better than to believe or do damnfool things, which brings me to yet another myth, perhaps the most pernicious one since damned near every book on writing, every article on writing, and every lecture on writing gives lie to it, and yet it persists. It is believed as fervently by newcomers today as it was back when you and I were breaking in forty years ago—and it is the myth that an agent can sell things that an unknown and unheralded writer cannot sell.

Now, there are a lot of reasons for having an agent. They have foreign desks, with contacts that would take the average writer years to establish. (Well, the good ones do.) They know the ins and out of contracts, and (especially) they know that killing such-and-so a clause will be accepted by Publisher A but is a deal-breaker at publisher B. They tend to be much more cognizant of the marketplace, and any changes and fluctuations in it, than most writers are. During negotiations they act as a buffer between the writer and the editor that he must eventually work with. They know of markets that are in financial trouble, and they know of potential markets that will soon be kinetic.

But despite the myth, an agent cannot sell an unsaleable manuscript. Not no way, not nohow.

They can get it out of the slush pile. No question about that. They can get it read faster. Absolutely.

But if the book's a turkey, the editor's not going to buy it simply because an agent—even an agent he deals with all the time—submitted it.

Now, part of the myth is that not only can an agent sell your unsaleable book, but also that an agent can get you a bigger advance—and if your book is not unsaleable, it's probably true. But if the publisher pays you 15 percent more, it's a wash; if he pays you 10 percent more, you're actually coming out behind after your agent gets his 15 percent commission.

There's nothing onerous about an agent making a living. The good ones earn their commissions and then some—but new writers who think that the extra $500 that an agent can get them on a contract is going to go into their pockets are due for a major disillusionment.

And new writers who think that an agent can get them one red cent for an unsaleable book are due for an even bigger one.

———∞∞∞———

BARRY: Quite right on agents. Also (and we have been at these dialogues for so long that repetition is becoming unavoidable, also unavoidable the harking back to those halcyon days of 1999 when I was so young and vigorous) a point that I made way back: the new agent you've taken on because the old agent has (you think) failed cannot invent new markets. She must deal with the same group of suspects as the old one; no agent is good enough to come with a completely new group of editors and publishers any more than the new divorce attorney can come equipped with an entirely different set of matrimonial laws from your state. Some divorce lawyers (and agents) are better at maneuvering through or around the extant situation, but all of us must live within the circumstances we are granted. Which is another way of noting that if your old agent can't sell the novel the new agent almost certainly can't. Mileage figures vary, of course.

Two more myths deconstructed:

1. Good work always sells, always finds a publisher. It may take much longer than it should, may bring less money but you can't keep a great novel or short story down, which is why writers should clutch passionately to Heinlein's Fourth Law: "You must keep it on the market until sold." Fred Pohl is fond of this one, has long propitiated. He does so most forcefully as part of a long contribution in the collected *PITFCS*.

Fred Pohl is and always will be admirable — great writer, superb editor — but he is wrong. Just not so. Good work does not always sell. The best novel of the thousands I read over my all too many decades in the Scott Meredith fee department never found a publisher. (For the record: *Beneath the Frozen Sea*, a mainstream novel by Herbert Brown, a then 51-year-old attorney in Cincinnati, 140,000 words.) It was in fact rejected for marketing by the Agency's senior editors (not my fault, boss!). That was 23 years ago and I have no evidence that it was ever in print. It's one of the forty or fifty best novels I have ever read. The *second* best novel I saw in the fee department (*The Resurrection Runner*, cannot recollect the author's name, borderline science fiction like Condon's *The Manchurian Candidate*, 100,000 words) *was* marketed by the Agency but took 40 rejections and was returned. Jody Scott's superb *Down Will Come Baby*, a novel set against the Berkeley upheavals of the mid-sixties, never sold as a book; I cut it in half and ran it serially in *Escapade Magazine* of which I was briefly managing editor 35 years ago and it was never heard of again. There are many, many other novels and even more short stories of great merit which I encountered at Scott Meredith and in other editorial capacities which never sold. "Talent is not disqualifying in this business," I noted a long time ago, but I wouldn't go much beyond that.

2. A corollary of the above: Because great work will always, eventually, find its way, it is possible for a writer devoid of personal connection to editors, publishers, the community of writers itself, to nonetheless have a significant career through simple, avid persistence.

Well there's Alice Sheldon and Paul Linebarger (that's "James Tiptree, Jr." and "Cordwainer Smith" to us) who in their working careers never met anyone associated with the field, worked out of post office boxes and nonetheless had records of brilliant accomplishment but these are the kind of exceptions which, flaunted by those who know better, sustain the myth. (Like the narratives of unpublished writers whose work was sold for great sums of money, the kind of narratives with which Scott Meredith festooned his fee brochures which over the decades were mailed to millions.) Lana Turner was purportedly "discovered" in a drugstore and Jacqueline Bouvier was an Inquiring Photographer with a Washington, D.C., newspaper too (of course, Ms. Bouvier had certain familial advantages) but as Damon Runyon would write, that is not the way the money goes. Most careers, particularly in our genre, are accomplished, propitiated, advanced by personal connection, by direct contact with editors, by a network of friendship and obligation (why do you think so many editors become writers?). There may come a time in the career of a few writers when the accomplishment and fame are such that they can become recluses and continue to sell — Thomas Pynchon, of course — but they are not exemplary.

It's as much of a contact business at its heart as sales. New writers fail to learn that at their peril. Fortunately most learn it relatively early. I did.

———*◊◊◊*———

MIKE: There are still a lot of myths to be debunked, so I think I'll handle a batch of them on this turn.

One is that a Hugo or Nebula will substantially increase your advances. Not so. If you're a new writer, and you've won one of those awards for your short fiction, and you go to sell your first novel, then yes, you'll get more for being a major award winner because you have no track record as a novelist. But once you have a few books out there, ten Nebulas won't do you as much good as earning $10,000 in royalties over and above your advance on your last book. Novels are a lot like racehorses: past performances don't necessarily determine winners and losers (though they're a good indication), but they sure as hell determine prices.

Another myth: the fact that Hollywood options your book or story means they're going to make a movie of it. Well, maybe they will, but the odds are still well over 100-to-1 against it, even after you've collected your option money. I've gone into this before, here and elsewhere, but let me repeat it very briefly: every Hollywood executive knows that he's better off optioning five hundred books a year and making none of them, than making the wrong one. At least half of the Hollywood execs are quite literally in the business of *not* making movies.

Let's shatter this myth too: the fact that an editor talks to you at a convention and encourages you to submit to his magazine or book company implies sincere interest. Nope. Never forget that the editor is there representing the publisher, at the publisher's expense. His transportation is paid, his room is paid, his meals (and those of anyone he takes out to eat) are paid ... and trust me, the publisher isn't shelling out that money so that the editor can discourage writers from submitting and send them off to sell to a rival.

Another one: you can campaign so subtly for an award that no one will be aware that you're doing so. Uh-uh. Forty years into the Nebula and half a century into the Hugo, every type of campaigning and vote trading has been seen so often by so many jaded writers and fans that you won't be fooling anyone but yourself.

And one that forms the basis of most contract negotiations: the fact that your book didn't earn out means the publisher lost money on it, and hence can't pay you as much for your next one. It's always possible that the publisher *did* lose money, but the fact of the matter is that the publisher's break-even point is a hell of a lot lower than the writer's. He can make a tidy profit before the writer ever sees a penny of royalties, and he counts on this argument when negotiating with an unagented writer.

Okay. Have you got some final mythtakes you want to address?

—⌇⌇⌇—

BARRY: Author of *The Resurrection Runner*, I now recollect, was Robert Wood Anderson (who wrote a little autobiography toward the Agency's unsuccessful marketing effort noting that he had once been a Doodletown Piper.) It is a myth that I can no longer remember details. I *can* remember details. Some of them. Granted time, patience and a stress-free environment.

Two more myths:

1. The "crossover" book. Best way for the genre writer to escape the strictures and limited audience of genre is to write something which will have a "broader commercial appeal," usually through the simplification of genre themes and a simpler, cruder plot structure. The audience for even terrible science fiction movies is much larger than that for most written science fiction; the "crossover" through that simplification will get some part of that audience.

Well, again no, it really doesn't work that way; most attempts by genre writers at such crossover fail dismally, being neither quite one or the other ... neither a satisfactorily rigorous and sophisticated genre book nor a work with mass appeal because the handling is uncertain and because publishers, sales divisions, retailers, and wholesalers are not comfortable with books out of category by writers already branded. Example: the late and very fine science fiction writer Rick Raphael (1919–1994), author of *Code Three* (Simon & Schuster 1964) and most highly regarded within the genre, decided in the early 1970s that he wanted to become Robert Ludlum. He didn't even manage Rick Raphael ... a spy technological thriller (the term "tekno-fiction" wasn't coined for another decade) for St. Martin's Press failed direly and a second attempt never even sold. Raphael then tried to get back to science fiction — sold a story to *Stellar*, maybe a couple in the 80s — but it was never the same for him again and at the time of his death he had been forgotten by all but devoted fans and a few anthologists. Raphael crossed over all right (as will we all), but not in the way intended.

2. A dandy myth is that the way for a writer in sales trouble (steady decline) to beat the computer is to adopt a pseudonym and start again. Sometimes — very occasionally — this works. Usually it doesn't. It doesn't because — I quote the agent Russell Galen here — "Unless the writer is able to come in with an entirely different kind of novel, the same pattern of failure will quickly replicate and the writer will be doubly doomed."

"Doubly doomed." Aha. How does that work as a proposed Gilbertian subtitle for this series. *The Resnick-Malzberg Dialogues, or Doubly Doomed"*? Oops. I meant "singly doomed of course."

———*◦✍◦*———

MIKE: One last myth to puncture before I prepare for a season of watching 16 other teams puncture the myth of the Cincinnati Bengals' defense ... and this may well be the one that hurts the most when it proves to be nothing but a myth.

The myth is that the editor is on the writer's side, and will go to the wall for a good book that the publisher doesn't want. The problem is that many editors and writers become fast friends, and many editors *do* fight for their writers—but the bottom line is that the publisher pays the editor's salary, and when it becomes a choice between letting a manuscript go or getting fired over it, the only editors who sacrifice their jobs and their incomes may well have had impaired judgment in other areas as well, like editing. When all is said and done, an editor (or anyone else's) loyalty lies with the guy who pays the bills, and all the friendship and convention dinners and shared gossip won't change that.

But wouldn't it be nice if it did?

18 Really Dumb Ideas

MIKE: So this past summer Hollywood turned a few really terrible television series into films, remade some movies that were either so good in the original that the didn't *need* re-making or were so bad in the original that only a fool would even think of remaking them, and then made a lot of films with Roman numerals attached to the titles.

And then they wanted to know why no one paid ten dollars a shot (and half again as much for popcorn) to watch this drivel.

It's easy to laugh at Hollywood, and at politicians, and at everything from Wrong Way Corrigan to the guy who invented the folding water bed.

But you know, the rest of the world doesn't have a monopoly on really dumb ideas. Science fiction has had — and still produces — its fair share. And since those who don't learn from history are doomed to repeat it (though hopefully not quite as often as Hollywood does), it might be interesting to examine some of the dumber concepts that our little field has given birth to.

And now that I've said that, and thought about it for a moment, there are so many I don't know where to begin. I have this urge to mention Sam Moskowitz trying to bring back Hugo Gernsback writers and artists with *Science-Fiction Plus* fifteen years after John Campbell thought he had dragged the field into the 20th century — but that was more a nostalgic hankering on Sam's part for his childhood than a truly dumb idea (though it was a truly uncommercial one; the magazine folded in 6 issues).

Wait a minute; I've got one. There's a proposal that just passed at the Glasgow Worldcon, and if it's ratified at LACon IV next summer it becomes Holy Writ. It seems that the book editors are tired of only winning Hugos posthumously (not a joke; the only two to win were Terry Carr and Judy-Lynn del Rey, both of whom died prior to winning their awards), and the motion was put forth that there should be two editing Hugos, one for magazine editors and one for book editors. And to make *sure* the new one went to a "real" book editor, anthology editors were lumped with magazine editors.

It's nothing new. Fanzine publishers got tired of losing to *Locus*, so they created the Semiprozine category, which *Locus* has won about seven thousand times ... so why shouldn't book editors do the same thing?

Many of my closest friends and most of my major sources of income are book editors, so I have no objection to it. But I read the wording of the proposal — which has already passed; I don't think they can change it and still make it law by the end of LACon — and nowhere did I see the word "reprint."

What does that mean? Let's consider it.

The new Hugo goes to novel editors. Let us hypothesize, for the moment, that I am the science fiction editor of a reprint house named BenBella Books (which I am in such spare time as I have), and that you are the science fiction editor of delTortam Books (which you are not).

Let's further hypothesize that the first year the new Hugo is in place, you purchase and publish thirty new novels — a total guaranteed to daunt anyone not named Donald A. Wollheim. Three or four of them are Excellent, and the others range from Pretty Good to Pretty Awful. And let's say that during that same calendar year, I purchase and publish eight reprint novels, two each by Heinlein and Clarke, one each by Asimov, Bradbury, McCaffrey and Le Guin.

Is there any question whose line has the better books? I'm not setting up a straw dog here: remember, there's no mention of the word "reprint" in the proposal that's been accepted. So based on the letter of the law, which of us deserves the Hugo — you, with your thirty books of varying quality, or me with my eight reprints, a few of them published before I was old enough to shave, but all of them brilliant or nearly so. If you're honest, you'll admit that the Hugo should go to me.

Really dumb idea.

But I see you standing in the starting gate, chomping at the bit, your nostrils flaring, your ears pricking forward, all but unable to contain yourself, so I will step aside and let you burst out of there full force.

———

BARRY: Seven issues for *Science Fiction Plus*, Mike, not six. Small difference but you know my fierce dedication to historical accuracy. After all, I am the man who placed the assassination in that Virginia parking lot of George Lincoln Rockwell in the summer of 1965, almost exactly conterminous with Johnson's flower-of-American-youth speech announcing furious escalation in Vietnam. So what if I was off by two years? Higher truth!

The Best Book Editor (seemingly modified already to "Editor of a Novel") seems to me to be a classically bad idea in the service (like the semi-pro fanzine category) of expanding the awards base, but I don't think it is pernicious, just misguided, and I wouldn't imagine that it would do much damage. There are certain awards or award winners which are so obviously misguided or corrupt that they fall from recollection almost immediately: most of the Pulitzer Prize winners in fiction before 1965 (*Guard of Honor* by James Gould Cozzens?) or some of the National Book Award Winners (*The Hair of Harold Roux*, by Thomas Williams, 1975). Ultimately, more award categories mean more winners, more happiness, more hype, more selling slogans (and also of course more recrimination, bitterness, envy and so on); any increase of this kind is probably not pernicious.

Having said that I will self-contradict immediately by noting what a spectacularly dumb idea the Retro-Hugos were. (I say were because there was such dissatisfaction toward the results of the three Retro-Hugo ballots to date that it seems unlikely that there will ever be any more.) The Retro-Hugos of course were a well-meant attempt to award Hugos for those years prior to the establishment of the Award and for the one year (the interregnum 1954, before the second round of Hugos in 1955 made for a tradition) missing. What happened was that the awards did not reflect the best work or the more prominent writers/artists of the year at issue but instead those who were *currently* best known. Kelly Freas, who had sold only a couple of illustrations, beating Cartier and Rogers and everybody else for the Best Artist Hugo of 1950. Hal Clement, at the time a minor, beginning writer, winning the 1945 Best Short Story Hugo over Kuttner, Moore, Van Vogt, Leiber and at least a dozen others. These Hugos were neither fair reflections of their time nor simply celebratory (Clement was one of the few living writers on the fiction ballot and it was moving to see him accept, but Ed Cartier is alive today at the age of 91 and surely would have enjoyed a Hugo as much or more than Kelly Freas who already had at least five "real" Hugos). That famous Fritz Leiber short story title "Try and Change the Past" can be read as a mocking dare; you really can't, and the Retro-Hugos appear to have collapsed into a glare of universal disinterest and spotty dissatisfaction. Exactly what purpose was this construction meant to serve? Did the Heinlein Estate need three more Hugos? (The 1950s retrospective.) Did *Destination Moon* really need memorialization? Who other than the surviving members of First Fandom and a base of perhaps a hundred dedicated collectors and bibliographers were either capable of making this judgment or caring about the outcome?

It's easy to take the Retro-Hugos apart, an essentially harmless occupation. But surely the energy could have been applied elsewhere ... perhaps the creation of a committee which would explore ways in which the bases of the Hugos might remain soldered to the rocketship and neatly aligned.

So far we have a couple of dumb Hugo ideas; I'd like to go somewhat further afield and discuss what we laughingly call issues of craft. There are terms which have become touchstones of science fiction reviewing and criticism which leave me bewildered. Am I alone in this? What in hell is the Singularity? The Singularity seems to be — like Damon Knight's definition of science fiction — anything you point to when you use the term. And what is post-modern science fiction? How can science fiction — how can *anything*— be "post-modern?"

If I write a story it's modern, right? If it were "post-modern" it wouldn't be yet written, isn't that correct?

Help me out on this.

———

MIKE: Sure. Which way did you come in?

One quick note for the record: Kelly won nine "real" Hugos and one phony-baloney one.

I have no answer about post-modernism. I do have an observation, though: it must bother the hell out of the post-modern writers that the pre-modern writers, many of whom are long dead and buried, outsell them dozens to one.

But back to dumb ideas. How about the Nebula for Best Screenplay rather than Best Movie? What percentage of the voters actually *reads* the nominated screenplays? And if it isn't a screenplay that was fixed up for publication after the film was released, just how many scenes and lines do the screenplay and the movie have in common? Based on the ones I read when I was toiling in Hollywood, not many. You can get full solo credit for a screenplay where literally half the lines and scenes aren't yours.

But let's get away from awards and into pocket books (lower case P and B). I used to wonder why the publishing business was still stuck in the 19th century while most businesses were heading hell for leather into the 21st. I mean, think about it: do car manufacturers or dressmakers or computer manufacturers accept—and give credit, yet—for the return of unsold items? Of course not. In every other field a product will stay in the store until it sells, and if it doesn't sell at $100, they'll offer it for $75, and then $44, and then $29, and then $15, and then $6, and eventually it moves.

But the book biz doesn't work that way. The publisher essentially subsidizes the book store. (Let's pluralize it: the publishers essentially subsidize every bookstore in the country.) The publisher pays the author. He pays the artist. He pays the typesetter. He pays the printer. He pays shipping. And then, if the book doesn't sell, he takes it back and gives the bookstore a credit for it.

How the hell did this come about?

Well, back in the late 1940s, before anyone ever thought of returns, someone at Macmillan had a Brand New Idea. They would run a six-month promotion, after which time they'd buy back any Macmillan book that didn't sell. And lo and behold, thanks to this Bright New Idea, within a week stores were *loaded* with Macmillan books, because they knew they could return for full credit any book that didn't sell. And the other publishers saw their own books being shunted aside to make space for Macmillan books, so they gave in to the inevitable and said "Okay, Bookstore Owners, we'll match Macmillan's deal." Which they did. And for five months everyone was happy.

And then it came time for the promotion to end. But Macmillan looked at Doubleday, who looked at Rinehart, who looked at Harper, who looked at

Putnam, who looked at Simon & Schuster, and each one knew that if they were the first to stop buying back unsold copies no store would stock them and the other publishers would take over their shelf/rack space and feast off their financial corpses ... so the returns stopped being a promotion and started being a cornerstone of the business.

It's ridiculous. Let me give you an example. Last Christmas one of the ten Cincinnati superstores decided to push a local author, so they ordered a thousand of her hardcovers, and built a lovely pyramid of them, right out near the coffee bar where everyone could see them. End result: everyone saw them, five people bought them, and the store returned 995 hardcovers for credit the next week. The author had a sell-through of less than one percent on those hardcovers, and how do you suppose that affected her next advance? And the publisher paid through the nose for a failed promotion on the part of a bookstore located almost a thousand miles away.

So why don't they all say, "After half a century enough is enough, and we will not honor returns starting at midnight tonight."

Easy. It's called collusion. (Every time the price of gas goes up a three cents at one station near my home, which is pretty damned often now that I come to think of it, it goes up three cents at the five closest competing stations ... yet somehow that's *not* collusion. Go figure.) Anyway, the bookstores would be in court in less time that it takes me to write this sentence.

So returns were a Brand New Idea.

And a Really Dumb One.

———ᘯᘰᘯ———

Barry: Me: "Help me out on this." You: "Sure. Which way did you come in?"

Very funny. Okay, I stepped into that one. "Have you ever heard Stockhausen?" someone asked Thomas Beecham, the British conductor. "No," he said, "But I have trodden in some."

Really dumb ideas, part the next: Multi-tracking at science fiction conventions. Hate it, hate it, hate it. No single issue has better symbolized and contributed to the atomization of the field, the loss of the center, the destruction of common language. Multi-tracking has done to the science fiction convention what Schoenberg did to classical music ... shattered it, left it in gasping sections. More practically, multi-tracking has, as Norman Spinrad wrote two decades ago, "made science fiction itself a small special interest at science fiction conventions."

Consider. At that 2001 Philadelphia World Convention to which I've made prior reference, there might have been—factoring in film, gaming, kaffeeklatsches, workshops, panels, readings, video, television episodes—twenty tracks running synchronously. There were 40 people in the room Saturday afternoon to hear a panel on the historic science fiction editors, a panel which included Fred Pohl. Forty people to hear Fred Pohl in Philadelphia at a World Convention in the post-millennium? "No foundation all the way down the line," murmured a character in Saroyan's play *The Human Comedy*. And please come back, little Sheba.

Many years ago you sent me the transcript of the proceedings at the 1962 World Convention in Pittsburgh: Theodore Sturgeon Guest of Honor, E.E. Smith special guest, Samuel A. Moskowitz chairman. It was to break the heart, to induce in me that feeling (there must be a psychiatric term for this) of nostalgia for a time and events I never knew. A single program, wending its way through the afternoon, speeches by Smith, Sturgeon, Moskowitz, other notables, panels on every aspect of science fiction, none of them in competition under that roof with any other official programming. Was this the time of the speech at Agincourt: "We happy few?"

Programmatic multi-tracking began in the early 1970s (you'll correct me on this if necessary) and by the mid-seventies had become the mode of all conventions ... even the smaller or more specialized gatherings supposedly devoted to special interests. It was impossible for all but a few events (usually the unopposed Guest of Honor speeches, the awards ceremony and of course the masquerade) to draw anywhere near what they would have had if the attendees had had a fair chance at them. The multi-tracking was not only toward the accommodation of discrete interests— gaming and the New Wave for instance — but within the interests themselves. It became a parody of convention programming.

I can mark the point at which I lost my temper: it was the Saturday afternoon of the 1993 Readercon, a convention dedicated to the published word, a convention which deliberately excluded gaming, costumes, masquerade and whose few panels on film or television considered these only in a strictly derivative context. Judith Merril was a Guest of Honor then, one of her very rare public appearances and her last I believe in the United States. She was scheduled as participant on a 2 P.M. panel on "1950s science fiction" while I found that I had been placed on a 2 P.M. panel on "The influence of modern science fiction."

I found the convention chairman. "This is insane," I said. "In the first place, I want to hear Judith Merril's panel as opposed to indulging in my own weary pontification; in the second place, anyone wanting to hear one panel would urgently want to hear the other, they are essentially the same subject. You are forcing choice upon people for no good reason and working directly against the very purpose of this convention.

"Furthermore," I continued, having managed to work myself into what is known in the United States as *a state*, "you are taking what is already a small, imperiled audience, those interested in literary science fiction, a tiny audience relative to the media science fiction fans, and you are then turning that audience upon itself. You are further atomizing those who are victims of atomiza-

to hear the most important writer-editor in the history of science fiction under such circumstances, then we have lost our history and are well on the way to losing our present. Telling me that I haven't kept up with the times is dodging the issue; let there be gaming conventions, science fiction film conventions, masquerades, jousting tournaments and computer simulations to any degree you want, but don't put them in competition with Fred Pohl and a panel on historic science fiction at a science fiction convention. Why do I have to make this argument to you, stern traditionalist and five-time fiction Hugo winner that you are? Perhaps you are being mischievous, trying to incite. Doesn't take much.

And a second piece of old business: yes, Laser Books was a dumb idea, Harlequin-Canada's misguided attempt to apply the romance novel format (interchangeable novels, interchangeable authors) to the far more author-oriented and idiosyncratic field of science fiction ... but this falls into a different category of dumb since it looked perfectly sensible to a sophisticated publisher on the front end. Only in retrospect did this format prove to be utterly misguided. There are two kinds of dumb ideas: those that are dumb but successful and those which are dumb and fail. In the nature of human affairs, it will be those in the latter category which become history's flotsam and the subject of merry commentary like this but dumb successful ideas can be no less dumb.

But before I launch into that sermon, quickly another indisputably dumb idea: *Vortex Science Fiction*, a two-issue magazine in 1953, limited to stories of 2000 words or less. Whose idea was this? I am sure that Marion Zimmer Bradley liked it—*Vortex* ran her first two published stories—but she was in a minority. But let me talk briefly of dumb successes which are, at least to me, no less galling (in fact they are a lot more galling) than the dumb failures. How about those shameless or shameful quasi-plagiarisms of Tolkien which entered the market in the wave of the great popular success of *The Lord of the Rings* and *The Hobbit* in the mid-sixties, quasi-plagiarisms which unapologetically recycled dwarves, rings, magic quests and Nibelung-like figures over and again, inaugurating a trend which 40 years later has—here we go bowing to Spinrad again — made science fiction a pendant to science fiction conventions, which have made science fiction, James Blish's true quill, a dwindling subsidiary within the larger circumscribed field occupied by fantasy. This constitutes an utter reversal of the publishing situation prior to Ballantine's reissue of the Tolkien books in the 1960s and has marginalized science fiction to the danger point. As any assistant to the junior editor in the paperback division now knows, as a truism, fantasy far outsells science fiction. Outsells science fiction on the average by a margin of two or three to one. Even the most successful science fiction titles, the most established science fiction writers are outsold by routine fantasy. Indeed, and from the economic standpoint, continuing science fiction programmatic publishing is an act of tribute and one which exists only through the power of editors (most of them over 40) who love science fiction and against all reason are committed to it.

Tolkien imitations published imitatively—the Ballantine list and format were copied by every publisher working within the genre, the great Judy-Lynn del Rey herself propitiated the most successful of those imitations—seems to me in the aggregate to be a really dumb idea. But it is a really dumb *successful* idea which, I am sure you will point out, is not therefore dumb at all. By calling this stuff "really dumb" I am allowing prejudice to overwhelm judgment.

Well, can't disagree with you there. Still, it's another way of looking at the situation. Here is another really dumb idea of more classic fit: in the 1950s someone was canvassing the Scott Meredith Agency for manuscripts to be considered by a new magazine called *Rejects*. No manuscript which had not been rejected to apply. The rejection letter or letters to precede the story as the published text. This one you will be astonished to learn did not fly, at least not in the genre. (There were a few scattered 1920s and 1930s magazines founded on that premise but they were operating within a milieu in which they were never expected to sell more than fifty copies.)

—*◊◊◊*—

MIKE: Uh ... let's back up a minute here. I don't remember science fiction being refused publication in favor of fantasy. In fact, some science fiction authors—we all know their names—did pretty damned well for themselves in the 1970s, 1980s, and 1990s. Some didn't. It's not the publishers' or editors' fault that today's audience dotes on quests and dragons rather than extrapolations. I don't know how you can blame anyone for that, any more than you can blame Hollywood for the fact that *Dumb and Dumber* has outearned *Lawrence of Arabia*. Fact of life.

Correct me if I'm wrong, but wasn't there a digest magazine maybe twenty years ago called *Unearth* which purported to run only first stories by new authors? I tried to find a copy before sitting down to write this section, and I can't, which would imply that it lived about as long as you would expect it to live.

Speaking of dumb ideas that worked, how about the Shaver Mystery? It worked so well that *Amazing* outsold every science fiction magazine before or since—and it worked so well that a lot of us had to hide *Astounding* or *F&SF* or *Galaxy* inside the pages of a more acceptable girlie magazine when riding on the bus.

I see by the clock on the wall that it's getting on to half past 4,500 words. Got any closing thoughts before we try not to think about Really Dumb Ideas for awhile?

—*◊◊◊*—

BARRY: *Unearth* was a pretty dumb idea of course, although its (retired) editors never tire of pointing out that Paul di Filippo's and William Gibson's first stories appeared there. Its contents were about as good as those of Martin Harry Greenberg's recent anthology of first published stories, *Wondrous Beginnings*, which is to say not very good at all. First stories usually aren't, although I like to point out that in 1948 *Astounding* published four first stories: "That Only a Mother"/Merril, "Time Trap"/Harness, "Dreams Are Sacred"/Peter Phillips and "In Hiding"/Shiras which are as important and memorable as any published that year and each probably the most memorable story of its author. And the year previous there was "E for Effort"/Sherred. *Unearth* must have looked in its inception more promising than it turned out to be.

And so this must be said for so many of us. So many of us—not you, Mike, you adorable five-time Hugo winner you—are dumb ideas personified. But we must go on nonetheless in our little boats, beating against the currents of space.

—◄◊◊►—

MIKE: Thanks for the flattery, but alas, Hugos are history about three hours after they're given out, and while we're writing this dialogue right after Worldcon, they'll be ancient history by the time it appears. You can brag for one night; then you have to go back to earning a living.

Obviously we've barely scratched the surface of Really Dumb Ideas, and as I consider which ones we've chosen to discuss, I find myself mildly surprised that we didn't go to the single greatest source of Really Dumb Ideas: John Campbell's editorials. How did we miss the Dean Drive, the Hieronymous Machine, dowsing, Dianetics and Scientology? They're worth more than another dialogue; they're worth a book at the very least.

But someone else will have to write it.

19 Abuses

MIKE: We're well into our tenth year of these dialogues, which are aimed at the science fiction writer, and while we've covered a lot of territory, there is one area that affects every writer and which we've only touched on in passing, and that is the economic abuses writers suffer at the hands of editors and publishers. Now, I'm not talking about emotional humiliations; they go with the territory any time your income depends on someone else's subjective opinion. I'm talking about the actual financial abuses writers suffer. I think we can easily fill up a dialogue or six naming and defining them, and also suggesting remedies, when possible.

Let me preface the first abuse with a little story. There is a publisher I've worked with (no, don't try to guess; at one time or another I've worked with every mass market house in the business) who has always been cordial to me, and to everyone else within sight and earshot. In fact, I have seen this publisher lose his temper only once. It occurred at a convention we were both at. I had delivered a book about six weeks prior to the convention, and had received my delivery check only five weeks after delivering — which is to say, five weeks after it was due. In my experience this was lightning-fast payment, and I thanked him for it. He had no idea what I was talking about, so I told him — and he got red-in-the-face furious, not at me, but at his accountant for having the temerity to pay me only four weeks after my money was due.

So the first abuse on the menu is promptness — or, rather, lack of promptness — of payment. You are supposed to get your signature advance the day your publisher receives the signed contract. You are supposed to get your delivery (or acceptance; it depends on the wording of the contract) payment the day you deliver or the day your editor accepts your manuscript. Most contracts call for royalty statements and payments to be made twice a year, usually on February 1 and August 1.

That's in the ideal world. Out here in the real world, publishers found out ages ago that you get can't go into a New York court with a non-payment claim (the amount is invariably too large for the prompt and lawyer-free Small Claims Court) in less than five months, and they know that if *you* know you're only going to get paid three or four months late, you're not going shell out the money required to get a hot-shot lawyer to represent you in court when there clearly will not be a case by the time the court date arrives.

As a result, most — not all, but most — publishers shell out those February 1 and August 1 royalty payments sometime in late May and late November, and take six to fourteen weeks to get your signature advance and delivery payment to you.

From their point of view it makes sense. *Your* advance or royalty payment doesn't come to much in the vast scheme of things, but a six-or-seven-month-per-annum float on maybe eight hundred payments ... well, that's the difference between profit and loss, or profit and bigger profit.

What can you do about it? Well, make a big enough fuss, and you'll get a prompt payment on the current contract and be an old man or woman before you see another. (Well, you wanted to be a writer, didn't you?)

However, there is something SFWA can do about it, and I've been waiting years for someone to suggest it.

Years ago — well, decades ago — we had the membership send in contracts so the Contract Committee could analyze and rank them, and as I remember Berkley had the most onerous one. And we pointed that out, in detail, in either the *Bulletin* or the *Forum*, I forget which — and lo and behold, when it was held up to the light of day, Berkley decided to amend their contract forthwith.

Maybe it's time for SFWA do to a survey showing the average length of time it takes each publisher to pay its authors, above and beyond the amount of time stipulated in the contract, and publish it in the *Bulletin*. Since a tiny handful pay on time, and abuse time varies for others, perhaps holding all the times up to the scrutiny of the membership will encourage the publishers to become a little less abusive before losing some authors they want to keep.

Or (this being the real world) perhaps not.

Okay, surely the author of *The Engines of the Night* and *Breakfast in the Ruins* has some abuses that are near and dear to his heart, or his intestinal tract, or somewhere. Fire away.

—◦◦◦—

BARRY: It's a maddening pursuit (I am hard-pressed even after all these years to think of writing as a "profession"): inequitable, unfair, unpredictable and overbalanced ... publishers regard writers as interchangeable, most writers in fact *are* interchangeable at least in commercial (selling) terms and therefore have no leverage. I have a few stories to tell myself, of course, and although I will give names only in the second case since both writer and publisher are deceased, I would certainly prefer to be more specific. But we are all, even unto the living dead, trying to stay alive in this business.

Two tales from the schoolyard:

In the late 1970s Leisure Books (the successor to Harry Shorten's Midwood/Belmont/Tower paperback empire) reverted, at my request, rights to three titles I had published under their imprint. The books weren't bad at all, and I had vague hopes (never realized) of selling them to another paperback house, but a few desultory efforts were unavailing and I dropped the idea. In 1982 Leisure's fall announcements indicated that one of those titles, *The Spread*, was scheduled for reissue.

That seemed unreasonable. I was able, surprisingly, to reach the publisher on the telephone and pointed this out to him. "You're absolutely right," he said. "I'm publishing a book which I have reverted. You have possession of the letter of reversion. There is no way that I can legally publish this book and I'll freely admit that.

"So," he continued after a short, unhealthy pause, "I can handle it this way. I can tell you to go ahead and get a lawyer and sue me, you certainly can do that, and I'll see you in court in about seven years and I'll have to settle with you for the amount of the advance then if I'm still around. But maybe I won't be or you won't be and in any case what do I care about what may happen seven years from now?

"But I'll tell you what," he said. "I'll pay you $1,500, the same amount as you got for the original advance. But that's only if you sign an agreement to forgo all damages you might claim."

I signed the agreement and not so many days later did receive the promised amount. In the context of modern publishing — and that means publishing in 1982 — this constituted a happy ending; the book had not been pirated by the publisher, nor had I been forced into a court action which would have been laborious and long delayed, and since it is doubtful that any lawyer would have taken this case on a contingency basis, the long-delayed settlement would barely have paid the lawyer's fee. In sum, the publisher had me absolutely stymied and his payment for a book he had absolutely no right to publish could have been considered a gift. At least, I looked upon it that way. Pretty good novel, incidentally, not that it ever had a chance; I needed fast money in early 1971— was trying to buy a house — and the fast $1,500 from a bottom-line paperback market for a paperback original which would never receive any kind of critical attention or coverage seemed pretty good to me.

In retrospect — well, heck, at the time — my publisher's original response seemed to be absolutely emblematic of publishers' positioning. You don't like this, sue me. I'll see you in court in seven years maybe. I don't care what you do. Having demonstrated to his satisfaction and mine my essential helplessness, having shown the knife in full view, the publisher then made an offer which under the circumstances I could only accept gratefully.

His attitude was very much like those of the contemporary publishers you do not name who understand so well that delaying advance payments or royalties comes utterly without penalty ... by the time the writer can get the publisher into court, even assuming that this course is wanted, years have passed and at any point along the way settlement can be made. The imbalance is absolute; the publisher utterly controls the situation.

Point the second, and it is possible that in a dialogue years ago I have already discussed this but it has been a long time and will be new to most of our readers and I am fairly sure that this is the first time I've dealt with the issue: In 1966, Ace Books commissioned Michael Avallone, for a flat fee of $1,000, to write a novelization based upon the pilot episode of the new television series *The Man from U.N.C.L.E.* The senescent among us will remember that this was one of the most successful of all the 60s shows, top of the ratings in its early seasons. Avallone's novelization, in consequence, sold in staggering figures, well in excess of a million copies, going back to press repeatedly.

Avallone did ask for a bonus but nothing was paid beyond the flat fee. A.A. Wyn, Ace's publisher, was adamant, Donald Wollheim told me. "I won't give this bastard a dime," he reported Wyn told him. "Who is he? Some lousy hack who we took off the street. *Anyone* could have written that novelization and sold the same amount of copies. We're not giving him anything."

Wollheim represented his position as being somewhat more forgiving. "I told him that it *had* sold a lot of copies and even though anyone could have written the book with equal success, we could give the guy something. $500, maybe. Throw him some money, just to keep him happy. It wasn't as if we couldn't afford it. But Wyn said absolutely no and that was the end of it. Avallone went crazy."

Well, I bet he did.

Here is all of it: publisher contempt, the interchangeability of writers, the essential irrelevance of the individual writer to the bulk of mass market publishing. Wyn — like Brisman — may have lacked the panache, the gloss of Bennett Cerf or Alfred Knopf, but in his downscale way (just as they in their upscale way) he was articulating the essential position of the publisher: You'll take what we give or you go away.

I think that every working professional writer has embodied within, whether admitted or not, this perception: that almost all of us are, in the view of the publishers, utterly dispensable and interchangeable. Under those circumstances the abuses of which we are writing are not only inevitable, they would have to be perceived by the publishers as necessary. Sound business practice, you know.

—◁ɷɷ▷—

MIKE: I think I'll leave the specific examples to you and concentrate on the practices in general.

One of them that seemed reasonable once upon a time was the practice of withholding a reserve against returns.

What does it mean?

Well, once a book is shipped out to the stores, it is theoretically sold until such time as the store decides that particular copy is not likely to sell and returns it to the distributor, who in turn returns it to the publisher. Seems simple enough.

So let's say the publisher, just to make the math easy, prints 30,000 copies of a paperback, and ships them all out. One day after publication, all 30,000 are potentially sold. In fact, 28 days after publication they are all potentially sold, since none have been shipped back. But of course no book sells 100 percent. Even bestsellers that go through five quick printings have damaged copies, lost copies, copies that a store holds for three months and then returns, etc.

So clearly the publisher is *not* going to sell every copy he ships. And some of them — let's say 4,500 copies, or 15 percent of the print run — stay out there for six, seven, ten months before they are returned. Comes royalty reporting time — always assuming he reports in a timely manner, which will surely happen when pigs fly and cows dance on the moon — he and even the writer realizes that there are some unsold copies out there. What is he to do? He certainly can't pay the writer for 100 percent of the unreturned copies. I mean, just *try* to get that money back from a writer.

So he holds back a cash reserve against returns. Absolutely reasonable in principle. When I got into the field, the industry standard was 23 percent for six months ... which is to say, the publisher held back 23 percent of the author's presumed royalties for a period of six months, a reserve against potential returns during that period.

As I say, it seemed reasonable. You'll probably sell 80 percent of what you're going to sell in the first 90 days, so six months made sense. And even though distributors can be as slow and mendacious as publishers, most publishers had a pretty good idea of how a book was selling after a few months. (These days, of course, they can track those sales almost hourly with Bookscan and through Amazon — and it drives them crazy that so can any writer who's got a friend in the publishing end of the business.)

Anyway, somewhere along the way, that 23 percent became 50 percent, and in some current cases as high as 79 percent ... and that withholding period, which should be shortened in these days of instant computer access to sales, is up to as much as two years at many mass market houses.

Is there anything that can be done?

Possibly. Almost no publisher lists the percentage or duration of its reserve against returns in its contract. Again, this might be an instance where SFWA doing a survey of its membership's experiences and making each publisher's practice public might encourage a few of the less reasonable ones to modify their practices.

Or perhaps not.

(Well, you wanted to be a writer, didn't you?)

—◊◊◊—

BARRY: Ah, yes, the reserve-against-returns racket. Know it well.

In those bad old days of the late 1970s and early 1980s (as opposed to the bad new days), publishers were holding back, on early royalty statements, as much as a 90 percent reserve against returns, dropping that to 60 or 70 percent after a couple of years. Under those circumstances, not only was it impossible to earn back an advance for several years if ever, regardless of sales, but the writer and agent couldn't even determine the true number of sales. That reserve-against-returns constituted a perpetually moving target. And as the director of distribution at now long defunct Popular Library, an old friend from our mutual pre-publishing days, told me in 1975, "Nobody knows squat about this stuff anyway. We just make up the figures, put down anything that looks good. How can the author challenge us?" Greetings, Stan, wherever you are; I read somewhere a decade ago that you had opened a delicatessen in Queens. There's a publishing story with a happy ending.

Reserve-against-returns is tons of fun and I have another: applicability-of-subsidiary-sales to the advance. That's a little beauty (as a Richard Yates character called all the stuff he had carried from his in-box to the bottom drawer of his desk). Let me explain this autobiographically with a big tip of the Hatlo Hat to my agent at the time, Robt. P. Mills. Mills (1920–1986), not a recognizable name I suspect to anyone under 50 reading this, was in his time a highly respected agent with a pretty good list: Walter Tevis, Robert Bloch, Daniel Keyes, Alfred Bester, Damon Knight, Nat Hentoff, Ward Moore, James Tiptree Jr. and many others at that level. And me.

Mills sold my novel *Universe Day* (1971) to Avon Books for an advance of $2,000. The publisher was granted 10 percent of foreign income, 10 percent of all performing rights. That seemed reasonable enough to me at the time; I was a young writer trying to get a foothold in science fiction and Avon's line, edited by George Ernsberger, was prestigious and represented a clear step north from the Ace Doubles and Lancer Originals which I had been writing previously. "Let's grab this deal, Bob," I said. (The Will Rogers of science fiction, I never met a deal I didn't like.) And so we did.

Two years later, Ernsberger's successor editor informed us Avon's foreign rights department sold *Universe Day* to a German publisher for an amount of Deutschmarks roughly equivalent to one thousand dollars U.S., significant money for me at that time and consequently very good news. "That's nine hundred for me and one hundred for you," I wrote Mills. "Can you please get this to me as quickly as possible?"

Well, in fact, no. I was reminded that the clauses dealing with subsidiary rights gave Avon not only the sole and exclusive right to license ... but the right to apply my share of the money received to the amount of the advance unearned. According to my most recent royalty statement, the novel had earned back approximately $800 of the $2,000 advance at the then-standard 4 percent royalty. That meant an unearned advance of some $1,200 and Avon would happily apply the $900 due from Germany to that unearned amount. Only $300 to go!

I never received a cent in royalties from Avon. Even with the $900 applied, the amount unearned continued to float above that point at which I would have been written a check. (Stan: "We just make up these figures any way we want. What is the author going to do?")

I fired Mills for having been so incompetent as to let a clause like this get past him (but he noted with absolute justice that my kind of blind trust was that of a fool; I should have closely read the contract myself). I managed to get along to this day without the $900 and under some pressure I signed similar clauses in contracts to come. But I never forgot what had happened. What a sweet dodge. Legalized theft.

But of course I was the fool who had signed the contract. Any business practice, no matter how corrupt, needs at least two participants: one to perpetrate and one to collaborate.

With a few exceptions, publishing makes collaborators of us all.

———

MIKE: Okay, here's one that established writers don't have to face, but I hear it from beginners all the time — and this time the villain is not the publisher, but the (usually freelance) editor.

You're a new writer of minimal credits and reputation. Most anthologies are by invitation only, but there are a (very) few open anthologies each year. You hear of one, and you submit your story.

And lo and behold, you don't get the usual form rejection slip, or even a personal rejection. Instead, you get a letter from the editor, telling you how much he likes your story, that it has made the first cut, that it is under Serious Consideration (capitalized, which is even more impressive than italicized), and he'll get back to you with a final decision when submissions close four months from now.

You feel thrilled. You've made the cut. You are under Serious Consideration. Pretty soon you can tell all your friends that you're in an anthology with Connie and Nan and Orson and that whole crowd. And maybe it'll come to pass.

But what the editor has just done is to "purchase" a free option on your story for four months. Oh, he'll buy it if nothing better comes along — but in the meantime he's telling you to keep it off the market for four months, to not let any other editor see it. After all, he is Seriously Considering it ... and he'll continue to Seriously Consider it right up to the day that he's filled up his wordage count with stories he likes better.

What can the new writer do? I truthfully don't know. If it was me, I'd say: You want a four-month option, which is to say, you want me to hold it off the market for four months? Fine. Give me two cents a word, applicable against the purchase fee, and forfeit if you don't buy it. The odds are he'll reject it that afternoon. I make enough sales so I can live with that a lot easier than I can live with word getting out that I'm willing to put up with this shit. But a beginner who needs that sale? It's a tough call.

(Well, you wanted to be an anthology contributor, didn't you?)

—◄~~►—

BARRY: Well, let's name some names this time, please. The editors at Bantam in the mid-nineties did this with *Spectrum 4* ... in the wake of Lou Aronica's departure as editor-in-chief there were a series of promotions and reshufflings, and this planned fourth volume of a successful, well-paying original anthology series got sidetracked. Months passed, then a year, and the stories lay in limbo. In response to queries and complaints, form letters were sent asking for just a little more time, moving right ahead here but reorganization, etc. Another year passed and finally, under pressure, Bantam killed the series and returned the manuscripts *sans*, of course, payment of any kind. Most of the writers had in effect granted a free open-end option which extended well past a year for consideration of no sort. There was a good deal of anger out there in the provinces, a lot of writers felt betrayed, but obviously there was nothing to be done. The editors certainly showed no sense of obligation. Just another publishing story.

Full Spectrum was an established series. More frequently, freelance editors have solicited material for anthologies not yet (and perhaps never to be) sold in the hope that an assemblage of manuscripts would be persuasive to a publisher. Thirty or forty years ago in a much different market, some of these anthologies might actually sell. More would not. The authors who had put their manuscripts into the hands of the editors, believing that they were dealing with a paying market, got quite an unpleasant surprise when they came to understand that they had been enlisted without their knowledge as part of a wholly speculative enterprise.

So there is a lot of that around. Has happened to me more than once — "This might be okay for the anthology, not sure, would like to hang onto it for a couple of months" — and in all cases I granted the free option. But this is a reference to time past, no one has asked me for this in a long time, and I would under no circumstances be inclined to cooperate. To address your question directly: I would demand some payment for option, perhaps a half of the amount upon acceptance. But — as you write — there is every possibility that the manuscript would be tossed away at such a suggestion. I am in competition with any number of people who can write acceptably and would gladly put up with such treatment. That is the principle of the interchangeability of writers, one which was certainly well understood by A.A. Wyn. ("Any bum could have written this for a thousand dollars and it would have sold the same.") The hard fact is that writers *are* in the main interchangeable, and there is no way for most of them to protect against this kind of abuse.

Donald A. Wollheim did this a *lot*. When I was his first reader lifetimes ago, he showed me a short novel which had already been on his shelf for several months. "Take a look at this," he said. "I *think* it can make a Double novel, but only if we don't have something ready to go for an open month. I've been holding it to see if I'll have any need for it. Take a look at this, would you? And tell me if you don't agree." At that point Wollheim had held onto the manuscript for a year. (The author, for the record, was one Nick Kamin.)

Wollheim, of course, had helped himself to a no-time-limit and exclusive free option with no expenditure whatsoever. Not bad business if you can get it, and then and now any publisher could get it if they tried. Ultimately what passes for a happy ending: Wollheim took the novel and paid $1,250. I don't believe that Kamin ever sold anything else, and under the circumstances who can be mystified?

With few exceptions, writers are powerless. They have no leverage. This need not apply for the duration of a career. After a while a good working professional has enough contacts and confidence to function slowly above the waterline of interchangeability. But it is a difficult form of limitation. In truth, our powerlessness may be overcome by what is our only strength: the strength to say no, to refuse the deal, to demand return of the manuscript, dismiss the derisory advance. But it isn't what professionals are supposed to do—the Statement at the Origin is "Get the Money"—and it isn't what they do most of the time.

————

MIKE: Let me consider one more abuse, minimally less common than it was before print-on-demand became widespread, and that is the reversion clause—or, to be more precise, the definition of "out of print."

A lot of writers, some of whom suspect they're being jerked around by their publishers when they ask for a book to be reverted and are told it's still available, others simply trying to acquire more copies of their books to send to overseas markets or give to doting maiden aunts, order from Amazon, Barnes, Borders, or the small local bookstore of their choice, and are told that (according to the publisher) the book is "indefinitely out of stock"—which is to say, there are no copies of the book in the warehouse, the publisher can't supply a single copy, and he has no idea when he can. Maybe sometime in the indefinite future. Perhaps. Possibly.

Okay, so what's the difference between "out of print" and "indefinitely out of stock"?

Answer: out here in the real world of the working writer, there is only one difference. "Out of print" means you can demand that the publisher revert your book, and "indefinitely out of stock" means you can't.

Now, with the advent of Lightning Press and all the other houses that can print up from one to ten books on a day's notice, it is conceivable that nothing will ever go out of print, so even putting wording in your contract to the effect that "indefinitely out of stock" is an unacceptable response and that if the publisher cannot get a copy to the bookstore that orders it in a timely manner it *is* officially out of print, all the publisher has to do is have his favorite POD house print half a dozen copies, deliver one to prove it's in print, and the book is his for another half year (or whatever time period the contract calls for.)

So I think it's time to realize that the traditional reversion clause is totally meaningless. What is to be done?

Obviously, every writer would like a term-of-lease contract, but not every writer has the clout to get one. However, we're paying dues to SFWA, so I don't think it's unreasonable for SFWA's Contracts Committee to come up with acceptable wording, maybe to the effect that a book is officially out of print when less than X copies are available, and the only way to make it officially *in* print thereafter is to print (and prove you have printed) Y thousand of copies. Otherwise, every book that is sold from this day forth is essentially the publisher's property forever, unless he feels like giving it back.

(Well, you wanted to be a writer, didn't you?)

We seem to have used up a little more than this month's allotment of words, and I'm just getting warmed up. But probably it's time to end with a word of wisdom or two, and perhaps pray that our current publishers aren't reading this. And since you have acquired a couple of more years of wisdom than I have, I think you should go first.

———◦ℛℛ◦———

BARRY: "Words of wisdom?" Wish I could help you and everyone else there. "All of our knowledge enables us only to rise to silence," I wrote Jack Dann a good many years ago. I am more knowledgeable now and silence ever beckons. What to say? What to instruct? We can convey — as we have — a good deal of information but the only summary advice I might have would be "Stay out of this business" and that is utterly stupid. I haven't, you haven't, most of our readers haven't. Furthermore, I don't have a few years experience on you; you were selling paperback originals sometime in the mid-sixties; my first short story sales came in 1965 and 1966 and I didn't get around to selling my own paperback originals until 1967. I may have a few years on you chronologically but you have more time in-service. It comes to more than forty years apiece which is probably a sufficiency.

My words of wisdom, if you insist, would be Damon Knight's at the conclusion of *In Search of Wonder*: Read your contracts, love your work, make friends where you can. We can't teach you how to love your work; friendship with editors (Knight's obvious point) is on an ad hoc basis, but you do the best you can.

The most practical advice here is to read your contracts. If I had in the

Avon instance, I might have saved myself some trouble, retained an agent, made a few hundred dollars more. Too late by far. At least do not repeat your mistakes. That's another word of wisdom right there.

Writers don't *have* to be stupid. It is the default mode of the profession, it seems, and our histories at times seem to be an endless procession of such ... but even if you have been a fool every day of your life you don't have to be a fool tomorrow. Reclamation is possible. Mark me as an optimist, then, as we await the commencement of our 36th dialogue in this Land of the Just.

———

MIKE: And here we are at the end of the dialogue, we've barely scratched the surface, and the hits keep coming. The latest has to do with acceptance payments. It used to be that an editor would read the manuscript, accept it (if it *was* acceptable, and 97 percent of those coming in on contract were), and then request any required changes, which the author would of course make. The new practice is to refuse to officially accept the manuscript until those changes have been requested and made, and if the writer is not a leader, just asking for the changes can frequently take from six to twelve months, which of course delays the writer's acceptance check by up to a year, sometimes even more. After all, what is the writer going to do— take back a sold book, breach his contract, lose a publisher forever, and hope he can sell it elsewhere before the sure-to-come blackball reaches the next house, just because he's getting paid (very) late? Ain't gonna happen.

Well, what the hell, there are traps and pitfalls in every business. If you're a hunter, you don't follow a wounded rhino or buffalo into shoulder-high grass. If you're a Wall Street operator, you learn very early on what a Ponzi scheme is. If you're a politician, you learn which colleagues and journalists you can trust and which will gleefully insert a knife the instant your back is turned. And if you're a science fiction writer, you put yourself at an extreme competitive disadvantage if you don't make yourself aware of all the abuses that you might suffer at the hands of most publishers and some editors.

It is clear that publishers do not want to kill the goose that lays the golden eggs. They just want to find a way to get a few extra eggs for a little less feed.

Can writers survive it? Sure. We've been surviving it since the industry began.

Should writers *have* to survive it? No.

Is there something that can be done?

I don't know. But I think it's up to SFWA to try.

20 False Doctrines

MIKE: I was recently on a panel at a convention with three other writers, all Hugo or Nebula winners, all in our 60s. It was a panel on how to break in and establish yourself, and as I listened I got this remarkable sense of *déjà vu*, because they were giving the same advice I heard when I was breaking in 40-plus years ago, and the same advice I've been reading and hearing ever since.

The problem is: it's wrong.

It wasn't always, but conditions change, and you would think award-winning science fiction writers would be the first to understand that change exists and is always with us. I get a feeling, having talked to a number of other writers about the subject since that panel, that we're actually among the last.

What's the standard advice we give to newcomers?

Start with short stories. Sell a batch of them to the magazines. Establish yourself. Build your audience. *Then* move up to novels, which is where, if you're good and/or lucky, you'll make a living. Every book on writing science fiction says that. Every convention panel I've heard says the same. I'd be really surprised if the writing workshops weren't in agreement.

Well, in 1954 there were 56 magazines and maybe four book publishers, and it made sense.

In 1964, when you and I were getting started, there were still about a dozen magazines, and Tor, Baen, DAW and a number of other book publishers had yet to be born, and it still made sense.

But this is 2008.

Take a look around. There are four print magazines in the USA. Three of them are hemorrhaging money, and are losing circulation every year. The fourth isn't a shining example of financial health. But healthy or unhealthy, that's it: four print magazines.

Now pop over to the book section. There's Tor, publishing over 200 books a year. There's Baen, ditto. There's Ace and Eos and Del Rey and Bantam and DAW and, if it hasn't gone over to a complete line of vampire romances, Warners. Look a little closer: there's Pyr, and Night Shade, and Golden Gryphon, and Tachyon, and Subterranean, and Small Beer, and a number of others.

According to *Locus*, and they probably missed a few, 2007 saw the publication of 623 new hardcovers, 534 new trade paperbacks, and 483 new mass market paperbacks. That's *new*, not reprint.

And we're still telling beginners to start with the magazines.

The magazines buy maybe six stories an issue. Go ahead, beginners: *try* to knock Connie Willis or Kristine Kathryn Rusch or Michael Swanwick or Allen Steele or Harry Turtledove out of that tiny handful of magazines. *Try* to convince a magazine editor whose circulation has been in a non-stop downward trajectory for 15 years that he'd really rather have your name on the cover than Orson Scott Card's or Nancy Kress's.

They're buying maybe 24 stories a month, total. And if they're stockpiling novellas, they're buying even less. Sell two stories a month and you'll never be asked to pay income tax because you'll be well below the poverty line.

But they are publishing 1,640 new books a year. Hell, you and Robert Silverberg in your heydays couldn't supply 2 percent of the book market's need, not even if you had Henry Kuttner helping you.

And we're telling beginners to ignore that market — one or two sales and you're paying some serious bills — in favor of the all-but-vanished and low-paying magazine market.

And these old established pros weren't trying to scare off the new competition. They thought they were giving valuable advice because, being established, they haven't paid any attention to any markets except their own for years.

And it made me wonder just how many promising writers listen to false doctrine about the field and are never heard from again.

You and I can't bring them back, but maybe we can point out some other false doctrines before too many more people fall for them.

—∾∾∾—

BARRY: Well, there are echoes here of a topic we pretty well parsed last year ... that of dangerous myths, lies and misassumptions; the *forma* of our trade which "everyone knows to be so" until we take a hard look and then they aren't so at all. Bad advice is certainly another form of mythmaking and there is as much bad as good advice floating on the Net or the Convention panels as was ever the case. In this era of the Net, in fact, there has *never* been as much advice of all kinds relatively available and the problem isn't obtaining that advice (as was the case in the golden old days) as separating the worthy from the worthless. Larry Janifer liked to quote an old line from the early 1900s, I don't know if it was George Ade or Elbert Hubbard or maybe (but he was a little later) Don Marquis: "It ain't what you don't know which kills you. It's what you *think* you know which just ain't so."

And it ain't so that the magazines are the engine driving science fiction; this has not been so for close to half a century and certainly will never be so again. And this is hardly the era of the short story in *any* genre of fiction, the short story (somewhat like the Confession magazines and the Western novel) got pretty well plowed under by television and soon became a marginal practice for a shrinking audience. It wasn't that way when *The Saturday Evening Post* and the pulp magazines ruled the land, when F. Scott Fitzgerald was being paid $4,000 for a story in the mid–1930s (representing the annual income of the average householder in this country) but it sure is now.

Still, I am not sure that your aged companions on these panels were giving the worst advice to an audience of aspirant writers. Short stories take much less time to write than novels and if one goes bad (they often go bad, even for the best of us) you've lost two days or two weeks; if a novel goes bad it can be two *years* before that becomes obvious. You can write a short story and get it through those four surviving prozines in about six months; six months for an unknown, unconnected writer would represent an extremely *fast* response from most extant publishers. Even with an agent, no easy acquisition in early career, an aspirant writer might get four responses to a novel in a year to a year and a half. The fate of a short story, at least, can be determined with relative promptness. Meanwhile, if the writer is sensible, she has already written one or two new short stories while waiting for a response to the one completed; these stories are available for quick follow-up submission and it is possible in this way (even through a series of rejections) to establish some kind of relationship with an editor. At least the editor will find your name recognizable. I cannot discern any possibility of building relationships when a novel can rest in a submission pile for six to twelve months.

And there are more than four markets ... a *lot* more, some of them paying. Of course I am now pointing toward the electronic magazines which are represented on the high end by your own *Jim Baen's Universe* down a descending scale of pay and exposure which might number forty to fifty. Most of these markets are edited with more optimism than shrewdness and they go in and out of publishing's evening like fireflies ... but they do, through their existence, represent a receptive market and constitute a reason to go on with short stories.

And short stories are good, they are a good medium and the bad ones take less time to read (or to obtain their rejections) than do a bad novel. So you see, your panel might not have been so bad after all. Don't feel guilty.

Instead, consider the matter of conventions and the personal contact they afford The Conventional Wisdom — which in this case is mine — countenances them as still invaluable and our advice through this series of dialogues to get to at least a few major regional conventions a year well meant. Have you changed your own opinion here?

———《◊◊◊》———

MIKE: The reason I expressly said *print* prozines is because the guys on the panel expressly said so ... and the reason they said so is that only one of them was even aware of *Jim Baen's Universe* or *Subterranean*, which are both in their third year, both solvent, and both paying more than the print prozines. These guys I shared the panel with know their markets — they've been around for an aggregate of a century and a quarter — and they're not interested in other markets at this late date, which is perfectly understandable ... but which of course colors the advice they give to newcomers. If you've never sold to an e-zine, or even seen one, why in the world would you suggest that a beginner submit to one? After all, *Omni Online* and *Galaxy.com* and *scifi.com* all folded five or more years ago, so you *know* there's no future in e-zines, right?

(Side note: one of *my* heroes, Damon Runyon, was making a dollar a word in the Depression, and most of his stories went considerably more than 4,000 words. So much for F. Scott.)

Nothing wrong with short stories. What was wrong was the advice: go compete with 75 well-known writers for 24 low-paying slots a month. Ignore the fact that the field is producing 1,600+ new books a year, most of them truly dreadful. You're not ready for the Big Time yet, kid; just keep trying to knock Bob Silverberg out of *Asimov's*.

Okay, that was the impetus for this column, but when I began looking around and listening — *really* looking and listening — I was appalled by how much misinformation we were feeding our beginners and wannabes. None of it malicious; all with the best will in the world — and much of it wrong.

For example: "Go to a few major regional conventions a year and meet editors."

OK, I've been to some regional conventions lately. Windycon (population 1,500) had Eric Flint and myself, and no other editors — and neither Eric nor I are full-time editors. Capricon (population 1,100) had part-time me and some-time-editor Bill Fawcett, and no others. ConFusion (population 800) had me and one other editor, an editor who doesn't want contributions but prefers to solicit those writers he wants.

Do you begin to see the problem? You could spend the money you make from your first ten sales going to regional conventions and never connect with an editor. Sure, it's good advice if you've been a fan for 20 years and know all the editors and what cons you're likely to find them at; otherwise it's useless.

You have to say *which* regionals draw editors. Only two or three do, in any quantity. You then have to take into account that mostly they're two or two-and-a-half-day affairs, and the editors have most of their meals and meetings scheduled before they get there, and there is a difference between *seeing* an editor and *visiting* with one.

I'm not against conventions for newcomers. I have always favored them. But, as I'm sure I've said before in these dialogues: start with the 6-day World-con, where your editor will have a little more time on his hands; make an appointment *in advance*, rather than counting on finding a couple of hours with her once the con begins; and if you've made an appointment for a meal, try to eat it away from the hotels, where you'll be interrupted by fans, pros, and literary supplicants every 90 seconds.

So ... go to a con is good advice, if you are *explicit*. Just "go to a regional and meet editors" is meaningless at maybe 37 of the 40 biggest regionals.

Also, I think it's defeatist to assume that the best thing about an agent is that he can get your novel turned down 4 times in 18 months. If you don't expect to sell, there are a lot of lucrative professions out there, just waiting for you. (I also think your turnaround times are wildly optimistic. An unagented novel takes about five years to get four decisions; if a short story gets four decisions in less than two years, that's lightning-fast.)

You've been listening to pros hand out advice to beginners for four decades now. Which one or two pieces most sets your teeth on edge?

—◁ΛΛ▷—

BARRY: So far, when we use the word "professionals" we've done it to describe writers on panels at conventions giving advice to would-be writers. This is a limitation of the discussion, a trap easily found. Writers are not the only kind of "professionals" after all. (And most of them, as you might admit privately, aren't all that "professional" themselves.) How about editors, writing instructors? Publishers? Chairpersons of University Creative Writing Departments? Publications like *The Writer's Digest*? They have plenty of advice for writers, some in fact make a very nice living that way (Richard Rosenthal, its former publisher, sold *Writer's Digest* for a very nice sum about ten years ago) and in my opinion most of that advice, actual or implied, is worthless at best, absolutely pernicious in many cases. The misinformation and misdirection coming from these sources gets me far angrier than an elderly writer on a Philcon panel suggesting that newcomers try the short story markets from the top rate down, beginning with *Playboy* and *Omni* and then sending the rejections to *Astounding, Galaxy, Fantasy & Science Fiction, Worlds of If, Planet Stories, Startling Stories, Super Science Stories*. That's essentially harmless after all and as an exercise in nostalgia has some primary value. Most of the panel audience in 1975, say, could figure out pretty well that George O. Smith or Raymond Z. Gallun, nice old fellas that they were, had very little refractory information on the market situation. George O. Smith was promising sequels to *Venus Equilateral* to an audience who might (understandably) have thought that George was giving the name of a favorite cocktail.

What kind of misinformation from the sources I've noted above? One could natter on at great length; I am almost intimidated by the sheer aggregate volume of complaint. Let me begin almost randomly with the Clarion Writing Workshop which we discussed glancingly in this column many years ago and which is science fiction and fantasy's counterpart to the Iowa or Stanford Writing Workshops ... the oldest and most respected such writing programs in the field.

What I wrote about Clarion in the mid-seventies and repeated on some panels in the 80s and 90s was that it was an institutionalized example of misdirection. Clarion in its early years was teaching students to write for original anthologies (*Orbit*) and magazines (*New Worlds*) which were avant-garde instruments somewhat on the margins of the field and due to go out of existence. The optimum Clarion story was an *Orbit* story and in fact many of them appeared in the anthology over the 10 last years of its existence (Damon Knight stopped acquiring in 1975 but there were at that time five or six full volumes in the Harper inventory and they limped into truncated existence through the end of the decade). Clarion's instructors were focused on a particular kind of short story which was never central to science fiction and for all purposes disappeared with the disappearance of *Orbit*. Plotless, filled with inference, highly allusive and focused on subjective response rather than objective extrapolation, versions of this story recur (like malaria) to this day, sometimes when a new market (*Full Spectrum*) appears, occasionally in *Fantasy & Science Fiction* or *Asimov's*. That the short story had become marginalized in science fiction by the mid-seventies was a fact that did not occur to Clarion's instructors or at least was rarely admitted by them ... in fact, until you were brought in seven or eight years ago specifically to teach the novel for one week, there was almost no instruction available in the form.

It was a dangerous and misguided exercise, in my opinion. Of course good writers, even splendid writers like Lucius Shepard or Kathleen Koja, were enrolled at Clarion, went on to have important careers (they learned how to produce novels) and their association with the program could only be to its credit as well as theirs. The astonishing success of these and a few others, in fact, could be said to have masked the real problems implicit in Clarion ... and in other workshops which were founded upon its model and therefore largely imitative.

I've never had any association with Clarion. As I noted in our dialogue years ago discussing the workshop, I never asked to teach there and I was never asked. But my experience as editor and critic of some of its students' production is that overall it has encouraged work which with exceptions is (as Wagner said of the operas of Meyerbeer) "effects without cause or consequence."

So much for this round. I'll talk about editors-on-Convention-panels and their insistence upon their absolute accessibility next time.

———❦———

MIKE: One correction. I wasn't brought in to Clarion to teach novel-writing. I taught short fiction like everyone else ... but I spent about two-thirds of my time teaching them how to read contracts, how and where to meet editors, how to make foreign sales ... the nuts and bolts of the business once they started selling. Someone did spend a week on novels one year; I think it might have been Beth Meacham.

You spent a lot of time talking about *Orbit*, which almost no one remembers. You're slowly oozing backward toward your favorite decade — the 1950s — and I think it's more meaningful to point out what advice is and is not valid *now*, rather than 30 and 50 years ago.

For example, thirty years ago, there were no blogs. More to the point, there was no John Scalzi — well, at least, not shaving and wearing long pants. But here's a guy who revolutionized the way to break in on top. He created a blog, began getting 25,000 hits a day, and then did something everyone older than him says you should never do: he posted a novel for free.

Hideous mistake. Sign of a hopeless beginner. Except he began posting a second novel, one of his readers alerted Patrick Nielsen Hayden, that second book became the bestselling *Old Man's War*, and John's career is doing just fine these days, thank you very much, all you naysayers.

Don't sell your best work to the online prozines, says conventional wisdom. Oh, they may pay as well or better than the printzines while they're in business, but the voters don't read them.

But then the voters gave Ellen Datlow a best editor Hugo while she was at *Omni Online*, and another one at *sci-fi.com*, and a couple of online stories won Nebulas.

Never ever post your work for free, say the pundits. (I will assume they're talking about previously published work, as opposed to John Scalzi's first efforts.) Yet Eric Flint and a number of other writers have been posting their work for free for a few years now, and each and every one of them says that their earnings have gone *up*, not down.

I have been hearing established pros give flawed advice about the internet to newcomers for almost as long as there's been an internet. Not five months ago, in one of the writers' groups, I heard someone state that no one was making any money from Fictionwise.com, the online reprint house. Everyone nodded their virtual heads sagely. No one challenged it — and none of them had sold to Fictionwise.com, either. I've made more royalties from reprint stories in eight years at Fictionwise.com than I made from the 13 novels, advances and royalties combined, that I sold to New American Library in the early 1980s. I mentioned it. No one asked me any questions about it. Three days later they were again sagely pointing out that no one could make money selling short story reprints online. If they don't want to try, that's fine by me; I can live without the competition. But there were probably a dozen new writers on that list, and my guess is they've been convinced to stay away from the internet.

Now, I don't think any of this bad advice is given maliciously, to keep newcomers from breaking into the field. I think it's given with the best will in the world ... and the worst knowledge of the field as it is currently structured.

So ... what other current bad advice to newcomers would you like to correct?

—◄~◊~►—

BARRY: I have not had your outcome with Fictionwise ... was paid $1,500 in 2001 for the use of ten stories and have seen nothing beyond that advance. Of course it's my understanding that Fictionwise no longer pays advances as was the case at their inception but only works on a royalty-only basis. This could also be an indication of your popularity relative to mine, the size of our respective audiences. I wouldn't quarrel with that at all nor find it objectionable ... as I noted long ago you write from the authority of success, I from the authority of failure. My saver has been to add "But failure can teach you things which success never will" and I hold to that but what the use of those lessons might be is quite another issue.

A cavil: *Orbit* was not an instrument of the 50s (although almost everything that emerged after that decade was in the penumbra of that period; I've maintained for a long time that the 50s were the most important shaping period for our field and certainly Damon Knight would have *liked* to have been editing his original anthology in the 1950s. He wasn't, however. *Orbit*'s initial volume appeared in 1965 and its 21 volumes were spaced through the next fifteen years. (I am not a hopeless anachronism. I am not a neo–Moskowitz. I can tell a hawk from a handsaw; this is 2008, not 1953, and *Iceworld* is not on the cover of the present *Astounding Science Fiction*.)

Misleading statements to would-be writers. You ask for more. Editors lie to writers all the time, at least in places of public congregation. "I'm always looking for exciting material from new writers." No, they're not, editors have enough material. They even have access to a fair share of *exciting* new material. What editors want, at least book editors, is something that will sell. The drive to keep up respectable sales figures (even though it fails most of the time) is the primary task of editors. Editors on panels "want work which isn't like anything already published, there's plenty of that around, I want work which is different, which shows me something I haven't seen before." No they don't. Editors want work similar to what is already around. It should be different enough, of course, to make sure that no one gets sued but it should conform pretty well to established patterns. That is why the sales conferences, catalogues and *Publishers Weekly* round-ups put a premium upon what must be called Publisherspeak. "This is *Jaws* out of *The Exorcist*; the shark is the devil." "This is a vampire chick-lit novel." "This is a *Sex in the City* with zombies." Everything is defined in terms of established markers; the term "high concept" evolved as a means of praising the kind of novel whose premise can be described at a sales meeting (and subsequently to chain-store buyers) in a single sentence. *Jaws* was praised before its publication as a great high-concept novel: "There's this big thing off bathing beaches which eats people." Anne Rice's *Diary of a Vampire*, now a cliché, was a great high concept... "The story of an immortal vampire told in the first person." Publishing is geared toward replication. It is, as George Ernsberger said to me in 1972, "The land of the self-fulfilling prophecy."

All that said, I think I must agree with you on your reproof: my suggestion that would-be and new writers make at least one and hopefully more of the major regional conventions for the purpose of meeting editors probably falls now into that category of bad advice. It was good advice decades ago (not as far back as the 1950s, though) but now there are simply too many writers, too many opportunities for editors to find what they need without resorting to direct contact, let alone active development of writers. Competition for the time and attention of editors is daunting now ... there have never been more writers now or potentially capable of writing acceptably for a level or declining marketplace. It is clearly a buyer's market. Editors don't like to give that impression; it tends to depress the room and alienate people best not alienated. And of course it is of no help to the editor's expense account if she lets it be known to the publisher that there is no need to travel or even solicit to be supplied with more acceptable writers and material than can possibly be used.

Still and to take the upside for once: Lies and misdirection feed optimism and optimism feeds hope and hope feeds the world itself. As Kurt Vonnegut would say, foma thrive even as the truth struggles with anorexia. Let us keep foma alive!

—◦◦◦—

Mike: *Orbit* is ancient history. Half the writers striving to break in weren't even born when Damon stopped editing it.

The problem is that not a lot of the advice givers are that young, or show the adaptability of youth. Panels on breaking in simply ignore the high-paying online magazines. They ignore the "medium press" that at least pays five-digit advances. They ignore the cross-pollenization between blogs and sales, online magazines building audiences for print novels, podcasting and the soon-to-be-widespread blogcasting and building an audience for professional sales.

They are, to a great extent, like elephants in a circus, each holding the tail of the beast in front of them. Go to lots of conventions. Sell the print magazines. Never post anything for free. Podcasting is for iTunes and Rhapsody, not science fiction. And cetera, and cetera.

Pity.

SECTION 3
The Field

21 Magazines

MIKE: I'm tired of starting each dialogue with a statement or a proposition. So this issue I'm going to start with four questions. (Don't panic; I'll answer the first three before I turn it over to you.)

Question #1—What do these magazines have in common?

Amazing
Astounding
Authentic
Avon Science Fiction & Fantasy Reader
Beyond
Cosmos
Dynamic
Famous Fantastic Mysteries
Fantastic
Fantastic Adventures
Fantastic Story
Fantastic Universe
Fantasy & Science Fiction
Fantasy Magazine
Future
Galaxy
If
Imagination
Nebula (British)
New Worlds (British)
Orbit

Original SF
Other Worlds
Planet Stories
Rocket Stories
Science Fantasy (British)
Science Fiction Adventures
Science-Fiction Plus
Science Fiction Quarterly
Science Fiction Stories
Space Science Fiction
Space Stories
Spaceway
Startling
Tales of Tomorrow (British)
Thrilling Wonder
Tops in Science Fiction
Universe
Vortex
Weird Tales
Wonders of the Spaceways (British)
Worlds of Fantasy (British)

Question #2 — What do these magazines have in common?

Science Fiction Age
Marion Zimmer Bradley's Fantasy Magazine
Amazing

Amazing (again)
Argosy
Omni Online

Question #3 — What do these magazines have in common?

Analog   Realms of Fantasy
Asimov's   Postscripts (British)
Fantasy & Science Fiction

OK, the answers:

Answer 1: Every one of these was a viable short story market in 1953.

Answer 2: Every one of these died (one of them twice) in the past half-dozen years.

Answer 3: They're what's left ... and I won't vouch for their health.

I answered the hard ones. Let me give you the easy one.

Question #4: How long before there are no magazines left, and where are we going to place our short stories on that unhappy day?

—◦◦◦—

BARRY: #4 is indeed a relatively easy question (although it is a laden trap) or pair of questions and I will endeavor to answer both succinctly. I would think that the present magazines are probably safe for another three or four years (you don't mention Ellen Datlow's *Sci-Fi.com* although you do include her *Omni On-Line* amongst the failures so I assume that you do consider such electronic publication a "magazine"), beyond that I have no idea and neither do the editors or publishers. We are all on a vast and darkling plain here; it is not, as has been noted over and again, a magazine era. The audience for genre fiction magazines has essentially departed. *Analog* sells 25 percent of what it did 30 years ago; *Ellery Queen* is off close to 80 percent. (There are reasons for this departure but you didn't ask me a fifth question.)

Second part: where will we sell our short stories? Almost everywhere, I would think. The magazine market is shrinking toward marginalization but on-line sources of short stories (a few of which are paying markets) proliferate and, more importantly, the original theme anthologies have held steady at perhaps a hundred a year for quite a while now ... think of all the Greenberg anthologies, Ellen Datlow's originals, the Writers of the Future and the one-shot anthologies like Al Sarrantonio's *999* or *Red Shift*, and surely that would be around the 100-a-year mark, giving space to 1500 or 2000 stories. That's not bad at all, considering that in the halcyon years *Analog, Galaxy, Fantasy & Science Fiction* and *Worlds of If* could amongst them publish perhaps 350 stories (including serialized novels) a year. Throw in all of the other magazines of that time and the total number of science fiction and fantasy stories published annually would be somewhat less than the present situation offers. The overall situation may be desperate, but it is not serious.

Of course the magazines offer what the theme anthologies do not ... an eclecticism of content, background, stylistic approach, and even the best theme anthologies by definition work within a narrower range than most magazines.

But these are aesthetic, not practical, judgments. The science fiction short story, seen in terms of raw numbers, may not be flourishing, but it is still a viable medium. Word rates, inflation-adjusted from 1953, may be pitiful but no one now writes short stories for money. Even in those halycon years, very few science fiction writers derived a significant part of their outcome from that medium.

It's always painful when a market collapses, and the roster of magazines in which I have published over the past 37 years which no longer exist could run for many pages. But the perceived end of our more serious problems. Dedicated students of these dialogues know that we find other issues of far greater concern.

———⟋⟋⟋⟋———

MIKE: Yes, I overlooked *Scifi.com*, probably because I still have a hard time thinking of electronic media as magazines. And that's a major mistake because Datlow pays top rates and certainly has a readership, as proven by her Best Editor Hugo and the Nebulas that her selections have won and been nominated for.

As for the anthologies, I don't know where you're getting your 100-a-year figure. DAW Books is the only publisher with a regular anthology program, and they produce one a month, most of them through Marty Greenberg. There are a few — a very few — in-house anthologies at Tor and elsewhere, but these probably don't come to half a dozen a year. And I'll grant you another half dozen a year, from Bill Fawcett, Lou Anders, or whoever. There are a couple more here and there. But I'd say the total of original anthologies paying pro rates is a lot closer to 25 than 100, and those that don't pay pro rates aren't germane to this dialogue. (Remember, we're not talking about reprint anthologies here, but about viable markets for new short fiction.)

Another problem is the non-sf magazines, and especially the men's magazines, that have all essentially stopped buying. There was a time when *Rogue* alone bought perhaps 20 to 25 science fiction stories a year. It's long dead. So are *Cavalier* and a ton of other sf-friendly men's magazines. Even *Playboy*, which has been the best-paying market in the world for the past 40 years, no longer buys any fiction at all. *Penthouse* gave up fiction a decade ago. I suppose we can place two or three science fiction stories a year with *The New Yorker*, and maybe, if we're lucky, one every other year with *Atlantic Monthly*, but I don't think that's solving our problem.

Another thing that's not solving our problem are the handful of science fiction magazines with pro rates and semi-pro distribution. There are a few of them out there, but they miss a lot of deadlines, and a guess is that they're in even more need of life support than the three remaining digests.

And the market forces are not becoming kinder to fiction magazines. *Argosy* was revived this year. The first two issues were excellent, as fine and broadbased a magazine as you could want, boasting science fiction, fantasy, mystery, adventure, humor ... and we've been waiting over half a year for the third issue. *Amazing* was resurrected yet again for the fifth (or was it the sixth?) time. It was in the hands of Paizo Publishing, which knows a little something about distribution (they also publish *Dragon* and one or two others), they could advertise it in all their other publications, they had an experienced staff, they went for the broadest possible audience by putting Spider-Man on the cover and splitting the issues between fiction, TV, movies and gaming — and they announced, three days before you and I began this dialogue, that *Amazing* is "going on hiatus," which sure sounds like it's died yet again.

Losing these two magazines so soon was a pity, not only because we lost two good-paying markets (they both paid more than the digests), but because they represented two distinct and different approaches than the digests, which have been in a downward circulation spiral for a dozen or more years, and in the long run (well, actually, in the very short run) those approaches proved even less viable.

It wasn't that long ago — at least, it doesn't *seem* that long ago — that most of the prozines were selling 100,000 copies or more per issue. I wouldn't be surprised to find that the combined circulations of the four remaining American prozines don't quite total 100,000. (And if they do, they sure as hell don't top it by much.)

So there's the problem. The prozines are dying by inches. The bold new experiments — and this goes back even beyond *Science Fiction Age*, to the reborn *Galaxy* of the late 1980s, and the resurrected *Worlds of If*, which lasted a single issue in 1986 — are all D.O.A. The anthologies still exist, but not in the numbers they used to; they're probably down seventy to eighty percent from a decade ago, when Marty seemed to be selling one a week, Bill Fawcett and Byron Preiss were forces to be reckoned with in the anthology biz, and a couple of dozen "independent" anthologies surfaced every year.

The outside markets, especially the men's magazines, are no longer viable for science fiction. The literary magazines might take a few, but half of them don't pay and the other half don't buy enough to keep one writer in business, let alone an entire organization of them.

There are solutions, of course. There are always solutions. Ours will require innovation, creativity, and maybe a mirror or two, but aggressive writers have always found a way.

Perhaps you'd like to take the first shot at it?

—◦◦◦—

BARRY: DAW does one original anthology a month — that's about 180 stories a year — and there are original anthologies from other publishers, throw in the Young Adult market, not inconsiderable, and the one or two very large original anthologies (*Red Shift*) which come out every year, and the number of new stories, although somewhat South of my all-too-enthusiastic original estimate, surely hangs around 500. Add the semi-pro publications like *Weird Tales* or what seems to be left of the other *DNA* magazines to say nothing of the ever-optimistic, ever collapsing on-line outlets which at least promise payment, and there is certainly more of a market for science fiction and fantasy stories than there was, say, in 1951, a year which gave us a good deal of important work. Or 1965 when *Amazing* was on an earlier "hiatus," *Gamma* had just collapsed and *Galaxy* was bi-monthly. I will conjecture that there were more short stories on the Nebula preliminary ballot this year than in 1967.

Which is not to say that the situation is good and your grim anatomization of the contemporary market — the attrition of the contemporary market I should say — is more or less accurate. (Well, *Playboy does* continue to publish fiction, one story a month, but it's almost always by Michael Crichton or Lawrence Block and if one science fiction story a year now appears in that publication it has been a good year, but in 1972 Robie Macauley routinely bought one sf short story per issue and occasionally a second.) It is not a good situation and the collapsing figures of the digest magazines—*Analog*'s most recent circulation statement records 38,000; when Ben Bova became editor in 1972 succeeding John Campbell he inherited a circulation of over 100,000 which got pushed to 120,000 through his years—are indisputable and for all to see. The digest magazine has, since *Astounding* went to that size in 1943, been the principal medium of the science fiction short story, perhaps the originating medium of science fiction itself. The end is now foreseeable.

But I have no remedy. I am moved by your confidence as you turn over the lectern and urge me to propose a solution; I have no solution. About 30 years ago Alexei Panshin proposed a new format — a large-format magazine with exploding graphics, fullscale importing from the popular culture, wild, colorful, hip stories appropriating that pop culture in a fashion like Lichenstein's 1960s paintings. "Call it *Gonzo* science fiction," he concluded and in fact *Vertex* and *Cosmos*, a couple of years later, were tentative moves in that direction; both failed quickly. *Omni* a few years later conceived of marrying cutting-edge science fiction to an expensive, colorful popular science magazine, it had an enormous budget, the distribution of its senior partner *Penthouse* and was never edited less than competently and often brilliantly. Initial sales figures, claiming close to a million per issue, were encouraging but the magazine slowly faded through the decade and even though it lasted 17 years (until 1995), it became a shriveled, downsized and eventually marginalized version of itself, a discouraging course even though the magazine's fiction was always highly regarded and attracted a great deal of attention through the last 15 years under Ellen Datlow when it was averaging little more than a story an issue.

A sad business in retrospect and *Omni* was perhaps the truest, fairest, best-budgeted and most extended test of the proposition that a science fiction magazine could reach its largest potential audience by being anything other than a

science fiction magazine. Certainly that was the thought behind Panshin's proposal. Most recently it was the conception behind this latest, revived *Amazing*.
Editorials in fact said so ... recognizing the nature of the market and the new,
media-oriented audience, a science fiction magazine could only flourish by
weighting against science fiction. Well, it seemed to make sense. Now they are
on hiatus.

I have no solution, really have no proposal. Anything I would try has been
tried, often by very competent and well-funded management. If someone were
to offer me a couple of million dollars start-up money to edit and publish a
science fiction magazine I'd tell the person to put the money into Certificates
of Deposit. I couldn't assure an appreciation rate of one to three percent. My
only guarantee would be eventual loss of principal.

So I defer. What would you do?

—*◊◊◊*—

MIKE: I'm more concerned with what the writers will do—but to get to
your question first, I think there are a number of things that can be done—
which does not mean they *will* be done.

First, I think the precipitous decline in circulation for *Asimov's* and *Analog* (as well as *Ellery Queen's* and *Alfred Hitchcock's*) can be traced to the fact
that they were sold by Joel Davis, who knew how to distribute digest fiction
magazines and made his living off those four titles, to Bantam/Doubleday/Day,
a hydra-headed conglomerate which is really Bertelsmann, a German giant ...
and when you consider that Bertelsmann actually bought (briefly) the New
York Mets in order to acquire Doubleday, I think you can see that the digests
pretty much fell beneath the corporate radar. Then they were sold again, as
part of a package with all the Dell crossword magazines, as throw-ins, essentially, to a company that had (and has) no real idea of how to handle them. So
the first thing is to find a publisher like Don Wollheim at DAW, or Tom Doherty
before he sold Tor to St. Martin's, a publisher who knows the field inside out,
knows how to maximize the potential of his publications, and makes 100 percent of his living off them.

Second, I think the concept of a loss leader needn't be confined to supermarkets—and indeed it isn't. For all practical purposes, *Scifi.com* is a loss leader
for the Sci-Fi Channel; it's certainly not showing a profit after paying Datlow's
salary and top dollar for the stories it runs. I don't think there's that much
overlap between magazine readers and book buyers, so why not go trolling for
new readers by publishing a loss leader magazine that is filled with the authors
whose books you're pushing? Horace Gold tried something remotely similar
(though in a reverse way) back in the 1950s, when he published Galaxy Novels
to draw readers to *Galaxy* magazine, which was the cash cow of the two (if that's
a proper expression when dealing with *any* sf magazine of the past half century.)

Third, I think some of the big-circulation sf/media magazines—you know, the ones with pointy ears and guys in colorful long johns on the covers—might be persuaded to start running some non-cutting-edge science fiction stories each issue. If it works, the rest will follow suit very quickly.

But that's a problem for publishers and investors. The problem for writers is different and more immediate: until one of the above methods is tried and succeeds—which could be years, or perhaps all eternity—where do we go to sell short fiction?

Well, first of all, as you mention, there are the mass market anthologies. I disagree with you about how many will be published this year or next, and almost all of them are mildly-restrictive "theme" anthologies, but there's no question: 25 anthologies times 20 stories apiece (they don't often reach 30) is 500 stories. Nowhere near what we want, nowhere near the markets of a few years or a few decades ago, but a start.

Then there's the "medium press," which is what a number of small presses have become. This year I was paid a dime a word by three different medium (or shall we say specialty?) presses for their original anthologies, which is better than the digests pay. Yes, you have to keep your ear to the ground, because the landscape changes faster at this level than in New York, but no one ever promised writers an easy time, and if they want to continue to be writers they really do have to morph into businesspeople the moment they write "The End."

There's the internet. We've certainly mentioned *Scifi.com* enough, but while it's the best-paying and longest-lived of the new fiction markets, it isn't the only one. They come, they go, one second they're there and one second they're not— but there's been a subtle change over the past few years. They used to promise to make you rich tomorrow if you'd just give them something free today; now at least they pay you up front, and if you get to the bank *very* quickly, you can cash their check before they go belly-up.

Here's another suggestion, for those with enough stories and enough reputation to sell a collection. (No, not to mass market; they really only want collections if you name is Ray or Connie.) Most medium presses can not only pay you a relatively competitive wage for your collection, especially if you've got an award winner/nominee or two in it—but frequently if they can advertise a Brand New Story Never Before Published, they'll pay you pro rates for it.

Another collection market: the college presses. Some of them pay with a hearty thank-you, but a number of them pay coin of the realm.

Well, those are a few suggestions. Have you got some more, I hope, I hope?

—◆◆◆—

BARRY: I don't have many suggestions. Not for the writers, anyway. Science fiction writers are, praise them, a resourceful group in the aggregate, but there's only so much writers can do and most of it devolves upon writing. If there are markets—eccentric markets, one-shot markets, crazy markets, point-

less markets—science fiction writers will rouse themselves and their manuscripts from the dead and exploit them as best they can. It's called "professionalism." What science fiction writers cannot do is *create* markets. Oh, a successful
writer can lend his name to an original anthology, can franchise a property for
an original anthology, that kind of thing ... but this isn't a programmatic
approach, not really; it's a one-shot business. Writers with lots of money and
a willingness to risk can become publishers but then again we know what happened to Mark Twain.

Your other suggestion, your "loss leader," is, however, a far more promising idea. A long time ago, when *Galaxy* was staggering in the late 1960s and
Amazing was leading its zombie's existence under Sol Cohen, Donald Wollheim told me that he had made a serious pitch to his masters at Ace Books, the
executives of Hanseatic Financial who had acquired Ace after the death of A.A.
Wyn. Wollheim tried very hard to sell them on acquiring either the *Galaxy* or
Ultimate Publications; the magazines could be tied closely to Ace, could function as publicity and house organs for Ace writers, could be used to serialize
or excerpt forthcoming properties, and could be used as relentless repositories
of advertisements for forthcoming Ace Books. Wollheim was convinced that
this was a no-lose proposition: even if the magazines themselves were not in
profit (which he thought they would be) they would serve such a useful publicity and pipeline function that Ace could not possibly lose.

Of course Hanseatic wanted no part of his idea. They had better ideas—
cut Wollheim's salary, fire Terry Carr, cut the budget for science fiction further, buy sexy "mainstream" novels for exorbitant advances, put a naked model
on the cover and call it "the hot new bestseller." Try to pay nothing less than
$50,000 for such novels. Their first acquisition was something called *Melinda*
about a nymphonmaniacal British novelist. I think it sold five copies, none of
them in New York City. Evelyn Grippo had a big poster for the novel on her
door. They printed about ten thousand of those.

But not to digress. Wollheim, as was usually the case, was both insightful
and brilliantly intuitive in a commercial way; I think that his idea would have
worked (and the magazine, edited in-house by him and/or Terry Carr, would
have had little extraordinary editorial cost). There is no reason that it could
not work today; if Penny Press doesn't want to sell its publications to Viking
Penguin or Bertelsmann, then those two worthies could delegate staff to start
a couple of titles. Really, what's the downside? A year's executive lunch budget
for these firms would probably cover most of their costs.

Well, I'm a writer, what do I know? I have to defer to wiser folks of the
kind who have managed in various and not-so-devious fashion to take the pale
but still viable magazine market which I confronted when I was but six and
twenty, and take those magazines on a 40-year odyssey into darkness.

—∿∿∿—

MIKE: Over the years there have been some interesting speculations and suggestions concerning the ever-contracting short story market. None of them came to anything. Maybe some of them should have, maybe not. I'd be curious to hear your take on them.

First, there was a period when every time *Amazing* died (and it always suffers a mild case of death, which never proves fatal), First Fandom toyed with the notion of buying and running it. My guess is that they'd have run reprints of Stanton A. Coblentz and David H. Keller and A. Hyatt Verrill and that whole crowd, but you never know, maybe they'd have bought some new stories.

Second, there have been mutterings that SFWA itself should start a magazine, maybe add $15 a year to the dues to pay for it and provide a captive audience. The main problems I see with this are that, if SFWA owns it, they'd better never run any stories by non–SFWAns ... and you're sure to get some members who feel that it's their dues-paying ghod-given right to sell to the magazine no matter what the editor thinks.

Third, there's self-publication online. (I hesitate to call it a vanity press, since "press" has nothing to do with it.) I know some romance writers have made substantial money selling peeks at their work online, and Stephen King pulled in a million dollars or so with the first few chapters of his online novel before it, too, went into hiatus.

Fourth, combining the last two, there's the notion that SFWA should start publishing stories online and charging for them. The problem here, as with so many electronic sites, is that there's no front money, and if no one wants to read an unknown or unpopular author's story, he's written it for (just about) nothing.

Fifth, just as First Fandom was in love with *Amazing*, which was available for peanuts at the time, I don't suppose anyone would expect a munificent sum for the rights to *Startling*, or *Thrilling Wonder*, or *Planet*, or (see the opening list). Could a compendium of pros and/or fans and/or investors be induced to resurrect one of the hallowed titles of days past? If the deal that SFWA worked out with Sol Cohen when he started running reprints that went with the titles he'd bought is the gold standard, these could run 50 percent reprints and 50 percent new stories and do it pretty inexpensively, especially with print-on-demand technology, which isn't limited to books.

Thoughts? Opinions? Howls of anguish?

—⁓⁓—

BARRY: When Bertelsmann put up the science fiction and mystery magazines (and the crossword puzzle magazines) some years ago, an offer for *Asimov's* and *Analog* was made from an important person within the field. That offer was peremptorily rejected; Bertelsmann wanted to sell all of the magazines. (This is not a rumor; I know the person who made the offer pretty well.) But then again, the conventional wisdom is that Penny Press—the publisher of many crossword puzzle magazines—wanted no part of the mystery and science fiction digests, that they took them on only because Bertelsmann would not sell the crosswords alone.

I will grant that these narratives are in conflict, make no concurrent sense. If someone within our field wanted the sf magazines, if Penny Press did not, why did Bertelsmann insist upon the outcome we know? Wouldn't it be better if the crossword people took on the magazines they understood, if the science fiction magazines were placed in the hands of those who really understood and wanted them? Maybe the two mystery magazines, *Alfred Hitchcock's* and *Ellery Queen's* were the breaking point here; they would have been orphaned. I simply do not know. What I do know is that the publishers of science fiction magazines in this era should be interests who really care for the field, who approach it with knowledge of its history and are able to take some kind of risk in order to propitiate the magazine. SFWA would on its face seem to be a good candidate for this kind of assumption, but as we explore the issue matters are less clear: there are obvious conflict-of-interest issues and also an editorial board, selected from the membership of the organization, would obviously be accepting some manuscripts and rejecting a lot more, and this might add to the conflict in an organization already riven with old and new enmities.

But I think that an SFWA project could at least be explored. Lying around, in public domain now for decades' lack of use, are titles like *Startling*, *Planet Stories*, *Worlds of If*, *Imagination*, even *Galaxy*, and there are still plenty of writers around who could edit such reconstituted titles within a real sense of the tradition. For me the science fiction magazines are, as I have said, the core, perhaps the soul of the genre, and if they are utterly lost they cannot be reclaimed. It is a strange thing that these suffering anachronisms can be called our soul but we all remember those science fiction stories of shabby Old Earth, a dingy, abandoned outpost circling a dead star, which yet excites wonder and trembling reverence in the hearts of all in the gleaming, dispersed Galactic Order.

———✴✴✴———

MIKE: I suppose when all is said and done, the operative question has to be: is there still an audience for science fiction short stories?

The answer can be found at Fictionwise.com.

Fictionwise.com is the most successful independent internet publisher around (I say "independent" because they're a start-up company, not an off-shoot of anything bigger). And against all conventional wisdom, Fictionwise. com has outperformed every other internet publisher while selling nothing (well, almost nothing) but reprints.

Wee Willie Keeler became immortal not for the way he played baseball, but for his advice to hit 'em where they ain't. I suggest that if you want to know where you stand in the hearts and minds of the general reader, hit 'em where they *are*—and that's precisely what gets done at Fictionwise.com. Science fiction competes on an even playing field with mysteries, thrillers, horror, Westerns, romance, erotica, and every other category, including non-fiction. SFWA members whose reputation barely extends past their front door compete with writers in other categories whose home address seems to be the *New York Times* bestseller list.

How do we do?

I'm writing this in the afternoon of December 28, 2004. I just accessed the Fictionwise.com bestseller page, where they rank their bestselling recent titles and their bestselling titles over the period of the past six months.

And what did I find there? In the recent bestseller category, in open competition with the novels and short stories of Dan Brown, Stephen King, Peter Straub, Louis L'Amour, Robert Crais, Robert Ludlum, Elizabeth Peters, Mary Higgins Clark, and the like, science fiction short stories hold 8 of the top 25 places. (And I hasten to add that none of these were classics; none are written by anyone called Ray, Isaac, Arthur, or Robert A.)

For the 6-month bestseller list, science fiction short stories—a different batch—again pull down 8 of the top 25 slots in open competition against novels and short stories of every category.

Fictionwise's Author of the Year Award — a combination of sales and reader ratings—has gone to science fiction writers 3 years in a row (though I suspect Dan Brown has cracked the code for 2004).

The point of all this is that there is still a clearly demonstrable market for short science fiction. And that implies that while it has fallen upon hard times with harder times still to come, the demand for it is so obvious that eventually a couple of competent entrepreneurs are going to step in and resurrect it.

I hope.

22 The Clueless (Part 1)

MIKE: I recently returned from a very interesting convention. I went down to the dealers room, as always, to check the tables and see if there was anything I wanted that I hadn't already ordered, maybe go through all the used-book dealers' stock and ditto.

Except there weren't any new book dealers (exactly; wait for it), and there weren't any used book dealers at all. Which is not to say there weren't a lot of new books for sale.

Table after table was occupied by one self-published author after another, sitting behind a pile of his or her own books, books they had paid to publish out of their own pockets. One girl told me she'd paid an "editor" over a thousand dollars to proofread her galleys(!). A guy explained that he got a real deal, only $600 for black-and-white cover art by this totally unknown artist.

And the interesting thing was that no one thought this was unusual. They were so clueless that they thought this was the way we all started. You spend your money, you pay a printer and an artist and an editor and maybe a proofreader, you pay shipping, you rent tables at cons and sell your books, and then maybe, if you're lucky, someday some hot-shot New York publisher or editor will chance to stop by your table, fall in love with your book, and reverse the cash flow from outgo to income.

A little later there was a panel on self-publishing — four self-published authors and me. If there'd been three loving spouses and an enraptured girlfriend in the audience I'd have kept quiet, made a polite noise or two, and gone back to my room to work on a story I was writing that weekend. But there were more than 20 people in the audience, all taking physical or mental notes, and these panelists were explaining, with the air of experts, where to find editors and book doctors, how to buy tables at conventions, and so forth. I kept quiet for about seven minutes, and then I couldn't stand to see that innocent audience submerged in a sea of misinformation, and I pretty much spoke non-stop for the rest of the hour, to the dismay and probably anger of the rest of the panel.

I could see by the audience's expressions that no one had ever spoken to them like this before. They seemed shocked. At one point I asked if anyone there subscribed to *Locus*. No one did. I next asked if anyone knew what *Locus* was. Not a single affirmative. My final question was whether anyone in the audience knew what the initials "SFWA" stood for. No one had ever heard of it.

Now understand: this was not a lecture at a high school, or at a public library for late-middle-aged biddies who thought it would be fun to write a novel about their cats. This was at a science fiction convention, one that actually flew me in on their dime.

All weekend long after that panel, one by one, hopeful writers would come up to me and ask the most basic questions. Nothing complex like: what is an option clause, or what is joint accounting, or how do I sell Czech and Polish rights? No, just things like: How do I find out who the science fiction publishers are? How do I submit a manuscript? Half a dozen of them have been corresponding with me on an almost daily basis since I got back home. I'm answering their questions, but it raises a bigger one: how did we fail them to the point where they truly believed that every writer began by self-publishing? How could every single member of an audience at a science fiction convention be ignorant of *Locus* and SFWA?

And — here, catch the ball, Barry — what can we do to change the situation?

—◦◦◦—

BARRY: Not to in any way dampen the festival ... but *why* should we help them? Isn't ignorance sometimes its best reward? More decades ago than I want to name, I would often pass up offered second helpings at the dinner table. "Good" my hardworking father would say. "More for me." In an Introduction to a short story collection 34 years ago I expressed my intention to write less in the form in the future and recalled my father. "'Good,' people should be saying all over the country," I wrote. "'More for me.'"

But science fiction writers have a long tradition of near-selfless collegiality; they not only help out one another, they seem driven to do so. The failure of a good story to achieve print seems to strike many of us as a personal insult; I know that you felt that way about Nick DiChario's "The Winterberry" when it came to you as a blind submission to your already closed original anthology *Alternate Kennedys* so long ago. You felt that it would be an insult to that brilliant story not to assist it into print, that it would be an insult to the then unpublished Nick DiChario if it (and he) did not become famous. You opened the volume for the sole purpose of accepting that story and, of course, it became a Hugo finalist and in its own small way has had a continuing impact. (As well it should. It is masterful. Heartbreaking. I will attempt no synopsis; may the membership make the effort to seek and find this.)

So you are driven to help your lost and by the wind grieved would-be science fiction writers and enlist me in their cause. What we are witnessing of course is one of the consequences of what I would call the *Writer's Digest* School

of Publishing Knowledge meeting science fiction ... with the essential collapse
of the paying markets for all but science fiction, a lot of writers who know very
little of our field are being brought to the genre hopeful of selling but knowing very little of its special techniques, its eighty-year history of writer-editor
relationships cultivated through its social network. To them marketing and
selling are what the *Writer's Digest* says it is ... self-publishing, self-promotion,
bookstore signings, subsidized printings, stamped self-addressed envelopes,
"market reports." How depressing it all is. That life, those assumptions, were
once mine. Over forty years ago I traded them in for a career or quasi-career
in science fiction and I have never been regretful.

The first step in a campaign to help these people would be to get them to
a convention where they can at least obtain some firsthand knowledge of the
actual mechanics and relationships of our genre. That your fellow panelists
seem to have negotiated. The second step would be to keep them off panels,
thus limiting the misinformation, and put them firmly in the audience in front
of people like you. The third step would be to ban them from any contact with
Writer's Digest for five years.

That at least would be a start. But granting that it would be pointless to
argue whether or why we should help them, what are the origins of our altruism ... *can* they be helped? Shouldn't perhaps the issue of education be addressed
before these people are launched upon an unforgiving and indifferent world?
Most if not all of your fellow panelists believe that true science fiction began
with Gene Roddenberry or George Lucas and could not name ten science fiction
writers who published before, say, 1950. Having hung around conventions
(although much less than you) I know as you that this is true. What should we
think of this? Does it have any bearing on the situation?

———◈———

MIKE: Why should we help them? I dunno; why help anyone under any
circumstances? Why toss a lifeline to a drowning man?

The simplest answer, and the truest, is that we should help them because
we *can*, and because they *need* it.

This field has been very good to me. I've been living a boyhood dream for
forty years. I can't pay back because those few people who helped me are rich
or dead or both, so I pay forward. Over the eons Bob Bloch and Bob Sheckley
and Gordy Dickson and Bob Tucker and Bea Mahaffey and others saved me a
lot of wasted time — years, probably — and made my professional life a lot easier, so why shouldn't I do it to the next guys in line? What point is served by
letting someone remain ignorant? Does he have to prove his love of the field
by sticking around after a dozen false starts and humiliations?

You are fond of saying that I speak from the authority of success and you
speak from the authority of failure. Leaving aside whether anyone who has sold
a hundred books and close to four hundred stories can be called a failure, why

do you want newcomers to make the same mistakes you did? Wealth is not a zero-sum game, and neither are book sales. If that newcomer never sells a word, or hits the *New York Times* bestseller list, it won't make one iota of difference to your own sales.

Your hardworking father was right when there was a limited amount of food on the dinner table. But does keeping innocent beginners in total ignorance really mean you're going to sell more books than otherwise in a field that, according to *Locus*, buys over 1600 new books every year?

I'll tell you something else, too. Pros network. We exchange market information. It helps each of us. And I get a hell of a lot more of it from the kids (well, most of them aren't kids anymore and haven't been for quite awhile) that I helped when they were starting out, than I get from my contemporaries. It comes back to what we discussed in our last dialogue: the field is changing, the markets are changing, even the methods of getting published are changing ... and the newcomers adjust to it a lot faster than the dinosaurs. They understand that the best markets, the quickest and highest pay, comes from the e-zines and not the digests, and when a new e-zine hits the scene, they are the first to know about it. They know there's a new tier between New York mass market books and small press. They understand selling audio rights can be pretty lucrative if you know what you're doing, and that comic book rights don't have to go exclusively to DC and Marvel. They know a *lot* that the dinosaurs don't know (or perhaps, being secure and a little slower than in their youth, don't care about) ... and why should they share any of this with writers who would not share with *them* when they were starting out?

So if you can't do it because you're one of Nature's noblemen, then you might think of doing it because it's in your self-interest. It just takes one Robert Jordan to keep a publishing house afloat in lean times. Maybe the guy you choose not to help is the next Jordan, and the company he would have sold to is the one you'd have sold your next book to—if they hadn't folded.

Over the years I have bought something like 45 first stories—and a hell of a lot of seconds and thirds—for anthologies I've edited. I didn't have to. It's not difficult to e-mail Kris Rusch or Nancy Kress or Greg Benford or David Gerrold or any of my other award-winning friends and say "Give me a story of X thousand words by Y date," and they always deliver and it's always a good story, and with a set word rate I don't pay them any more than I pay a first-timer. And I *do* e-mail them and solicit stories from them —for maybe two-thirds of the anthology. But their purpose is to be trumpeted on the cover and produce the stories their fans know they *can* produce, so I can give a shot to some new writers whose names can't be used to sell the books.

Was it worth it? Eight of "my" writers have made the Campbell ballot. Surely that benefited the field ... and I tell you true: half of them would still be clueless if I, or established professionals like me, had not disabused them of all the false conceptions and misinformation they possessed.

Did I owe it to them? I think I did. Did it cost me a penny to help them? No. Did it make me any extra money to help them? Yes. Some of them have stuck around long enough to be able to buy stories from me, or suggest me to editors I hadn't previously dealt with.

So if we don't help them for altruistic reasons, maybe we ought to remember the old adage: what goes around comes around.

—◦◦◦—

BARRY: Of course we should help would-be science fiction writers. Collegiality, mentoring, the nurturing of new writers are qualities profoundly integral to science fiction; our record in that regard is unmatched in any field of writing and perhaps in *any* creative field. The generosity of science fiction writers has long been noted; as Charles Platt once wrote, "It is science fiction's great gift to itself ... any would-be writer can meet professionals on equal terms." When you compare the state of relationships in science fiction to those which exist in the so-called mainstream, the truly pathetic state of the latter becomes clear. Carter Scholz recalls a friend of his, an unpublished writer, carrying around for months (and showing to everyone) a form rejection slip from a quarterly on which the editor had scrawled *sorry*. "Compare that to science fiction," Carter wrote. "I knew then that this was a place I wanted to belong."

So do not understand me too quickly (as Mailer liked to quote Malaquais); I am all for helping would-be writers or what we might call "underpublished" writers and I have long felt that I have a decent record on this account, one for which I need not apologize. In my pitifully short tenure (six months) at *Amazing* and *Fantastic* so long ago, I published the first story of P.G. Wyal, the first science fiction story by the mystery writer Edward Breese, Jody Scott's third sf story, a work by Jack Wodhams which he had been unable to sell to his one market, *Analog*, which I think is his best. Lafferty's "This Grand Carcass Yet" appeared in a best of the year anthology. And we know that Fred Pohl and John Campbell, better editors at better markets, published an astonishing number of first stories over the years. They set the bar for the rest of us.

But the *Writer's Digest* Displaced Persons who pontificate on convention panels about the wonders of self-publishing or "slanting" their work toward markets do try the patience; they have, in the last ten or fifteen years, brought to science fiction a certain kind of amateurism with which the field up to that point had not really encountered. Up until, say, the mid–1980s, science fiction editors would see a lot of dreadful material in the feared and famous slush pile ... but most of it was written, however ineptly, by people who had some familiarity with the form, who could differentiate among Theodore Sturgeon, Edmond Hamilton, Richard Shaver. It was an insider's game not from parochialism or clannishness, but because anyone who essayed to write fantasy or science fiction felt compelled to have some knowledge of the form and at least a little bit of reading background.

That began not to be the case when, as I noted in my first contribution here, the broader commercial paying markets for fiction virtually collapsed in the 1960s and left stranded a huge number of writers who were driven from the few remaining markets by sheer competitive pressure but still wanted very much to place their work. Science fiction, according to the *Writer's Market* (published by the *Writer's Digest*), presented a number of markets which at least nominally needed fiction. That large sampling of writers turned right at the nearest corner and ran, did not walk, to our neighborhood.

Everything that the Science Fiction Writers of America accomplished in its early years to professionalize the genre, to carry that professionalism to the provinces, was counteracted and often stymied by this influx of writers in no way familiar with the genre or the nature of writing or the markets. Some of these writers and their attitudes spilled into the convention scene ... and in the end you found yourself a flabbergasted panelist on a dangerously misleading panel. We all (or at least most of us) want to be helpful. I received a good deal of help in early years, but there are an increasing number of writers around now who I would say are beyond help.

My nominal mentor in the Syracuse University Writing program long ago was George P. Elliott (author of the brilliant "Among the Dangs"/*Esquire* 1958, reprinted severally in science fiction anthologies and *The Magazine of Fantasy & Science Fiction*). I liked George just fine and miss him (1918–1980) still, but as I once observed to my wife of George the literary writer as opposed to George the science fiction writer he really wanted to be, "He's a literary writer. He doesn't have colleagues ... he has connections."

—*◊◊◊*—

MIKE: Okay, so we're agreed we should help new writers; at least that's out of the way. You seem, and I'm sure you'll correct me if I'm wrong, to be concentrating on their lack of talent, and most new writers in *any* field abound in lack of it. I'm more concerned with the total cluelessness of so many hopeful writers, those without talent and, more importantly, that small handful with enough talent to sell, or to learn and then sell, if only someone would explain to them that you do not enhance your career by self-publishing, or writing for penny-a-word magazines, or by hawking your own books at a table at a convention, or by hiring the first agent who goes trolling through your literary neighborhood for clients even when that that agent is located 1,500 miles from the action and doesn't have a recognizable name in his or her stable.

Yes, the stuff's available to SFWA members—the books and articles on contracts, on writing and selling science fiction, even the sff.net forums on those rare occasions they're not too busy abusing each other. There's Editors & Predators, there are all kinds of things ... but how does a hopeful (and let us postulate: talented) writer in South Carolina or North Dakota or New Mexico learn that the information is there?

You can sit on some panels like I have, and destroy some dreams and argue with some hopeful writers who don't want to be told the truth, but what do you reach? Twenty people? Thirty? And if they even knew that a convention existed, they're already ahead of the rest of the hopeful writers out there.

How do you tell them that this field, above all others, requires you to be well-read and creative — and then explain away 500 Tolkien ripoffs, some of which are bestsellers, and 750 vampire romances (oops, can't say that: they're "paranormal" romances), many of which are bestsellers?

I just spoke to a girl in Cincinnati a couple of days ago. She's pretty clueless (though she had the gumption to find the local pros and the local fan club), but she's clearly going places. She just made an eight-book sale of a young adult fantasy series, for *very* good money, especially for a beginner. She knew enough to go to a couple of conventions this winter and try to network with writers. The science fiction writers looked down their noses at her (no wonder — it's not even fantasy, but *young adult* fantasy), and the one YA writer she found wouldn't share any knowledge or information with her because in his mind they are competitors, not colleagues.

Okay, the problem can't be fixed solely through SFWA because if you're in SFWA you are no longer that clueless and you know where to go for information and help. But like the group I spoke to (at a science fiction convention, I have to keep reminding myself), there are a lot of hopeful writers out there who don't know what SFWA is, have never heard of *Locus*, and a couple of years ago would also not have heard of *Science Fiction Chronicle*.

Waste bothers me, and that includes waste of time and talent. The losers and the talentless are going to be losers and talentless no matter what, but how do we help the others, who don't even know they need help, let alone that it exists? (Right. I didn't mention it before, but none of the self-published beginners were hawking their books because they didn't know what else to do. They were publishing and hawking them because they thought this was the way *everyone* started, and nobody had told them otherwise.)

BARRY: I guess the easy answer here — at least it is the easy answer for *me* — would be this: Gather all of our dialogues to date (this is the 38th and when published will bring us to just short of 180,000 words) in one or two enormous books, have them published — with appropriate fanfare — in trade paperback, send them out into the world and wait for the improvement of the breed, to say nothing of our enormous royalty income. This would be a good solution but it is one essentially out of our hands and in those of others. I have to concede — and I wonder if you would agree — that in an essential sense we have for the past 10 years been preaching to the choir, bringing fish to the Fulton Fish Market ... members of the Science Fiction Writers of America by virtue of that alone are at a higher level of sophistication — and have been put in the presence of a range of advice — than almost all of the clueless panelists who function as the inspiration for this column. It might be useful to see our message taken to the provinces.

Useful but not practical for a whole list of reasons we can defer for another time. Here is another, perhaps equally self-serving suggestion ... let the dialogues or something very much in their spirit become a regular feature in one or more of the general writers publications, carry a practical message to an audience which has had little enough access to it, at least in relation to the genres. *Writer's Digest, Poets and Writers* (which latter could be called the *Writer's Digest* of the quality lit set) ... this would be a kind of mission to the Eyeless in Gaza which might have some real outcome.

I doubt the possibility, however. The publications I have noted (and their lesser imitators) specialize, as the Scott Meredith Agency's instruction sheet to prospective Fee Department employees urges, in "Helpful, Optimistic, Supportive Advice," they make money by misrepresenting the market as being far more accessible than it really is and their articles (and even more importantly their advertisers) hawk a mythology rather than reality. To no small degree the *Writer's Digest* is a promotional instrument for the *Writer's Digest* (correspondence) school and it is that image of eternal accessibility which keeps the treadmill going outside and the rent payments inside. A genuine portrait of the market and professionalism might be vastly more helpful but like an honest fee report to the 90 percent of fee clients who were talentless, it would be manifestly bad for business.

Well. Your turn again, your final turn I suspect for what I also suspect will be the first of a two-part series. My last advice to the would-be writer-electorate and perhaps of equal practical value ... study my career very carefully, with particular attention to be paid to my various essays on the markets and my own career management. Internalize my characteristic approach and its apparent motivation. And then in every case do the opposite. This in the spirit of Mickey Mantle's last press conference in 1995, shortly before he died. "Do you want a role model? Don't be like me. That's a role model."

—⁓—

MIKE: Okay, you realize your fondest dream. We sell a collection of the dialogues— probably *not* to *Writer's Digest*— and lo and behold, it sells 7,500 copies, phenomenal for a how-to-write-and-sell book.

Your worked the fee desk for Scott Meredith. How many clueless writers were so desperate they would pay hundreds of dollars for Scott's form — excuse me: plot skeleton — letter? Five thousand a year? How many needed help and didn't or couldn't shell out the money? What percentage was that of all the clueless beginners who desperately need help, not in their writing, but just with a basic, even kindergarten-level understanding of how the field works? Two percent? Certainly not more than three percent?

Do you see the problem? Create a book that sells above any reasonable expectations, and three years later better than 99 percent of those it was aimed for remain totally in the dark.

Well, I see by the clock on the wall that we've run out of words—imagine that! Writers running out of words—and we'll have to make this a two-parter. On the other hand, that gives you eight weeks to come up with a perfect, foolproof solution to this conundrum, on the not-unreasonable assumption that one eludes me. A world of cluelesss writers who don't know that you, or I, or SFWA, or this magazine exist is waiting.

(In fact, what they're mostly waiting *for* is to shell out their hard-earned money on editors, artists, and printers, and *that* is why we really need some solutions.)

23 The Clueless (Part 2)

MIKE: Okay, last issue we defined the problem — said problem being the hundreds of thousands of clueless wannabees out there and how to reach and educate them — and this issue we're supposed to at least make some reasonable suggestions aimed at solving it.

The logical first step is to say: Well, let's urge SFWA to start a web page aimed at beginners, something that will answer their most basic questions, maybe with a Q&A section that can be addressed and updated every day.

The problem, of course, comes back to that convention I mentioned last issue, the one I attended in the spring of 2008. I was on a panel that was there to educate the audience on the glories of self-publishing (until I began forcefully voicing the opinion that money is supposed to flow *to* the writer, not *from* him) ... and at one point I looked at this mystified audience — mystified because no one had ever suggested there was an alternative to self-publishing — and asked if any of them knew what the initials "SFWA" stood for. No one did. At a science fiction convention.

It rather suggests that a SFWA web page is not going to reach the largest possible audience.

We can go out of our way to work with beginners, and most of us do. Over the years I seem to have accumulated perhaps 40 of what Maureen McHugh calls "Mike's writer children." Most of them have sold, and some of them have won awards and are now making a full-time living as science fiction writers.

But if I've personally helped 40, that's probably 199,960 I *haven't* personally helped. I did a Q&A column about the business aspects of the field called "Ask Bwana" in the Hugo-nominated *Speculations* for a dozen years, but I doubt it reached 1,500 readers with the best-circulated issue it ever had. I collected the first seven years into a book titled *The Science Fiction Professional*; I haven't looked lately, but I'd be flabbergasted if it's sold 3,000 copies. That is a *lot* of clueless newcomers that, with the best will in the world, I have nonetheless failed to reach.

So, since you've had a whole two months to ponder the problem, perhaps you'll share your sure-fire solution with me.

—•◦◦◦•—

BARRY: I've pondered this for a good deal longer than two months. It's a real problem and what makes it so troubling is that it is endlessly self-renewing ... like the parable of the Marching Chinese impossible to count because they reproduce at a greater rate than the line moves (Cyril Kornbluth helped himself to this idea for his most famous story), the influx of ignorance is self-renewing. There are more people interested in writing and selling science fiction than there ever have been ... perhaps ten thousand times as many as there were in the 1940s, an even less conceivable multiple of the number in 1935. There are many reasons for this and I have alluded to some in Part One of this dialogue: the collapse of the commercial markets for literary short stories and novels, the crumbling of barriers between the genre and the mainstream, the mad proliferation of graduate writing programs and adult education writing courses. The pool is ever larger (or more watery) and it deepens every month. Educate one class at the New School (Charles Platt and Shawna McCarthy taught science fiction writing there some years ago) or New York University Adult Extension Program (Carol Emshwiller taught there for many years until recently) and there are six or sixteen new classes beginning next semester.

I see a few ways to deal with this but most have already been tried and the cultural penetration is not great. The *Writer's Digest* is still kind of a dismal publication slanted toward amateurism but it has, probably unwillingly, become more hip in recent years. *Poets & Writers*, which is kind of a *Writer's Digest* for the quality lit crowd, has occasionally had some useful information. The panels for new writers which are now present at most science fiction conventions are (depending of course on who's paneling) of some use although as you have noted the proportion of the population in need of such instruction reached by these panels is minuscule. The Chinese who march do so determinedly but there are all those others snuggling in the secret compartments.

Here's one idea: I would like every Clarion six-week seminar to enlist for one of its weeks a hard-bitten experienced editor who would not only review manuscripts from the standpoint of market needs and realism but who would educate writers on the hard practicalities of the business ... double-spacing, fake agents, the snare of vanity publishing (under various new guises) and so on. My principal quarrel with at least the earlier Clarions is that they were teaching writers how to prepare accomplished stories for markets that no longer existed. Most of what writers come to learn about marketing and career questions comes *after* they have left the Graduate Writing Workshop, the late Theodore Solataroff pointed out in a bitter essay published over a decade ago. Only when writers are forced to trade the false pleasures of collegiality and immersion for isolation, rejection and the hard reality of the marketplace do they learn what accomplishing a career might entail. It might be useful (as an extreme instance) to put a Harlequin Romance editor on the faculty of Stanford or Iowa and assign writers to produce acceptable portions and outlines for that category (and, if contracted, completed novels). Anything propelling the writer toward some approximation of the true professional experience would be useful. Clarion's now 40-year history is littered with writers who sold one or two or ten or even twenty stories and then did not know where to go. (I'd argue that this outcome can be more personally devastating than a simple failure to sell at all. My friend Joseph Kornfeld, who attended Iowa over four decades ago, noted that 85 percent of its graduates ended as high school English teachers and were almost certainly the better for it.)

Complicated issue. I'm sure you have some ideas more practical than these.

———✺———

MIKE: Well, let's look at the problem, and that is that there are literally hundreds of thousands of totally clueless wannabee science fiction writers out there, some self-publishing, some tossing their stuff up all over the internet, some bragging to real editors about penny-a-word sales, and so on.

Clearly conventions don't reach them. Clearly they don't know to contact SFWA, have probably never even heard of SFWA. There have always been a couple of useful fanzines for hopeful writers—*Empire* and *Speculations* come to mind—but the average untutored writer probably thinks a fanzine is something with Brad Pitt and Angelina Jolie on the cover ... and besides, the biggest-circulation fanzines of all never reached five digits.

But there's something that reaches millions. It's called television. And there's something that reaches at least a few hundred thousand of those millions, and that's the Sci-Fi Channel. They've done okay with known writers before; as I recall, Harlan Ellison used to do a regular commentary on it, and I know some of us have appeared there after being taped at various Worldcons.

I have no idea if they'd go for it, but it couldn't hurt to propose a half-hour weekly or bi-weekly show featuring a different well-known SFWA member every episode, explaining all the things these clueless would-be writers need to know. And to sweeten the pot, ten or twelve minutes could be turned over to a screenwriter — we're not without them — explaining how you write, or try to write, for the Sci-Fi Channel.

It would cost them bupkis: travel expenses and a couple of meals every two weeks.

And maybe they'd say No. But it's the easiest way to reach the largest number of the people we want to reach. I'd say it's worth a shot, before we get down to smaller cures for a rampant disease of ignorance.

Okay, that doesn't work? Then how about a massive e-mailing to colleges offering writing courses, offering them — and their classes— access to a series of articles by SFWAns (certainly enough already exist) explaining exactly how the business works, how to break in, and just as importantly, how *not* to break in.

Or, assuming the new generation of would-be writers prefers watching to reading, simple make a DVD containing a few hours of pertinent advice from a dozen of our better-known and more successful stars, notify every college that teaches writing, and make it available at cost. (Which isn't prohibitive: these days blank DVDs run about a quarter apiece, often less; and even postage will be well under a dollar.)

The trick, of course, is to reach one hell of a lot more people — in fact, large multiples of the people we're already reaching. These are some suggestions. I trust you have more, and that they're more likely to receive a massively favorable response?

— ◁/◁/◁ —

BARRY: Your television idea is a good one although I can't conceive of what would be in it for the Sci-Fi channel; your college idea is equally good but in this case I can suggest what would *not* be in it for the colleges ... they would be opening the academic environment to outsiders who were not part of academia and this might be taken by some members of the English faculty as a direct threat. One of the most important aspects of academic and departmental politics has to do with the defense of turf at all costs and allowing outsiders to set and express an agenda might be a fearful thing to the junior faculty.

There's been a question lurking through the earlier installment of this topic and it is no less pressing in this second part; asking it does not endear me to the readership or (for that matter) to you but here goes: Exactly why should we be so dedicated to bringing enlightenment to that clueless population who largely does not seek enlightenment and who, at best, we would be helping at some possible cost to ourselves? Historically science fiction writers have been more collegial, more helpful, less protective of their own position than writers anywhere else ... as Harlan Ellison wrote somewhere long ago, we seem collectively to be a group who are dedicated to putting ourselves out of business. If you can potentially write better and sell more easily than extant writers, then you can be pretty sure that most of those writers will work frantically, teaching you how to displace them. This says wonders for our altruism and overall karma but from a career standpoint, it has to be seen as at least questionable.

Here is perhaps the more basic issue: the present situation in at least the fiction marketplace is a direct reversal of what prevailed during science fiction's so-called Golden Age. There were not in the 30s and 40s (and perhaps even to the mid–1950s) enough competent science fiction and fantasy writers to fill the available space ... there was more room than there were acceptable stories and novels. Editors had to scramble to develop writers and they also had to let a lot of marginal material get through. This was a specialized and demanding literature by the mid–1940s, even lower-ranking magazines like *Thrilling Wonder* or *Planet Stories* demanded fairly specialized skills. Editors at the second-rank markets who knew better had to often stretch a point, simply to maintain sufficient copy. Writers were *really* ill-paid then, but writers had a kind of leverage because the markets needed them more than they needed the markets.

Of course that isn't the case now. There have never been more competent writers, there has never been more acceptable copy seeking outlet; writers, always regarded as interchangeable by most editors, are seen by some as wholly dispensable. "If you give me any lip," an editor wrote in the Science Fiction Writers *Forum* decades ago, "you can be replaced by the script just above yours in the stack or the script just below. Maybe this won't be true when you become a Modern Master of Science Fiction but it certainly is true now."

What this means in practical terms is that writers in the aggregate have lost the kind of leverage they had long ago when not too many people could produce this kind of thing at all. Now so many can produce acceptably that even the on-line or semi-professional fiction magazines are filled with copy which meets professional standards of composition. For those editors cluelessness and amateurism are qualities which become their friends; unestablished writers are so desperate that they will accept almost any set of conditions in order to place their work.

So we are faced with a situation which inherently resists professionalism. Professional writers have expectations, professional writers tend to make demands. The clueless are only too happy, however, to accede and therefore the contemporary market situation tends to militate against professionalism.

Science fiction writers as a group really want to help beginners, indeed seem dedicated to teaching themselves out of business. Well, good for us. But many of the audience for your panel probably likes the situation as it is and would resist a standard of instruction which would teach them to be difficult. Who wants to be difficult? Those are the people who don't sell.

———❧❧❧———

MIKE: Briefly, what does the Sci Fi Channel (or any local PBS channel) get? A free program (most cost six digits, a tiny handful cost seven), and — given its audience — a free name. Okay, in terms of television in general, most of our membership couldn't draw flies at a watermelon party — but in terms of shows aimed either at hopeful writers or, preferably, hopeful science fiction writers, we've got a couple of dozen members with sufficient name recognition.

And if colleges minded, then why do I and so many others get asked (and paid) to travel the circuit and give lectures on just what we're talking about? Can there be half a dozen colleges in the country that don't drool over the prospect of guest lecturers?

But as to your main topic — and I believe you hinted at it last issue as well: why do we owe these clueless beginners anything? I can't speak for you ... but I owe it to them because, as I also mentioned last issue, old pros like Bloch and

Sheckley and Dickson probably saved me five to ten years of cluelessness and discouragement and false starts, and they're not around to thank, so I'm thanking the field by helping the next generation, just as they did when *I* was the new kid on the block (and I was far from the only one they helped).

This will not be the first time I have noted that the 1950s seem to be your favorite decade in science fiction, which I find somewhat mystifying since you and I both broke into print in the mid–1960s … but that's neither here nor there. What I object to is using them as a template for today.

Yes, in the mid–1950s, there were so many magazines being published that there were enough competent writers to fill them up, and today that is no longer the case.

To which I reply: look at Barnes & Noble, or Borders, or Books-A-Million, or Amazon. As I keep pointing out, *Locus* reports that there were over 1,600 new science fiction books published in 2007. *New*, not reprint.

And are you, the greatest pessimist since Eeyore, suggesting they were all so competently-written that there is no place in the field for talented new writers? That we are filled to the brim with such superb writers that helping talented newcomers is an exercise in futility?

I refuse to believe it. I have personally helped dozens of writers break into print in our field. In the past four years I've helped three sell their first novels and two others resurrect moribund careers. Neither you nor anyone else suggested that this was a total waste of time and effort. Their success harmed no one, affected no one else's sales; as I have pointed out time and again, this is not a zero-sum game. All I want to do is explore ways to get vital information about how the field works out to those who don't know, and depend on such totally useless things as *Writer's Market* and creative writing courses taught by equally clueless failed writers to inform them.

Are most of them beyond help? Sure. But so are most would-be athletes. Does that means we should eliminate all college and minor and instructional leagues? That if a 20-year-old can't hit a ball like Ken Griffey Jr., pass like Peyton Manning, shoot like LeBron James, or putt like Tiger Woods, we should just give up on him? Do you know how many superstars were *not* superstars at age 20?

Go to the bookstore. Browse some of those 1,600 titles. If you can honestly tell me that every one of them is well-conceived and well-written, that they're all page-turners, that there is no room for any more talented writers in the field, then I will withdraw all my arguments (or sadly recommend you for electric shock therapy, whichever comes first).

—*∿∿∿*—

BARRY: Ah, but what you've done now is to have lurched in a new direction. I thought we were discussing clueless beginners lacking knowledge of how to start and conduct a professional career and *you* have raised the issue of 1,600 new published books of science fiction and fantasy. Are they all so lacking in ineptitude that no authors are in need of lessons in the art of writing?

Well, no, most of those works are hardly lacking in that area. There is no Ineptitude Scarcity Crisis in modern writing (or anywhere else for that matter). But I thought that we were dealing with the distribution of basic information ... *not* with teaching the technique of composition. These are two entirely different areas. Those 1,600 works listed by *Locus* were, after all, published. Whereas you began a column and a half ago lamenting a roomful of would-be writers who didn't know *how* to get published. They weren't present at your panel to learn how to *write*. That was another panel down the hall, most likely diabolically counter-programmed as these things always tend to be now. You began a column and a half ago not by complaining about the limitations present in 1,600 books. You had an entirely different complaint. You're asking me now to go to the provinces to teach writing, not selling, and although I have nothing against the provinces this was not (when we began dialogue 38) the campaign for which I signed.

That's an entirely separate issue anyway. As you and I know, there is no synchronicity to excellence and success. (My own summary aphorism for the business has always been "Talent at least is not disqualifying.") We could both cite a long list (there might even be overlap) of well known, successful modern works of science fiction and fantasy which we feel to be severely unaccomplished. But our audience has no more signed up for my literary judgments than I signed up for giving them. We should, accordingly, try to stay on-topic.

(I am a bit bemused by your statement that you and so many writers have been invited by colleges, at a fee, to lecture on writing and markets. I've published a few books myself and that has not been my experience. In over four decades as a functioning professional, I've been a Writer in Residence at a University twice [for one week each time], I've given two college lectures, been paid [minimally] to appear at a few seminars and in front of a couple of college classes, and was paid $25 by Paramus High School in 1973 to address an English class for an hour. Is my experience so at variance with those of most writers? I have found that English departments at both the secondary and collegiate level are frantically territorial and often *resent* writers taking the place of regular faculty. Of course all of this is moot if you are or were Arthur C. Clarke, Isaac Asimov or Neil Gaiman but most of us are or were not.)

Well, that's an extended digression. To return, however perilously, to the topic at issue: we've emerged with some good suggestions and possibilities. The problem is that most of them (I except your Sci Fi Channel idea which is in fact a very good one) have been tried over the many decades without, it would seem obvious, notable success. Our own dialogues have been helpful (or at least were so intended) but of course we are in a sense already preaching to the converted; most of the readers of the *Bulletin* are writers who have negotiated their way to at least minimum standards of professionalism. I yammered intensely enough through my Writers in Residency and classroom appearances but the outcome of this process reminded me of what Donald Barthelme once wrote about the act of publishing short stories in the United States: "It's like dropping feathers into a well."

Almost summary time. Do you think we've had any success in addressing this question? Or is ignorance, in all its loveliness, eternally self-renewing (deep bow to the collected works of Cyril Kornbluth.) I'm reminded of something Donald A. Wollheim once told me long ago, a story which had been passed on to him by a friend who worked at a vanity press ... said vanity press had been sued for fraud and a civil trial had awarded substantial damages to the aggrieved plaintiff/author. That result had been announced in a rather extended story in the *New York Times*. Two days later, the manuscript of a novel was received by the vanity publisher with a covering letter which began, "I just read all about you in the paper. I hope you like my work."

―◄◊/◊/◊►―

MIKE: I'm sorry you haven't had pleasant and lucrative experiences speaking to colleges while a number of SFWAns have. I've yet to run into anyone who experienced resentment on the part of the people who invited them to speak, and the fees, unless you're a celebrity, are usually pretty standard, school by school.

As for the rest of it, I mentioned the 1,600 books because your favorite template seems to be the 1950s, and the case you seemed to be making was that there was room for everyone, competent and otherwise, in the 1950s, due to the abundance of magazines, whereas that's not the case today. And if we take your template at face value, that's absolutely true: there were 56 print magazines then, and there are four print magazines today.

But of course, as I keep pointing out every couple of dialogues, this is *not* the 1950s, and those 1,600+ books offer a lot more space and a lot more money than the magazines of the 1950s did.

Which is neither here nor there. I was answering you, and I should have been addressing the problem. And you know something? The magazines could help.

Not by buying from beginners. That helps individuals, but it doesn't educate the rest. But if the magazines, as a public service to those who wish to become part of the field, could each run a display ad directing them to the proper web pages—"Predators and Editors," the SFWA pages, and the rest—it wouldn't cost them a thing, and it might show another 30,000 clueless beginners how to start becoming less clueless.

It's ridiculous to think that the book publishers give enough of a damn to do the same thing—but it wouldn't cost them a penny to have a little note on their web site, somewhere in the "how to submit" section, telling potential writers about SFWA and the various useful web pages. One of the beauties of the electronic age (and one of the pains, thank you, spammers) is that you can reach ten million people for the same minimal cost as reaching ten people.

And I think we're going to have to use that fact to reach the broadest group of clueless beginners. We may make our living from print publications, but let's be honest: either of us can reach more people with a couple of e-mails than we have with the total number of books we've sold in our aggregate 80+ years in the business. So can television. But a magazine can't, and a book can't, and a convention can't. Possibly the approaches I suggest here won't work, but we need to keep trying, and clearly the internet is the key. What we need is a database of wannabees, and I'm open to anyone's suggestions on where/how to get it.

They're out there, those wannabees—and among them are the next you and the next me. They need instruction and education. And it seems to me that the best way to reach them is not through the medium that they want to work in — the printed page — but through the media that are slowly but clearly driving the printed page out of business (but hopefully not before you and I are peacefully in the grave).

24 Change

MIKE: I just got back from DragonCon a few days prior to writing this, and I have come to a conclusion: the world —*our* world — is changing.

Consider: Worldcon, held three weeks earlier, drew 3,600 warm bodies. DragonCon drew between 35,000 and 50,000, according to which estimate you believe.

No Worldcon book has ever sold out at the convention. DragonCon printed 1,500 copies of an original anthology of stories set at DragonCon. It sold out in less than three days.

Worldcon, as anyone attending this year knows, took very small parts of seven hotels, spread all the hell over downtown Denver. DragonCon filled four huge hotels to overflowing, taking every room, every suite, every function space.

DragonCon flew in dozens of writers, actors, artists, even bands, at their expense, and comped rooms and suites for all of them. Worldcon flew in their Guests of Honor.

DragonCon had its annual banquet (which Worldcon hasn't had on a regular basis since 1976, and only twice since then). It filled a very large room.

DragonCon is primarily for media, anime, and gaming fans, but that didn't stop them from inviting me, and Harry Turtledove, and Josepha Sherman, and Kevin Anderson, and Carole Nelson Douglas, and Bill Fawcett, and Jody Lynn Nye, and John Ringo, and Eric Flint, and Rebecca Moesta, and Michael Stackpole and Toni Weisskopf, and a bunch of other writers and editors— and almost all our panels and readings played to full houses. These weren't fans who disdained written science fiction; they were just the latest generation who were brought up on movies and TV and computers, and didn't know anything about written science fiction — but they were eager to learn, and just as eager to spend their money on books once they knew a little something about the writers.

And I suppose I should point out that a month earlier, ComiCon drew 135,000 attendees, and that more and more publishers are showing up there.

I go to Worldcons to line up my next year's work, and to visit with old friends ... but I find I can do a different kind of business at cons like DragonCon: I can meet and address 5,000 people over the weekend, people who have either never heard of me or at least never read me, and talk maybe a third of them into buying one or more of my books, and *that* is business too.

Worldcon used to be the biggie. Rarely does World Fantasy Con draw over a thousand people. Boskone once drew in excess of four thousand attendees; when I went two years ago I was told they pulled about 1,300. Those numbers are dwarfed by DragonCon which in turn is dwarfed by ComiCon.

I still prefer "real" science fiction cons. They're what I grew up with, and where most of my friends go.

But it's pretty hard to ignore these massive cons where the literature is not ignored, but is seen as just one facet of science fiction. More and more major writers seem to be agreeing (as well as top artists), and so too are the publishers (Baen and Tor both were major presences at this year's DragonCon).

So ... are these — and probably a dozen new ones just like them — the cons of the future? If not, are they at least cons we'll find it beneficial to attend as often as the traditional cons?

Science fiction writers extrapolate change all the time. Do you think we can comfortably adapt to it in the real world? And will it become necessary as more and more fans come to science fiction through routes other than the literature?

—⚹⚹⚹—

BARRY: It's changing. It is really changing And just as we predicted in the 40s and 50s (but I don't think we ever truly believed) the change is an accelerating process. The change is ever more rapid and I wonder if much of what we now know — both as writers and as part of the sf community — would be even recognizable to that version of myself who stumbled wide-eyed through a few hours of the 1967 New York World Convention. (Attendance about 500. The Statler-Hilton Hotel across from the then unbuilt third Madison Square Garden. Shared the Statler-Hilton that weekend with a Scientology Convention.)

I wasn't at Denver this year. As you know I am rarely anywhere near a World Convention. Not a recluse but I suppose a mild agoraphobe, I have not been at a World Convention since Philadelphia in 2001 (about 6000 there) and before *that* Baltimore in 1983 (about the same number). But I keep informed and when Joshua Bilmes told me that he had estimated the attendance at 3500 my immediate response was to yet again quote Norman Spinrad's unnamed Parisian friend of the 1990s: "Science fiction, that is a dying thing." The World Convention attendance peaked (please correct or confirm) in Los Angeles in 1984 with an attendance of approximately 9000. Hasn't gotten near that again. In a 1971 novel, *Gather in the Hall of the Planets* set at an imaginary New York World Convention, my characters used exponential figures to predict the future. Twenty thousand by the end of the century. Another triumph of prognostication to put in the box with my assurance that Edward Albee was incapable of writing a successful play of more than one act.

What happened? Well, that is another sermon and it is one which I have delivered in various venues, this column included. That's not where we should go with this. The question which you raise is a better way to open a discussion and it contradicts the sometimes desperate pessimism which many regard as my calling card. Where do we go from here? Are DragonCon and the huge ComiCon really visions of desperation ... or do they represent opportunities to be seized? If our readers won't follow us, we must follow our readers. If potential readers don't like or are not aware of what we are about, then should we make ourselves available to them? Your statement that these two enormous conventions are populated by many who may know little of the so-called True Quill but are quite eager to learn is one I would like to seize upon, one I would like to believe.

To amend our anonymous Parisian: Science fiction may *not* be a "finished thing." Instead it is science fiction *as we have narrowly perceived it* which may be finished. Publishing history is replete with examples of both kinds. The historical Western novel, which was still a viable category in the mid-sixties when I entered publishing, has in practical terms died: there is no publisher bringing out a line of Westerns, the aging audience for the category is vanishing through mortality and it is not being replaced. The historical Western, that is a finished thing.

But the narrative of vampirism — a kind of transmogrification of the horror novel — is undead and flourishing, expanding in all media. If it bites, it's right. Alan Ball's Home Box Office series, *True Blood*, premiered in early September; it is based upon a series by Charlaine Harris and the premiere received *Gone with the Wind* type publicity and coverage. Anne Rice's *Interview with a Vampire* was published thirty years ago in an atmosphere of general disdain or reluctance: "that *Dracula* stuff *again?*" I think we could misread our potential at our peril.

So at last an agreement: There is hope, there is a way perhaps to remake science fiction by placing it before a huge potential audience. But can we do this without the kind of pandering represented by the franchise and media spin-off phenomena of the last three decades? And exactly how could this be done?

Or is outright pandering — I speak now to the politically-oriented among us — the only way to go?

—*ᴧᴧᴧ*—

MIKE: There was one Worldcon that came close to the 1984 LACon: ConFrancisco in 1993 drew about 8,700. But they haven't been getting larger. You would think that after the Worldcon goes overseas, the next year it'd be huge, since most pros and fans don't follow it across the ocean, but that is no longer the case.

Clearly a convention that specializes in *all* aspects of science fiction is going to far outdraw the traditional convention, which only caters to those interested in written science fiction. You might also make a case that when you don't change venues—DragonCon is always in Atlanta, and ComiCon is always in San Diego—and you don't change dates (think of the recent Worldcons, which are all over the late summer calendar, whereas for decades they were on Labor Day weekend) you figure to draw better.

There's another consideration. One of the things the people running DragonCon knew was *which* writers to invite. I've never seen Laurel K. Hamilton or Sherrilyn Kenyon at a "regular" con, but they were at DragonCon, and they drew thousands of worshipful fans, some of whom wound up talking to me and a few other authors who don't live on the bestseller list. Kevin Anderson, fresh from a new 3-book Dune contract, was there; so was Anne McCaffrey. And so on. In other words, for the most part they invited names that the average attendee had either read once upon a time, or at least recognized. (Yes, there were some exceptions ... but our kind of conventions are the flip side: how many bestsellers are among the 300 writers who attend Worldcon? Five? Six? Surely less than ten.)

Sherrilyn Kenyon also (at her own expense, I'm told) set up a large display booth in the dealers' room. Was it cost-productive? I have to assume so. She did it last year, too—and if you doubt the efficacy of her self-promotion, just run an Amazon Title-Z search on her.

But attending such cons also makes you wonder: what else are we overlooking, what new audiences are out there that we're not trying hard enough to reach in this changing milieu?

I know I've picked up a lot of new readers by selling podcast rights, and of course Audible.com and its subsidiaries and competitors are scooping up science fiction and fantasy novels by the hundred—and it's probably not the kind of thing where you can record one of your books and sell it yourself, since it requires major distribution channels. But there have to be other avenues, avenues that will let us reach those 50,000 kids in Atlanta (and tons elsewhere) who are not clueless, but merely uninformed about the literary end of science fiction.

I don't think ads in program books are the answer, and I'm sure booths like Sherrilyn Kenyon's aren't cost-productive unless you sell like Sherrilyn Kenyon ... but maybe, instead of making a pained face whenever someone mentions vampire romances (excuse me: paranormal romances), we might tell them about *An Old Friend of the Family* or *I Am Legend*. I know a bunch of the fans we met there—I hesitate to call them non-readers; let's dub them not-yet-readers—expressed surprise that people like Harry and Kevin and I were so approachable. Evidently their tastes have been spat on just enough by contemptuous literary writers that they *knew* there was nothing in the literature for them ... until they met some writers at their convention and decided we were human after all, and that some of us even had interesting things to say (and possibly interesting books to buy).

So am I saying everyone should attend these and other gigantic cons? No, not really. My gut belief is that if enough SFWAns attend them, they'll hang out together in a small group and never do the interacting with fans that should be their primary reason for attending. Face it: it's more comfortable to be with 50 friends than 50,000 strangers who don't know you from Adam.

So ... along with conventions, are there other ways to meet these not-yet-readers, or at least to let them know you're alive and they'd love your books? With fannish non-readers (as yet) outnumbering readers dozens to one, how do we contact this vast untapped and potentially friendly and lucrative market?

—◦◦◦—

BARRY: There are of course the conventional responses, most of which we have parsed in earlier dialogues. Local bookstore signings and readings. A website of professional appearance and content (paying someone to prepare that website in the many cases when we are not capable). A blog, of course, a strong, constant online presence to increase reader awareness. As much local press coverage as we can find. Publication tours for the few of us a publisher will finance. There's a set protocol which has evolved over the decades and the differences among us in terms of publicity have mostly to do with the varying degree of sophistication with which we approach those protocols.

Is there a way to go outside of this? The key to the modern bestseller of course, from *The Da Vinci Code* to *Catch-22* and anything in between, is to break through the barrier separating "readers" from "non-readers," to find a way to sell a book to an audience far beyond that of book buyers. *The Andromeda Strain* was a science fiction novel whose publisher found a way to sell it in quantity to non-readers of science fiction. The Thomas Harris Hannibal novels were police procedurals which sold way beyond the audience for police procedurals (or for gross-out horror books) and so on. The task is to sell reading material to non-readers and this outcome translates to almost all other media. The Picasso and Matisse exhibitions at New York City's Museum of Modern Art in the 80s and 90s drew enormous crowds, 80 to 90 percent of which had never before been in the museum. The film *Titanic* grossed over 600 million dollars, still a record, and much of that income came from the repeated theatrical attendance of adolescent girls who wanted to see ever more of Leonardo DiCaprio.

That is the challenge facing what is left of science fiction in the new millennium. If it is to be preserved (let alone flourish), its product is going to have to be sold well beyond the borders of the extant science fiction audience. There are those that say that this could be done only at the cost of turning that science fiction into *The Andromeda Strain*, something neither original nor particularly imaginative. If that were to become the approved method of marketing, would we be destroying the village in our attempt to save it?

Perhaps we would. I have heard and read arguments that good science fiction, what James Blish called "the true quill," is by definition a specialized form of limited appeal. Only a relatively small amount of readers have the patience and sophistication, the sheer *knowledge* to truly appreciate this material. So-called cutting edge science fiction has become increasingly arcane and self-referential in the last twenty years; much of it will make absolutely no sense to most of the audience. You're not going to be able to sell Stephen Baxter or Paul MacAuley, Greg Egan or Neal Stephenson to the attendees of Comicon or DragonCon. Some of them in years to come might find their way to these writers, but they haven't done so yet and in the main they are not interested. I don't know what good in their case any attempt to raise visibility or create publicity would manage.

As Norman Spinrad noted well over 20 years ago (and I have quoted him so many times as to be half-convinced that we stumbled independently into the insight), "Science fiction itself is a small special interest at modern science fiction conventions." Fantasy and media tie-ins have certainly dominated the author list and dealers rooms of DragonCon and most of the conventions now, and there seems no way at all to change the situation.

So long ago, in the early 1970s, Larry Janifer compared science fiction to the Elizabethan Theater in the middle of the 16th century: "There are a whole bunch of us working for some kind of an audience, all of us are waiting for our Shakespeare." That may still be true. But whereas both he and I were convinced that our Shakespeare — if she ever came — would doubtless save us for immortality I am not sure that this would be the case in today's DragonConified climate.

———⚘———

MIKE: I'm not totally convinced that we can't reach a mass audience with quality books. Certainly Bradbury, McCaffrey, Asimov, Heinlein, Herbert, Gaiman, Simmons, and a number of others have managed, and they can't all be writing yard goods. As for the cutting edge, I've never been convinced of its commercial value, and only occasionally of its artistic value. The trick is to let that mass audience know the books exist, which in turn means identifying that audience.

Back to the conventions for a moment. (Yes, there's a connection.) One of the things I have noticed at Worldcon, and at most of the traditional regional conventions, is the graying of fandom (and prodom, for that matter). There aren't the plethora of young people at these things that there once were. Some, yes, but not the percentages we used to see.

But at DragonCon, if there were 50,000 attendees, I don't think anyone would argue that well over 40,000 were under 30 years of age. Surely 100,000 of the ComiCon attendees were under 30.

And that says something to me: it says that our writers and our editors are to a great extent writing for each other, and their own generation and milieu, and ignoring the millions of potential buyers who grew up after science fiction had become a respectable mass market phenomenon, when most of the top-grossing movies are science fiction or fantasy, when science fiction has its own cable channel (regardless of what anyone may think of the content), when most of the top-selling games (a *huge* market) are science fiction, and when the term "sci-fi," which most of us old-timers hate, is in common usage.

There is an enormous, mostly-untapped new young audience out there, one that is predisposed to like science fiction, that doesn't have to be convinced that it isn't that crazy Buck Rogers stuff—but the publishing establishment, which includes writers, editors and publishers alike, has to be made aware that it *is* there and not to be ignored or viewed with smug superiority. This is not a potential audience that has to be won over, so much as one that has to be made aware that science fiction exists as literature as well as movies, television, games and comic books.

Kevin Anderson understood that early on. He's been going to DragonCon for over a decade, and to ComiCon, and I'm sure 99% of SFWA would love to trade royalty statements with him. Others are starting to court this audience as well—David Weber, David Drake, Sherrilyn Kenyon, Harry Turtledove, Laurel K. Hamilton, John Ringo, Anne McCaffrey, and Eric Flint have shown up at one or both of the last two DragonCons ... and they all have one thing in common: they don't have to worry about where they're selling their next book.

I think the education process here is a two-way street: we have to educate the next generation, already committed to science fiction, that the literature is a vital and fascinating part of it, well worth their time and money; and we have to convince the publishing establishment that this is a huge and friendly audience that needs cultivation, and that we ignore it at our economic peril.

———⟨/\/\/⟩———

BARRY: Well, yes, education is a "two-way process," and I interpret that a little differently ... you are thinking of it as educating two audiences, the DragonCon attendees and the publishers. (The publishers, I quickly note, are already semi-educated: what do you think those three Star Wars/Clone Wars novelizations just published mean? What do you think all of the other film novelizations, the endless Star Trek knockoffs and spin-offs mean? The publishers since at least the advent of Judy Lynn del Rey are hip to media sprawl and exploitation.) *I* think of it as the need to educate science fiction writers to the reality of the contemporary market. Most of them are still resisting that reality.

This is of course one of your own principal topics and it feels strange to propound this; I feel that I am not only channeling you, I may *be* you. But it must be made clear in this context: the majority of the audience we are addressing in the *Bulletin* does not want to come to terms with the fact that 90% of the audience for science fiction is not interested in what they write or want to write or read. Just as contemporary professional athletes are increasingly separated by income, lifestyle and fear from the fans in the bleachers and the press, most science fiction writers are separated from their audience. They are addressing one another, they are addressing some skewed image of what science fiction might be, they are addressing some imagined past. They are uninterested in or contemptuous of the 90% of readership or potential readership who could not name five Nebula Award winners, who are not aware of the existence of magazines, who are — if they intersect with them at all — confused and alienated by the contents of current Best of the Year anthologies.

There is no way that these readers or potential readers can be wooed by the contents of the contemporary Nebula Awards anthologies. They are simply not interested in the main and many of them, juxtaposed with this kind of material, react with hostility. What the magazines are publishing simply isn't being read by that audience, and it never was.

There are only a few magazines remaining now and sales of these survivors have been in steady descent for decades. (I am not claiming that I could edit those magazines any better; they are in fact magnificently edited in terms of the field's history and our own expectations, and I am in fact indebted to Gordon Van Gelder, who has paid me more honor than I deserve. But the magazines and the Best of the Year anthologies represent the past, not the future. It was a wonderful past and we face a very bleak future. But we cannot be borne ceaselessly into the past, beat our little oars as frantically as we may. And science fiction writers should be surer of this than any other brand of American.)

You have addressed these issues in your own essays and the 2007 edition of Nebula Awards Stories which you edited includes a commissioned essay by Kevin Anderson which states the case in the bluntest terms. Change or die. The key to real change, perhaps, is to understand that however contemptuous we may be of the DragonCon population and the content of its dealers room, we are going to have to live with this, work on its terms or die.

Some of us would prefer to die, of course, at least in literary terms. Or sequester ourselves with the first five *Galaxy Readers* or a pile of collections from NESFA Press. I'm not only sympathetic to those members, I'm probably one of them.

But if education does not run two ways, science fiction in less than twenty years is going to be as one with the Western novel or the category light-in-the-window Gothic.

———*♫♪♫*———

MIKE: There's a lot of uncomfortable truth in that. Though I would argue that whoever's publishing Trekbooks and Wookiebooks is not exactly keeping up with the times— don't forget, *Star Trek* debuted at Tricon, the 1966 Worldcon, 42 years ago; and *Star Wars* hit the screens 31 years ago— which means these things were old when the current generation of readers we want to attract was *in utero*. That's part of the problem; you can't ignore the fact that *Star Trek* and *Star Wars* , and not Heinlein, not Asimov, and not Bradbury, are the icons that 99% of the public is aware of. I would doubt that as much as 4% know any of the above-named writers.

But those icons are merely pointing the way. *Lara Croft* was selling millions of games before she became a movie, and sold millions of tickets before she became a series of novelizations. Publishers are no longer innovating, at least not in a commercial way — or so the conventional wisdom goes.

Me, I disagree. They *are* innovating, just not in a direction you and I care for. I don't see anything romantic about an unclean *thing* drinking your lifesblood, but whether because of a young Frank Langella or a younger Buffy, quite a few million readers, most but not all of them women, disagree with me — and they put their money where their passions are. I would guess that paranormal romance novels grossed *far* more money than science fiction novels last year.

Am I happy about it? Of course not. I don't write paranormal romances and I don't plan to ... but I'm enough of a realist to say, well, if that's where the readers are, how can I blame Warner's and the other publishers for cashing in on it?

Put it another way. William Gibson started a trend called cyberpunk, and some of our finest writers tried to expand upon it, and the critics went wild over it, and the publishers pushed it — and with one or two exceptions it never sold out of the ordinary, and you'd be hard-pressed to find half a dozen people still writing it, and their sales are as good a reason as you need to explain why it vanished from the racks.

Anne Rice started a trend, too: sexy vampires. If it's not a billion-dollar industry yet, it's close. What can one do — shake the reader by the ears and say, "No, read *this* stuff instead!"

Fantasy quest novels outsell hard science novels. Action/adventure science fiction outsells social science fiction, and political science fiction, and satirical science fiction. We don't seem to mind when we can claim it for our own ... but when it starts elsewhere and invades our field, we ignore it for as long as we can, which is economically too damned long, since others do *not* ignore it.

And I'm just using paranormal romances as an example. How many journeyman science fiction writers can name ten video games? Yet the average video game has about $20 million of development money sunk into it while the average book has a copy editor and a quarter page in *Locus*, and a decent-selling game's royalties dwarf anything this side of Stephen King.

But I'll bet that more than half the fans at DragonCon and ComiCon could name a dozen games, and if they read at all they'll have shelled out coin of the realm for paranormal romances and movie novelizations, and they can give you the casts of half a dozen mediocre "sci-fi" shows on television —*and they aren't ashamed of it, and they are resentful as hell when "real" science fiction writers and old-time fans look down their noses at them.*

They're out there, they love science fiction (or at least their notion of it), and they're going to patronize whoever cultivates them.

I don't know about "change or die"; it's all part of the same huge tent (even if a lot of writers and publishers don't acknowledge that).

But it's certainly a case of: adapt or die.

25 Tailspinning

MIKE: Hi, Eeyore. I've got some figures that are right up your (philosophical) alley.

Try this one: $13.00 and 67 cents.

Know what it represents?

The $13.00 is the 52-week high for Borders stock. The 67 cents is the price it's going for today (December 8, 2008), as we begin this dialogue. In the parlance of Wall Street, that makes it a junk stock ... or, of you prefer, a penny stock.

Got another figure: $65 million. No, it's not what the New York Yankees pay Alex Rodriguez every 2½ years. (Well, actually it is, but it's something more germane as well.) It's the total current capitalization of Borders, which once upon a time was worth well over a billion dollars.

OK, those figures would even depress a hyena. Let's look at some brighter ones.

Try these: $38.42 and $16.62.

Right. That's Barnes & Noble's high for the year, and its price today. Less than half its best value this year ... and it's coming back. Its low for the year, hit a few weeks back, was $10.77. Its market cap (which is to say, its total capitalization) is $860 million, not quite equal to the golden parachutes of the top half-dozen oil execs, but getting there ... but it used to be more than two billion dollars.

A number of mass market publishers got flooded with unexpected returns from Borders this summer and fall. Not that sales were down — according to industry figures, book sales were *up* between 10 and 11% through the end of October — but Borders returned millions of books for credit (expecting most of them back in a month or two) to improve their balance sheet (so conventional wisdom said) so they could find a White Knight.

Maybe they tried and failed, maybe conventional wisdom was wrong as it so often is — but for whatever the reason, four days ago they announced they were no longer on the market.

Now, when these two behemoths came along, they managed, in a relatively short time, to put 90% of the independent booksellers out of business, including a number of chains such as Little Professor. Pretty soon not much

240

else was left except Waldenbooks, B. Dalton, Crown, and Books-a-Million, all lesser chairs—and lo and behold, three of those four chains were owned by Barnes or Borders.

This was the face of bookselling's future. No one could stand against them except Amazon (and while Amazon has the advantage of being able to "stock" six million titles, since they're not paying for finite space in commercial venues, they have the disadvantage that one can't really browse online, despite their numerous pro-browsing innovations).

Anyway, suddenly Barnes and Borders were calling the shots, either themselves or through their distributors. If an author didn't sell they could (and often did) issue the edict that they wouldn't stock his next one — and an awful lot of authors began hiding behind pseudonyms as these corporate bean counters essentially usurped a number of editorial functions.

They never seemed to think much of category fiction. Romance may be over 50% of the fiction market, but it's always been a poor cousin at the superstores. Science fiction and fantasy get a lot of shelf space, but rarely in the front of the stores or near the coffee shops, the two prime locations. The superstores specialize in bestsellers—but they have to give such huge discounts to compete with each other, with Walmart, and with Amazon, that they don't make any money to speak of from bestsellers, which almost become loss leaders.

Okay, that's the situation as of today, December 8, 2008. You and I — and almost everyone who will read this—make our living from writing, and in almost every case from writing science fiction or fantasy. You've seen the figures, so use that science fiction background and start extrapolating. Is this a momentary glitch in a generally expanding economy (which began contracting, worldwide, this fall)? Will independent bookstores, stores that *care* about books, make a comeback? Will Amazon emerge with a 75% market share? Will there even *be* a Borders in two years—and does it matter? If Borders and its 1500+ locations fold, will some bookseller, maybe Barnes, maybe a brand-new entity, move in to take over those locations (or create new ones)—or is it a well-managed company that has proven there simply isn't a market in America for 3500 superstores plus Amazon?

And most important of all for readers of this publication, how does this affect the membership of SFWA? If Borders folds and isn't replaced, how many careers might fold and not be replaced?

Can you, with your lifetime of experience as a writer, editor and agent, find an upside to all this, if not this year, then up the road?

—⁓⁓—

BARRY: If it is possible to find an upside in this news, we're going to have to sneak our way around the subject and try to find an open flank. There's no rapid optimistic response. We — and by "we" I mean not only the writers to whom these dialogues are nominally addressed, but the editors, the publishers, the entire "industry" such as it is— are in serious trouble. A couple of pre-liminary observations:

1. As you note, we are beginning this dialogue on December 8. That is 28 years after the murder of John Lennon in the courtyard of the Dakota by an assassin disguised as an acolyte. I will leave the petite symbolism to others; it is an uncomfortable conjunction. There are many who felt that the hopes of more than one generation died on those stones.

2. Just last week, Random House and Doubleday, two subsidiaries of the gigantic German conglomerate Bertelsmann, announced (Happy Holidays, folks!) substantial layoffs amidst rumors that the Doubleday, Dell and Bantam imprints, ancient and honorable imprints all, may be abandoned. The publisher of Random House announced his resignation; it is not clear if this was his decision. Synchronously, Houghton-Mifflin went on indefinite buying mora-torium. That means no acquisitions for an indeterminate period of time. "Acquisition moratorium" historically is a euphemism for "imminent dissolu-tion." Okay, Houghton-Mifflin is too large and has too much of a backlist to die. But it is not too large and backlisted to be sold to another conglomerate. (Which may do to H-M Co. what Bertelsmann seems likely to do to the Dou-bleday and Dell imprints.)

That's just a little bit of background or synchronicity. Another way of sneaking our way into this topic is to consider what Barnes & Noble, in its (approximately) twenty-year-old incarnation as a conglomerate manque might have thought it was doing when in the 1980s it elected to expand from a rather sleepy (but profitable) textbook distribution business with a limited number of bookstores to the ravening literary Starbucks which we now know.

Like every good, power-driven and venal conglomerate, Barnes & Noble had a systematized plan ... expand, build more bookstores, stock the bookstores to the roof with trade and text (with some specialization amongst the stores), entice the public inside with across-the-board discounts and coffee shops, undersell the independent bookstores so severely that they would be driven out of business and *then*, having established a commanding position, raise the prices, consolidate the advantage and conquer the world. Borders, a consider-ably smaller but no less carnivorous animal, could work the territory as well; there would be time enough later to absorb them. The first target was, how-ever, the independent bookstore. Tomorrow the world.

Worked in the early years very well. Independents died a variety of deaths: some slow, some fast, some colorfully, some quietly. New York City, a petri dish, enacted the perishing in all ways, sometimes quite dramatically. Down went Brentano's, Scribner's, the Doubleday chain. Down, spectacularly, went Book-masters. Goodbye Shakespeare & Company. So long Eeyore. It wasn't pretty but — as Jimmy Breslin observed long ago, covering the death of the *World Jour-nal Tribune*— journalists are energized by the deaths of newspapers, publishers, bookstores. They identify. In fact, they over-identify. It brings out the gifts of blood like *Death in the Afternoon* brought out the poetry in Hemingway. The bullfight is a magnificent spectacle for everyone except the bull, as the observation goes.

Meanly but brilliantly enacted by Barnes & Noble, the transition had in passage and then retrospect an air of absolute inevitability. As Emma Rothschild (writing of the automobile industry) observed in *Paradise Lost* (1974), "What we take to be vast and intractable social movements are really only the consequences of the decisions of a small band of greedy, powerful people."

Barnes & Noble however — sound D Minor descending triads, the leitmotif (in Beethoven's Ninth anyway) of hubris — had made a fundamental miscalculation. Functioning in the traditional mode — like, say Alfred P. Sloan of General Motors in the 1950s — they came very quickly against something which General Motors and its similar methods had been spared for more than fifty years. The market itself was completely reconfigured. Everything changed for them (and little brother Borders) even as they stared with disbelief. The Net. Amazon. The crumbling of the "brick and mortar bookstore."

Suddenly being Alfred Sloan was not such grand fun any more. They were victims rather than perpetrators of Sloan's most famous dictum: "Dynamic obsolescence."

Eeyore off the orator's box for a refreshing few mouthfuls of hay. Carry forward the story, Mr. Bear.

———

MIKE: How it happened is someone else's concern. Even if we'd seen what was coming in 1980 we couldn't have stopped it then, and if they pull another such blunder in 2020 we can't stop it now. The trick is how to deal with it — and indeed, *can* it be dealt with if your name isn't Butcher or Hamilton or Koontz or some such thing?

The first thing to acknowledge is that the world *has* changed. People are buying more books now than ever before. Clearly they're not buying them from Borders, and not buying as many as they used to from Barnes, and I don't see Books-a-Million or Joseph Beth cutting into their business ... so where *are* they buying them?

Well, of course, the first thing that comes to mind is Amazon, and clearly that's one bookseller that's not in any trouble. But Amazon isn't picking up *all* the business the superstores lost, so where is it going?

There wasn't an internet back in 1980, not so's you'd notice it anyway. Today the internet probably is the conduit for over $100 billion in annual commerce, strictly within America. Amazon's the 900-pound gorilla, but run a web search on any title and you'll find a *lot* of online bookstores carrying it. In fact, you'll find some physical bookstores, like the huge Powell's in Oregon, that are now also online stores.

A lot of publishers—especially the small and medium presses (who aren't hurting as badly as you might think, since they never got much distribution or display in the superstores)—are selling direct to the public online. Makes sense, too. You give a 10 or 20 percent discount for a direct online sale, that's still a hell of a lot better than the 45 to 55% (and sometimes more) it cost you to get into the superstores (without posters, without dump displays, without anything but the book, stuck anonymously in a cavernous store with tens of thousands of other books, all but a handful put there to live or die on their own).

Fictionwise.com was the first to start selling reprints in electronic form online, and once they proved that it was a totally viable enterprise, publishers have started making e-books available. Webscriptions is probably the best-known in our field, but there are quite a few others.

These reprints convinced entrepreneurial publishers, who had entered the field a little too early and got burned, that it was time to try again—and the better ones seem to be doing just fine. The top three paying short fiction markets are all e-magazines. The book market has been waiting for truly convenient readers—I think Kindle may still be a generation away—but as soon as they're here, I don't think there's any doubt that you'll just be a couple of years away from making comparable money for an e-book as a paper one. (No, not at the top ... but at the bottom and lower midlist. Again, as we've discussed before, the economics favor electronic publishing: no paper costs, no color separation costs, no printing and binding costs, no shipping costs, no national and local distribution costs, no bookstore costs, no warehouse costs.) Maybe the advances won't be quite as high, at least for a few years ... but no traditional publishing house is going to match the 30% and 40% royalty rates you'll make from e-books.

And then there's audio. How much do audio books cut into the superstores' sales? Well, a year ago I'd have said: microscopically. Then Amazon shelled out something like $300 million for Audible.com—and Amazon doesn't throw that kind of money around if they don't see a market.

So clearly the world is changing, and readers are going to find new ways to get their literary fixes.

The problem is: we're not readers (well, not for the purpose of this dialogue, anyway); we're writers, and if a couple of thousand superstores vanish, clearly it's going to cut into sales, and royalties, and advances, and careers, at least in the short run, before the emerging markets can get the word out to a very conservative public (by which I mean, it is still estimated that half the people who buy computers have no idea how to work them; it's kind of like buying Stephen Hawking's bestseller of a few years ago and letting it sit on your coffee table, the least-read bestseller in history).

I know all the usual advice: go to signings, give interviews, start a blog, speak at schools, go to conventions, promote yourself when your publisher won't (or even when he will) ... but that was advice people were giving out five and ten years ago, when there was no hint that a third of the commercial shelf space in the country might vanish momentarily. Is there anything you can suggest for the (probable) coming hard times?

—*ΩΩ*—

BARRY: I think that we're well beyond the standard advice (which of course we've given so many times). Establish a Web Site. Make it professional. Get a blog. Carry your books to conventions and display them on panels. Send flyers to local bookstores. Use local media opportunities. Yes oh yes oh yes. Such advice may have been useful for a long time but I don't know how useful it is today. Would be like telling General Motors to get back to tail fins and breast-like bumpers. Advertise 400 horsepower Rocket acceleration. It's a bit late for this and if the present five or six conglomerate publishers give indication that within a few years they will amalgamate into one or two it will be later yet. I'm not suggesting that the conventional wisdom is wrong or even hopeless. But it does have an aspect of dining out at the apocalypse.

I might find my way into some advice of my own later in this dissertation. But let me, having engaged in the pause that refreshes, return to the interrupted line of my discussion.

Barnes & Noble was operating with business methods which had proven perfectly viable through four-fifths of the twentieth century; these methods had led General Motors and International Business Machines and McDonald's to riches and seeming unassailability. But the appallingly swift and utterly unanticipated emergence of the Net and its penetration into every aspect of business and culture changed everything so rapidly that—in business terms—the huge bookstore chains had not even formulated the language to come to terms with the situation. The system which delivered written material to the public had been utterly reconfigured and so quickly that the reconfiguration was occurring more rapidly than the evolution of a series of procedures to understand it.

There had been, at least since the advent of the Industrial Revolution in Western society (let us put this somewhere in the last decades of the nineteenth century), a standard model for the delivery of written material. Dependent upon paper and print distribution, it worked pretty well and with increasing sophistication deep into the era of conglomerate takeover of publishing (which began somewhere in the mid–1960s). Bookstores, magazine distributors, newspaper distributors, subscriptions, book clubs, advertising as the sustaining economic factor in magazine and newspaper publishing. And suddenly there was television which from its outset in mid-century attacked the magazines and newspapers at the most fundamental level (larger audiences could be targeted and reached at less expense) and then there were the chain bookstores and then of course was the Net. Everything changed and (unlike the circumstances surrounding the penetration of television) there was no visible, agreed-upon next step. The entire print delivery system had been smashed and yet there was no clear replacement, there were only a series of alternatives, all in embryonic form, some of them definitely headed for failure, others not necessarily heading for failure ... but it was *impossible to sort them out before the fact*. Meanwhile, in recent years, trade sales have dropped dramatically and the sale and consumption of new fiction, outside of forty or fifty highly promotable writers or properties, have fallen even more dramatically than those of nonfiction.

Perhaps Yeats' "new and terrible beauty" *is* about to be born ... but no one knows where or how. No wonder Borders seems headed for receivership. No wonder Barnes & Noble stock has been pounded. And certainly no wonder why — here at the populist near-bottom of the food chain — most of our current membership are clearly taking the consequences.

"This is no comedy, it is a situation serious," as one of Poulenc's cops in *Mamelles de Tiresias* points out, waving his baton (no, not that baton) in reproof. I don't think that convention signings and flyers to local bookstores really address the circumstance. Panic in the end exacerbates chaos, as we know. But a little dose of panic at the beginning might help us understand that the standard model of publishing, as you and I came to understand because we were formed by it, is finished.

***Apropos of nothing or everything, I went to the local library of this pleasant New Jersey town of some 40,000 in search of Ross Macdonald's *The Barbary Coast* or *The Zebra-Striped Hearse*. And learned that these were not available. In fact, not a single title of this Grandmaster of the Mystery Writers of America (1916–1983) is catalogued here.

—*◯◯◯*—

MIKE: Of all the many MacDonalds who wrote mysteries — John D., Gregory, the rest of them — I always thought Ross was head and shoulders the best. I put him behind only Chandler, Hammett, and (on his good days) Ellroy among all mystery writers.

Which, alas, does not address the problem, except perhaps to say that being a Mystery Grandmaster is not necessarily a viable career path a quarter century after your death.

Getting back to more immediate and pressing concerns, *if* the industry figures are right and *if* book sales are up — well, prior to the banking collapse and the deep and sudden recession in which we find ourselves — then I wonder if the loss of Borders (assuming we lose it) will be quite the cataclysmic event many writers anticipate. These superstores seem to follow the drug stores' edict (which started with lawyers ages ago): one starves, two prosper. It's a rare Barnes or Borders that isn't within a couple of miles of its opposite number. So one of the meaningful questions is: how many readers won't travel that extra mile or two? 5%? 80%? I don't know, but I suspect the number isn't as big as some fear.

I'm more concerned with the effect on publishing if Borders stays in business without making unspecified (by me, anyway) changes that will make it more viable.

Why?

Well, I can anticipate a number of strategies, and I don't like any of them.

They can discount all their books, not just their bestsellers, even more heavily to remain competitive. This makes their profits vanish, and then they die — unless they can convince publishers to offer books to them at an even bigger discount. You're a publisher. You don't *want* to sell Borders your entire science fiction line at 40% of cover price — but if you don't and your rivals do, you've just lost a couple of thousand outlets. (And if you do, we all know whose advances and royalty payments will be eight months late instead of the usual four months as the publishers try to adjust to this new attack on their cash flow.)

They can order fewer titles and push the ones they order more. Which puts most of the remaining midlisters out of business.

They can return unsold books much sooner — not quite like the 24-hours-and-out airport stores of the Good Old Days, but not like the current model, where just about any paperback lingers for close to a year. This will hurt an author's sales and sell-through, and the publisher's balance sheet — and when a publisher's balance sheet suffers, we know who suffers more. (As the immortal Pogo Possum once pointed out, when you starve with a tiger the tiger starves last.)

They can expand their restaurants, set aside larger areas for CDs and DVDs, start selling computer games, even more knick-knacks, and see what is and isn't profitable, what saleable items they might have been overlooking — but every time they display anything but a book in a finite bookstore, there is less carrying capacity for books.

They can close the least profitable half of their stores, but that just cedes the local business to Barnes, which will *not* order and display 50% more books because of it ... but until they figure out how to make ends meet, I have no more confidence in the top half of their outlets going into profitability than I have in the current situation.

They can liquidate. After all, they own a lot of buildings and a lot of prime real estate — but this is probably the worst time in 75 years to be selling property, with or without buildings on it.

So as a writer and a reader I hope they stay alive, and I hope they keep all their stores going ... but as a realist I have to say that *no* scenario is appealing, so the question is: where can we replace the income we are likely to lose through the superstores' collapse or contraction?

I'll tell you where not to look: independent stores, which once littered the landscape. Even special interest stores have taken a hit. I remember about twenty years ago Michael Kube-McDowell made up and posted a list of all the science fiction specialty bookstores, and the number, as I recall, was 57. I'd be surprised if ten still exist. And I truly don't think the mom-and-pop local bookstore is coming back. Would *you* invest your savings in one with the knowledge that Barnes, or the successor to Barnes, could come along and wipe you out within a week of opening anywhere within four or five miles of you?

So, as I've been saying here since long before the current crisis, the answer for the writer who needs to replace real or potential income is to look to nontraditional sources. I'll name some in my final turn, but I see you're chomping at the ever-decreasing bit, so take it away.

—◦◦◦—

BARRY: "Non-traditional sources." Well, yes, I would think so, because the standard model is broken. GM didn't figure it out until 2007 (or maybe they still haven't figured it out) but big cars, breast-like bumpers, flash and dash and pizzazz don't really work any more. They'll never work again. Even if gas goes down to a dollar a gallon (the plunge from $4.50 to $1.50 over the last couple of months has been astonishing) the Suburban Utility Vehicle is as dead as the Cadillac Eldorado convertible.

The so-called brick-and-mortar bookstores are heading the way of the Eldorado and so are the newspapers in which Knopf with a great flourish used to take half-page advertisements for the new Ross Macdonald novel. I am not sure what will replace them but my money would be on direct authorial sales through the Net, the sales driven by blogs, by chat groups, by free samplings, by personal rather than publisher publicity. I expect bookstores—and I love them too—will be as anachronistic twenty years from now as forty-five rpm records and record stores. As *Your Hit Parade* would be if one of the networks were dumb enough to revive that now half-century-old weekly format. Vinyl doesn't work any more, cassette tape works only in specialized limited instances, and the compact disc is on the way out. The iPod may be as stale five years from now as the compact disc seems today; the delivery systems of the entire culture are in meltdown. From these ruins something or many somethings may be born but in the meantime no one from the movie studios to the book publishers to the record executives knows what is going on. Everyone is faking it, living or dying by inches and ready to go into reverse on a day's notice. Perilous times. Displaying my books (if I am still publishing books) in front of me on convention panels isn't the answer.

Has there ever been an answer? Publishing is a fluid business. Grub Street may be timeless but will become New Grub Street and New New Grub Street and Old Grub Street within a blink of time; signs are always being changed. All that writers can do to hang on is to be resourceful, to understand evanescence, to trust in little but their own resourcefulness, and to understand that not only is no model permanent, it is in these times barely temporary.

Damon Knight's envoi to aspirant writers in concluding *In Search of Won-*

der was "Love your work, read your contract, make friends where you can." To which I would add "Keep the hybrid car fully fueled and be prepared to try another town at an hour's notice."

You and I: over the past 40 years we've done okay. (Well, I've done okay, you've done a lot better than that. Authorities of success and failure, you know.) I wouldn't even for the gift of being 40 years younger want to be trying the wheel now.

———•◦◦•———

MIKE: Just for the record, I have never told anyone to show off a pile of their books, or even a single cover, on a convention panel; I think it's bush league.

And also for the record, while no one suggests that the Big Three auto manufacturers know their asp from their Elba, the fact remains that Congressional mandates have been forcing them to make green-friendly cars that no one wants to buy. Yes, they make them badly, but I suspect making them well wouldn't encourage all that many more people to buy them. Including me; if I'm going to spend that much money, I'm going to get what *I* want.

Okay, back to our problem.

There are non-traditional sources showing their heads almost every month. I'll name some, and I'm sure I'll miss even more.

1. The "medium press," that handful of non–mass-market publishers that nonetheless will pay five-figure advances.

2. Professional podcasts. There's Escape Pod, and Podcastle, and Drabblecast, and four or five others now, and more soon.

3. Personal podcasts. A few people are running their own podcasts on their blogs to promote their books. Some are selling podcasts of their stories. Others are "blogcasting," producing audio blogs to promote themselves.

4. Audio sales. Professionally produced and narrated CDs (as by Blackstone and others), and/or professionally produced and narrated book downloads (as by Audible.com and others).

5. E-books and e-zines, both new and reprint, all of which we've discussed already

6. Online sale of your books. (I'm opposed to this personally; I think my time is more valuable writing ... but if your time is currently *not* more valuable, then there are a *lot* of online venues for your own autographed books.)

7. Believe it or not, there's a market, and a handsome one, for original manuscripts. I had no idea until George Alec Effinger (now deceased) phoned me one night, all breathless, to tell me he'd decided to put the manuscript to *When Gravity Fails* up on eBay, and got a 4-figure offer. That was good enough for me. I put my next one up and found that he was right — and a few of us have been selling them on eBay and other venues ever since. I'm still kicking myself for throwing the first hundred-plus away.)

8. There's also a collector's market for contracts. Honest.

9. There's probably more money in games right now (and definitely more in video games) than in all of category fiction. Most science fiction writers know little about the field and have no contacts; that is not the gaming industry's fault.

And there are a number of other non-traditional ways of keeping afloat. What amazes me is how few writers are willing to look into them.

There are things we can't control, such as the Borders situation (and if they survive this year, that doesn't mean they'll be around next year, or the year after that), and there are things we *can* control, such as finding and dealing with the very forces that have pushed Borders to the edge. Most agents have large stables and haven't got time to hunt up all these non-traditional markets, so we have to do it ourselves—and the writer who doesn't adjust to that has no one to blame but himself.

26 Google

MIKE: Well, the Google settlement, such as it is, has been postponed for a few months, which allows us to get in our two cents' worth.

Basically, the settlement, negotiated by the Authors Guild, about whom I'm sure we'll have more to say later, comes to this: Google pays $125 million and everybody shuts up.

Well, actually, I'm sure it wasn't worded *quite* that way, but that's the gist of it. If you want to make an objection, you must opt in by the deadline. And — and this is going to be fun when some author without a computer, or one who's been living on Bora Bora for the past decade, hears about it — if you don't actively opt out, you are automatically in. And if you opt in, you get a maximum of $60.00 for every book Google "confiscated" (there's a better word, but Google has more lawyers than I do).

I'm sure we'll go into all the details before this dialogue is done, but just for the record, I opted out. And so there would be no mistake, I listed every single thing I've had my name on, back to my starving writer days when I was busy being the redeeming social value between nude photo spreads in men's magazines. (I didn't list the endless "adult" novels I did under pseudonyms; if Google wants 'em they can have 'em, and I never wanted my name associated with them, then or now; all I asked was that it was spelled right on the check.)

Anyway, there are a lot of legal reasons why I opted out, and we'll come to them. But there was a more important reason. Maybe it'll cost me money, maybe it'll damage my career in other ways, but I will *never* agree that any novel I ever signed my name to is worth only $60.00.

Where did you come down on the opting, and why?

———〰〰〰———

BARRY: I think the Google "settlement" is going to be delayed a great deal longer. This "postponement" of a couple of months could well be years. In fact, there seems a good chance that there will *never* be a settlement. Google tried to rush this through as a done deed, gambling that insufficient attention would be paid and writers, that notoriously clamorous but disorganized group, would never be able to get it together in time to stop the railroad. And that seems in fact to have been the case ... its not the writers' groups or individual actions which have put on the brakes, but the government. Which has had a lot of questions and seems to have caught Google by surprise.

If I am right and if this process is stopped on the tracks, dead in the water, shot at sunrise, pick your figure of speech, then our own take could well be mooted. I know that the Science Fiction and Fantasy Writers of America for whom we are such constant advisors has itself taken no position on the situation; it's all been relegated to committees and "further study" which of course is, parliamentarily speaking, the best way of making an issue go away without seeming to want to make it go away. Our members are as split on the settlement as they are on almost everything else, and government by fiat clearly is not going to work here (as it has worked so well with the revision of the Nebula rules). Whatever position might be taken collectively would be overtaken by individual response.

That said, I think that there is a powerful argument for accepting the settlement and if I were ever given the choice, I find myself inclined toward that acceptance. It is a cynical argument, the offspring (as are so many of my positions) of despair, but no less viable. You state that you will be damned if you will be party to any agreement which holds your books to be worth sixty dollars apiece, and I feel the same way about my own (a tip of the Hatlo Hat to my critics), but as between sixty dollars a title and no dollars at all I am strongly inclined to take the sixty.

Here's why: the Web, as we know, is uncontrollable. It cannot be satisfactorily policed. In fact — and taking the longer view — it cannot be policed at all, as many tyrannical governments throughout the world are now learning every day. There are so many pirate sites, there is so much sheer violation or appropriation of copyright, that our own monitors can be aware of only a fraction of it and the situation is fluid; there is new piracy every day. Within the last week I was informed that at least a hundred of my works (novels and short stories) exist on a new pirate site. This is not the first or the tenth time I have been so informed.

Copyright and its limiting clauses are apt to become as much of a fiction in the times ahead as your Galactic Midway series. Under those circumstances, Google's offer — as a huge corporation now with an outstanding public relations department — to at least come into the tent may stand as the best offer we are likely to get. They are at least proceeding from the position that the author of a copyrighted work has *some* recognizable rights.

Sixty dollars is an insulting offer but it's better than no offer at all and if it is seen as voluntary, as an originating proffer, it does leave some room for negotiation. The flat rejection you seem to be arguing (correct me if I am wrong) leaves us with nowhere to go other than public domain, the land where everything published in this country before 1922 goes to die.

—◦◦◦—

MIKE: I think the Authors Guild caved, and I think there are going to be enough people saying so in court that the settlement will never stand.

However, to address your last point first, Google didn't offer to pony up $125 million solely for future use of titles. Don't forget, they're not only offering sixty dollars a book but also royalties, however minimal. No, some of that money is for past indiscretions (my own choice of words would be "abuses") for making available copyrighted works—mine, yours, everyone's—to which they did not, of course, own the rights.

Therefore, those who opt out *do* have some recourse for getting a better settlement: it's called a lawsuit. After all, Google is certainly culpable or they wouldn't be offering $125 million to make the problem go away. Am *I* going to hire a lawyer and sue? Of course not. I'd spend more on legal and court costs than I'd ever win.

But if fifty, or one hundred, or two hundred, prolific authors get together on a class action suit, I'm sure we'll find some competent lawyer to take it on a contingency basis (i.e., no retainer or charge up front, probably ⅓ if he wins), and indeed a number of us are looking into it right now. My 60 or 70 books aren't worth a top lawyer's time, and yours aren't, but 200 of us times 60 or 70 books and suddenly you're talking about a real incentive for a class action lawyer. (Is there a statute of limitations? Probably. But since the damned thing is still in court, we have years. And why sue now when the case isn't settled, and indeed the Justice Department has recently decided to look into Google's actions in this area?)

Once you're public domain, you've lost all rights to your book. But I don't think anyone in SFWA, indeed any living writer, copyrighted his work eight and a half decades ago, and I'm a lot less concerned with them — the "orphan volumes" Google nobly promises not to consign to oblivion — than with the non-orphan volumes they're trying to grab.

I also want to disagree about taking the sixty dollars because it's better than nothing. Leaving aside my refusal to ever agree that a novel I've written is worth only sixty dollars, I think a clear case can be made, not that it's a choice between sixty dollars or nothing, but rather that it's a matter of sixty dollars *and* nothing.

Let me explain. I have never sold foreign rights to any of my novels in any country, even such tiny markets as Bulgaria and Latvia, for less than five hundred dollars apiece, which is as lowball as you can get. But lowball or not, each of those advances is four hundred and forty dollars more than Google's offering, and once your book is on Google for anyone in the world to read, why should any publisher anywhere in the world pay you to publish it? It will kill your English-language resale, especially as each new generation prefers reading screens to reading printed pages— and as Google itself comes up with better and better translating programs (and they're improving all the time), there will be no reason for a foreign publisher to buy translation rights.

Will it all happen this year, or this decade? Of course not. But if it costs you a single domestic or foreign resale, no matter how small, taking that sixty dollars is not only humiliating, but it's not cost-productive.

———ανν———

BARRY: As always you make a powerful statement and one which on its surface seems unexceptionable. In fact it *is* unexceptionable. Who can argue that $450 isn't more than $60? Who could dispute that Google's appropriation and distribution worldwide of books would severely affect and possibly destroy the entire concept of foreign rights? The Web is instantaneous, the Web is everywhere ... if Google digitizes a novel it is as easily available in Latvia or Poland as in Brooklyn, New York. Sure, there would be translation costs involved for foreign publishers ... but those could be accomplished by individual enterprises or individuals. For that matter, if there isn't such a thing as a "translation machine" already available, I would suggest that one might be within the next ten years ... it might not parse like Faulkner or Hemingway or with the eloquence of your faithful perpetrators of this dialogue ... but it could make the work accessible, at least on the plot level and sufficiently to pass an undergraduate exam.

But you have elided the central point of my opening statement.... Google is many things (choose your adjective) characteristic of a huge corporation, soulless or otherwise, but Google is at least making an attempt to be law-abiding. They want to come into the tent. What I fear more than Google are the outlaw appropriators, hundreds or thousands of them, who *don't* want to come into the tent, who refuse to even acknowledge the presence of a tent. They lie utterly outside of the Authors Guild, of contingency lawsuits, of publishing attorneys working on contingency. They lie outside of our organization and the Mystery Writers of America, outside of appeals to conscience, decency, ethics, morality. Picture them if you will as a widely-scattered population of kid geniuses in garages with frightening computer skills, no assets, and what they think is a revolutionary mentality. You'll never bring them in. They'll break camp at the first sound of the cavalry's hoofs ... and they'll set up camp (which consists of a couple of tin cans, a few incendiary devices, and a field mess kit) in another part of the forest.

Google represents—as new style as it would like to be, as free and easy on the draw as its public relations department would have it—a more conventional model; they have set up a camp they cannot easily break if at all, and they have indicated a willingness to negotiate. They have already—under very little pressure—made the most fundamental concession, that authors (or in some lamentable cases publishers) own their copyrights and the benefits thereof. They cannot be ignored, elided, circumvented. This is a place to begin and a class-action suit for hundreds of millions of dollars is *not* a beginning; this kind of antagonistic position should be taken only if negotiations fail and only then with the understanding that the pirates have nothing to fear from the courts because the courts are not in their world.

Your response may be that I am showing an unseemly willingness to collaborate with Google rather than take an adversarial position. I concede this. I will also paraphrase Damon Knight, our spiritual father, who wrote fifty years ago in Theodore Cogswell's *Proceedings* something like: "There is much to be said for science fiction writers as a community, but they show a lamentable tendency to roll over and show their soft underbelly at the first waving of a check." That is a statement which I have had occasion to use in argument myself more than once. But Google is an adversary — and, yes, for writers they are an adversary — of a nature and dimension which we have encountered only within the last ten years. The Web has changed everything; the old standards simply do not apply.

I don't know what *does* apply. We are in a frantic redefinition now, all of us. Talk of situational ethics!

———*๑๑๑*———

MIKE: I'm coming around to Eric Flint's point of view: pirate sites cost me very little income, and probably equal what they take when people who otherwise wouldn't encounter my writing read it there and then go out and buy some of my books.

Most of the pirates are small potatoes. Often they're kids who just want to share stuff they like with others, and don't know the law. It's been a couple of years since I found a pirate site that was actually *selling* my books or stories rather than giving them away for free. They're *little*, and the harm they do is relatively minor. Hell, even after I know one of them's got my stuff, and I want to check it out before writing them a harsh letter (if it's short fiction or out-of-print novels) or letting my publisher do it (if it's in-print novels), *I* have a difficult time finding the site — and I'm *motivated*. Usually a call or an e-mail to the server is all it takes to get a site taken down. Piracy's a bother, and of course you fight it every time you encounter it — but it's simply not an economic disaster.

Compare piracy as we know it to Google. If there are two billion computers in the world, every one of them has access to Google. Even the censorship deal Google made with the Republic of China didn't affect science fiction. How many hits a day does Google get? Ten billion? Fifteen billion? How many do all the pirate sites currently carrying your stories or books get? Seventy? Two hundred? And how many visitors to those sites download your titles rather than someone else's? So you tell me: who can do you more harm?

"Google is making an attempt to be law-abiding." Yeah, *now* they are — but they weren't until they went to court and learned that the copyright on your books belongs to you and not them. I hope you don't think they approached the Authors Guild and said, in essence, "We feel so guilty about appropriating all these tens of thousands of books to which we have no legal right that we want to throw some serious money at you to make amends." They got caught with their hand in the till — or on the copyright page — and they made the best deal they could. And it's such a sweet deal that it's almost sure to be struck down. The writers— well, *some* of the writers— aren't the only ones who are challenging it. You want a more formidable foe? The Harvard University Library is fighting it, and I'll bet they have almost as much money behind them as Google — maybe more in this current economy.

If the statement you are so fond of quoting is accurate, and I have no reason to believe it isn't, some of us don't want to be Damon Knight's spiritual, please-hit-me-again-sir children. Google is trying to become a monopoly, which is bad enough, but they're trying to do it at our expense, and that is worse. When you see something like that happening, in politics or economics or anywhere else, and you *don't* stand up to it and say "This shall not pass," then you are the architect of your own demise. Totalitarian states don't come into being by subjecting *all* the people to superior power; they do it because too many people who know right from wrong stand by and do nothing.

Or say: "It's too much trouble to fight this. Give me sixty bucks, hit me again and may I please have another, sir, and we'll call it quits."

—◦◦◦—

BARRY: Well, I take your point as I hope I can persuade you to take mine. My underbelly is clearly showing. My take-the-money-and-run principle which guided me through the twenty disastrous years of what I no longer call my "career" has certainly made its way into this dialogue and in fact may have dominated my point of view. As I seem to recall writing long ago, near the beginning of these dialogues, which are now in their 44th installment and twelfth year, I am putting forth a point of view here; I am not asking that others subscribe to it. As I *clearly* recall writing long ago, in the Introduction to *Engines of the Night* in fact, my career was to be viewed as a kind of outcome of a certain approach in a certain period; the book was the record of a journey. I am not suggesting that our readers blindly follow my advice which — put succinctly — is to accommodate Google because the alternative is the obliteration of copyright. I ask only that they give it some consideration, place it against yours, and make a decision. What I *can* write is that like some evil lawsuit, this situation is not going to evanesce. It won't vaporize. Ignoring the situation will not make the situation go away. The googles will get you and they bite.

What I do believe is that we are in a situation of complete reconfiguration. Everything is up for grabs now ... copyright, medium of delivery, audience, everything. The old idea of copyright as a kind of restraint is an anachronism. It's back there with Martha Foley and Plotto and the *Writer's*

Digest books of advice. ("Always use first class postage both ways and address your query to the appropriate editor.") The situation is maddeningly fluid; it changes almost daily.

Everything has changed. Here is one small example: Caesar Franck's *Symphonic Variations for Piano and Orchestra* is a nice 19th century work of some minor import. Its primary interest, at least to me, is that the opening theme of the allegro ten minutes in sounds like *Honeysuckle Rose*. Pursuing the Honeysuckle Rose musicological theory, I ventured (without optimism) to see if YouTube would yield a performance. A quick search yielded *two* performances immediately, both by first-class French pianists, one of them with the first-class Orchestra of Paris. Took me ten seconds to find them, fifteen minutes (apiece) to play them with good definition and fair sound on a home computer. Cost? Nil. Copyright/performance protection for the pianists and orchestras? None.

The Society of Composers and Performers can't fight this and to the best of my knowledge haven't even tried. Do you think that the Science Fiction and Fantasy Writers of America are stronger than *ASCAP?* Just asking.

Vernor Vinge's complete short stories are available as the result of a simple Google search. So are the complete works of H. Beam Piper.

As Jonathan Schell made clear in his 1982 *The Fate of the Earth,* once the knowledge, once the technology is out there in the world, it can never again be suppressed. Never.

We can block Google, perhaps, at the cost of extended, difficult litigation. The outcome is uncertain. But if we succeed there we are *not* going to get advances for our work in any way equivalent to the standard established by print publishing. Google is not going to pay four-figure advances for reissues. That would make no economic sense whatsoever. (I could attempt the arithmetic on this, but I leave it to wiser minds in the hinterlands.) We might get a hundred and sixty instead of sixty, we might get some kind of royalty arrangement but it would be on a spotty, limited basis. Forced to pay four figures, Google will withdraw interest in at least 90% of the titles they have digitized. I am sure of this.

So what's the answer? The digital era is the answer. How's that?

—*♪♪♪*—

MIKE: The answer is that you never cave when you know you're right. It's like the old joke: Will you go to bed with me for a million dollars? Yes. Will you go to bed with me for two dollars? Certainly not; what kind of girl do you think I am? We've already settled that; what we're arguing about now is the price.

The second you take the offer, *any* offer, when you know you're right — six dollars, sixty dollars, six hundred dollars, it makes no difference — you've told Google what you are, and now all you're arguing about is the price.

And I repeat: Google lurks in every computer in the world. Letting them publish your book for sixty dollars — which, I should note, even Google agrees

you won't see for years, and that's if the settlement stands—is far more detrimental to your book's future earning power than all the pirate sites in the world
multiplied by a hundred. It's really as simple as that.

"Forced to pay four figures, Google will withdraw interest in at least 90%
of the titles they have digitized." You say that as if it's a *bad* thing. I say that if
they won't pay a fair price, to be agreed upon between the two parties (and the
second party is *you*, not the Authors Guild of which most of us are not even
members and was certainly not authorized to speak for you and me), then
Google's withdrawing interest is a consummation devoutly to be wished.

Heinlein agreed with Jonathan Schell, pointing out in "Solution Unsatisfactory" that you can't embargo knowledge. In fact, we didn't need Schell and
Heinlein to point it out; as I write this (June 21) the streets of Tehran are running red with blood because you can't embargo knowledge, or information (or
Facebook, or YouTube, or Twitter).

But that doesn't mean you roll over for them when they come a-calling—
or a-grabbing, as is the case. Do we have to make a stand, and possibly go to
court, and fight them to retain ownership of our intellectual property when it
would be so much easier to take their offer? In somewhat different circumstances Neville Chamberlain didn't think so, and aren't we all happy that eventually *someone* stood fast and said, "No, this shall not stand."

The internet is here to stay and is more and more a part of our daily lives.
So of course is digitation. I don't think there's any question that electronic publication is going to become more widespread with every passing year and for
every new generation, and that the printed page is embarking on a downward
trajectory—just look at the magazines' circulation (and the number of new e-
zines paying pro rates), or at the average midlist print runs, or any other cri-
teria you choose. We are indeed at the dawn of a new digital era—and if you
let the 900-pound gorilla in for a pittance now, when even the court decrees
that he's abused the law and his power, who do you think is going to make him
pay a fair price later, when he's the only game in town?

BARRY: Sure you're right. Your basic position is unassailable. You shouldn't
cave if you know you're right (of course that leaves us open to a discussion of
subjectivity) and you should place enough value on your work to fight for or
defend it. I seem, all unwillingly, to have been pushed by this discussion into
a position I do not really like: I am recommending appeasement. You compare
my position to Chamberlain's and I take your point and neither of us have to
be reminded that it didn't, in the end, work for Chamberlain. It did not, in
fact, even work at the beginning.

Whether Google is Hitler is another argument, however. I don't think that
corporation is monstrous; it is just selfish and aggrandizing and monolithic
and (in the PR sense) duplicitous and deceitful in the way that corporations

tend to be. Underlying much of their performance is the same insecurity that drives, well, freelancers; its Chief Executive Officer, Eric Schmidt, is quoted in today's *New York Times* as noting (in a defense of the very subject we are arguing) that "We are one click away from you going to one of our competitors." The Internet is very powerful; it is also frail. The movie projector can get jammed at any point; the police can enter the darkened theater without a warrant and drag the projectionist away. Google's behavior—which is at best one of appropriation—can be ascribed more to insecurity than that "evil" which they state it is their principal to avoid.

What I have been trying to make clear in this dialogue is only this: That the old verities do not apply. In fact the old principles do not apply. We are now well into an era of absolute reconfiguration. Everything is up for grabs: copyright, distribution, information, the educational system itself. Libraries. Mass media. What function will a library have in perhaps less than 20 years when a home computer will provide access which will dwarf the Alexandrine Library? What function will a librarian have in the age of Google and instant information? What function will the concert hall have when I can summon Franck's *Symphonic Variations* to my home computer in thirty seconds, watch and hear it played before an audience by one of the world's great pianists and orchestras? Do I really need to go to Avery Fisher Hall for the experience? (And will the experience be available in Avery Fisher Hall? The piece has been programmed once in the Tri-State area in the last twenty-five years by the New Jersey Symphony and Andre Watts. The New York Philharmonic has never programmed it within this period.)

The old posture: reflexive and ferocious "protection" of copyright by its holder is no longer possible in this new configuration. The old system is broken irretrievably; Yeats' rough beast is shambling toward Bethlehem to be born. We have to be reborn in order to deal with those consequences. We have to consider this situation as if for the first time. History—even evoking Neville Chamberlain—is not going to save us.

All that said: I find your position most appealing. I wish you well. Maybe there *are* eternal verities.

—◦◦◦—

MIKE: I persist in thinking it's a simple situation: either your intellectual property is yours, or it is not. If it isn't, then you are, in essence, doing work-for-hire using characters and concepts that you have no legal claim to, despite the fact that they originated between your ears. If it is, then if someone wants to publish it in any form, he has to negotiate fairly and openly with *you*, not with some organization of which you are not a member, which doesn't represent you, and which signed off on an agreement stating that no book you've ever written is worth more than sixty dollars of front money.

If the agreement stands—and I have just enough faith in the court system to believe it won't — you can opt in, take your sixty bucks, and file objections from within, and we all know how far that'll get you. Or you can opt out, fight for your rights in an individual or class action suit, look Google or anyone else in the eye, and say, "This is the fruit of my intellectual labor, and if you want it, you have to come to *me* and make an offer I find acceptable."

I think it's really just as simple as that.

Index